Ireland

A Short History

Ireland

A Short History

JOSEPH COOHILL

ONEWORLD

OXFORD

For Thomas Patrick Coohill

IRELAND: A SHORT HISTORY

Oneworld Publications
(Sales and Editorial)
185 Banbury Road
Oxford OX2 7AR
England
http://www.oneworld-publications.com

Oneworld Publications
(US Marketing Office)
160 N Washington St.
4th Floor, Boston
MA 02114
USA

ISBN 1–85168–238–4

Cover design by Design Deluxe
Typeset by LaserScript, Mitcham, UK
Printed and bound in Great Britain by Creative Print and Design

Cover photographs: nationalist John Hume (left) and
unionist David Trimble (right) join Bono from the group U2 in
campaigning for the 1998 Good Friday Agreement, © Pacemaker, 2000.
MS 58 fol. 130r. Opening words of the Gospel of St Mark,
Irish (vellum) Book of Kells, (c. 800)
The Board of Trinity College, Dublin, Ireland/Bridgeman Art Library.

Contents

Acknowledgements

Many people helped me with this book, and I am very grateful to them. My students at the Oxford summer programmes of St Bonaventure University and the University of Massachusetts helped me understand how to present Irish history to a new audience. Chris Belshaw, Margaret Braker and Seena Fazel read chapter drafts and offered many good suggestions. Rebecca Clare, Helen Coward, Novin Doostdar, Juliet Mabey and Victoria Warner at Oneworld have treated me as well as an author could be treated. The anonymous reader for Oneworld made vital corrections and excellent suggestions. Meg Davies produced the index and was an excellent and patient copy-editor. Jillian Luff drew the map of Ireland, Deborah Martin proofread the final product and Barry Riordan provided great help with the pronunciation guide for Irish words. Joan Rough not only read and commented on chapter drafts, but was a true neighbour during the time it took to produce this book. Most of all, though, Nicola Coohill read every word of every chapter several times, offered many insightful suggestions and gave me immeasurable support.

The book is dedicated to my father, an Irish-American in the best sense of the word. He'll be surprised and, I hope, pleased.

Preface

Ireland is fortunate to have had a great many excellent historians, and their work shows the deep complexity of its history. In addition to countless specialized studies and works concerned with the pre-1800 period, Irish history is well served by three outstanding modern histories. These are: Roy Foster's *Modern Ireland 1600–1972* (1989), Alvin Jackson's *Ireland 1789–1998: Politics and War* (1999), and Theodore Hoppen's *Ireland Since 1800: Conflict and Conformity* (second edition, 1999). Each of these books, however, presumes some knowledge of Irish history and is, as Alvin Jackson wrote, 'not a primer'. This book is a history of Ireland (concentrating on the post-1800 period) that will provide students and general readers with enough background to tackle these more sophisticated works. There are also good recent surveys of interpretations of Irish history, which have influenced this book greatly. The three best are Ciaran Brady's *Interpreting Irish History: the Debate on Historical Revisionism* (1994), D. George Boyce and Alan O'Day's *The Making of Modern Irish History: Revisionism and the Revisionist Controversy* (1996), and John Whyte's *Interpreting Northern Ireland* (1989).

In order to keep this book as accessible as possible, I have dispensed with traditional references in the main text, but the context should make it clear from where my material and quotations have been gathered. Full details of the books and articles mentioned in the text, as well as others of value, are listed in the Bibliography and Further Reading section at the end of this book. A close reading of the books mentioned above, however, should arm any interested person with everything needed to discuss Irish history confidently.

Pronunciation Guide for Irish Words

A number of Irish words appear in this book, and this pronunciation guide gives phonetic help using ordinary English words and sounds rather than formal linguistic phonetics. For instance, Sinn Féin is listed here as pronounced 'shin fain', and Éire as 'air-uh'. Words of more than one syllable have been divided by a hyphen where it is felt this will help good pronunciation. The full list of Irish words in this book is presented below, along with pronunciation guides. Phonetic guides are also given when each word appears first in the text. English translations are also given for both the literal meaning and the way the word is used today. For example, 'taoiseach' comes from the old Irish word meaning chieftain, but today refers to the Prime Minister of Éire (the Republic of Ireland).

Irish words	Pronunciation	English translation
Connacht	conn-uckt	(western province of Ireland)
Connradh na Gaeilge	conn-rah nah gale-geh	Gaelic League
Cuchulainn	coo-cullen	the mythic warrior and 'defender of Ulster'
Cumann na nGaedheal	cummann nah gale	party [or group, society, circle] of the Irish
Dáil Éireann	dawl air-un	council [or gathering] of Ireland (the lower house of the parliament of Éire)

Irish words	Pronunciation	English translation
Éire	air-uh	Ireland
Fianna Fáil	feena foil	warriors of destiny [or soldiers of Ireland] (political party in the Republic of Ireland)
fine	finna	family [or group, race]
Fine Gael	finna gale	tribe of the Irish [or Irish race] (political party in the Republic of Ireland)
Gárda Siochána	garda shee-eh-caw-nah	guardians of the peace (the police)
Leinster	lenn-ster	(eastern province of Ireland)
Munster	munn-ster	(southern province of Ireland)
Sinn Féin	shin fain	ourselves (political party in the Republic of Ireland and Northern Ireland)
taoiseach	tee-shook [or tee-shock]	chieftain [or leader] (Prime Minister)
tuath	too-ah	people or community
Ulster	ull-ster	(northern province of Ireland)

Introduction

History is important to most societies, and nowhere is this more true than in Ireland. Irish history does more than give the story of an island off the western European coast: its interpretations have provided various groups of people living there with justification for their ideas of nationality and identity. One of the most important things this book attempts to show is how diverse Irish history and culture is, but also how starkly different readings of that history have shaped its politics and society. Perhaps in no other country has the work of historians gained such importance in the popular mind. Interpretations of Irish history, from whatever period, ancient or modern, seem to have an immediate relevance to modern Irish society. This is because the issues raised by that history, particularly those issues raised by Ireland's relations with Britain, run in parallel with contemporary questions about the political and cultural make-up of Ireland, and what it means to be Irish. There are several reasons why interpretations of Irish history have been so different. One is that history has often been used to bolster political ideologies. Another is that, as in many countries, the writing of history became more professional in the twentieth century. But perhaps the main reason is that Irish history is very complex, and is, therefore, also compelling, and historians have never ceased to find new avenues for exploration and interpretation. *Ireland: A Short History* tries to present both a general narrative of Irish history (concentrating on the modern period) and a guide to the interpretations of major historians and commentators. If this book shows how difficult it is to make solid generalizations about Ireland, the Irish and Irish history, then it will have accomplished its main goal.

Chapter 1 provides a brief history of Ireland before 1800, chapters two to six examine specific periods and events in the nineteenth and early twentieth centuries, and chapters seven and eight complete the history of the twentieth century. Each chapter contains a section entitled 'Interpretations', in which the main arguments of historians and other writers are discussed. These interpretative sections cannot hope to be comprehensive, but try to address some of the major and most interesting questions from each chapter. The discussion of various interpretations is necessarily brief and the definition of the schools of thought cannot be considered strict.

These interpretative discussions may also give the impression that historical arguments change with every generation, and there is some truth to that. A very broad generalization of interpretations of Irish history would point to three major schools – the traditional, revisionist and counter-revisionist. Traditional interpretations are generally those produced from the late 1800s to the end of the 1940s; revisionists took over from the early 1950s until the late 1980s and early 1990s, and we are presently under the spell of the counter-revisionists. This is, of course, an over-simplification, but it is not entirely incorrect. Histories written in the 'traditional' period did share many characteristics. They were generally not the work of professional historians (partly because that profession, at least in Ireland, appeared slowly in the twentieth century), they often had a strong underlying political agenda and they did not use historical sources in an extensive and sophisticated way (as later twentieth-century historians would claim to). To many traditionalists, Irish history was either the noble and tragic struggle of the long-suffering Irish against their British oppressors (which is the nationalist version), or an equally strong struggle of Protestants in Ulster to retain their separate identity from the rest of the Irish population (which is the unionist version). The traditional nationalist interpretation has generally received more attention than the traditional unionist interpretation, partly because it was propagated through nationalist writings published in Ireland, Britain and the United States.

'Revisionists' were those historians who trained more professionally in the first half of the twentieth century, analysed more sources and treated them more critically than some previous historians had done. They often came to the conclusion that Irish history was much more complicated than either traditional school would have it. Further, the actions of the British government towards Ireland were not universally hostile and oppressive, and their motives were not always wicked. An important strain of the revisionist interpretation has been known as the 'liberal' or 'inclusivist' interpretation. These liberals and inclusivists have stressed the broad sweep of Irish culture and the diversity of Irish identity, as well as the deep complexities of the Irish past. 'Counter-revisionists', however, generally think that the revisionists have gone too far in their willingness to relieve the British of blame for Irish problems. Since the counter-revisionists share the same degree of historical professionalization and critical methodology as the revisionists, they do not see a need to reinterpret the previous generation's work simply on the basis of higher-quality analysis. This, they would argue, has freed them from a reluctance to analyse the motives and morals of historical actors.

Again, these are generalizations, and would not stand up to specific scrutiny. The first problem is that all historians can claim to be 'revisionists', in that they constantly reinterpret the past as well as the work of other historians. Secondly, not all members of each of the schools mentioned above would agree with all the other members of that school. Revisionists quarrelled with each other as much as they did with traditionalists. Finally, the generational divisions are too sharply drawn. Historians of different turns of mind have lived and worked in all periods, even if the long lens does seem to reveal a generational tendency.

Irish history has attracted a great deal of public notice, especially since the beginning of the Troubles in Northern Ireland. Much of what Irish, British and American politicians and commentators have to say about contemporary Irish problems has been given a historical gloss. The problem, however, is that the work of professional historians has not received adequate attention in these quarters. In many countries there is a great difference between popular and professional ideas about history. In Ireland, however, some popular ideas about history have been used to justify political extremism and even violence. Many myths and misunderstandings have become solidified into different types of history that can be used to justify contemporary actions and attitudes.

Finally, if the issue of interpretation were not complicated enough, there needs to be some clarification of terms and geography before embarking on chapter one. Ireland has been traditionally made up of four provinces: Ulster [ull-ster] in the north, Leinster [lenn-ster] in the east, Munster [munn-ster] in the south and Connacht [conn-uckt] in the west. At present, the island is divided politically between Éire [air-uh] (the Republic of Ireland) and Northern Ireland. The Republic is an independent country made up of Leinster, Munster, Connacht and three counties from Ulster (to make twenty-six counties in total). Northern Ireland comprises the six north-eastern counties of Ulster and is part of the United Kingdom of Great Britain and Northern Ireland, and is governed from London. In late 1999 and early 2000, an Assembly was founded in Northern Ireland, under the provisions of the Good Friday Agreement. Although it was suspended in February 2000 over disagreements, it was re-established in late May and early June. Chapter 8 provides a history of this process up to the time of going to press.

There are several terms which appear throughout this book which need to be explained here. They relate mainly to politics and religion, but it is essential that they are understood early on. 'Nationalist' refers to someone who desired independence (in varying degrees) from Britain. Nationalists have ranged in opinion from those who wanted Ireland to have control of its domestic affairs but to share the monarchy with Great Britain, to those who wanted an Irish republic, completely independent from Britain. Those with the latter view are called 'republicans'. 'Unionist' refers to someone who wanted to retain the link with Great Britain, but even here there were different opinions about how strong that connection should be. 'Loyalist' refers to someone who was loyal to the English crown as the monarch of Ireland as well. Loyalists are now also unionist in political opinion, but this has not always been the case. Generally speaking, 'loyalist' is used today when referring to terrorist groups who oppose a united Ireland. 'Catholic' refers to someone who believes in the Catholic religion.

Many Catholics were nationalist as well, but some were not, and it is very important not to assume that these two words are synonymous in Irish history and society. For instance, even the venerable *New York Times* refers to the nationalist Social Democratic Labour Party (SDLP) in Northern Ireland as 'the Catholic SDLP'. While it is certainly true that most SDLP members are Catholics, and that the SDLP has fought for equal rights for Catholics in Northern Ireland, it is not, strictly speaking, a religious party. 'Protestant' refers to a member of a Protestant religion. While many Protestants (especially those in Northern Ireland) were unionists, this was not universally the case. In fact, many of the most important Irish nationalists from the late eighteenth century to the late nineteenth century were Protestants. Recognizing this subtlety in politics and religion is not just a historical concern. The popular perception of the Troubles in Northern Ireland as a religious conflict is inaccurate because it can give the impression that the two main groups there are fighting over theology and religious doctrine. While religion has played an important part in the Northern Ireland difficulties, the situation is much more complex than that. Politics and culture are at least as important (perhaps more so) in explaining the divisions there, as the Interpretations section of chapter eight makes clear. Finally, the 'Church of Ireland' referred to in chapters 1–6 is not the Catholic Church (the majority religion in Ireland), but the Anglican Church of Ireland, allied to the Church of England since 1536.

ONE

Ireland Before 1800

Understanding Irish history before 1800 is a difficult task. Diverse geography, different groups of settlers and invaders and complicated relations with Ireland's larger and usually more powerful neighbour make easy assumptions untenable and simple generalizations impossible. There are, however, several important themes that stand out. One is geography, the second is the diversity of settlers and invaders over the centuries and of the cultures that they brought, and the third is the distinct lack of inevitability in the complicated power struggles between groups in Ireland and between them and powerful English monarchs, warriors and settlers. These themes will be discussed generally in this chapter, before slowing down the narrative, starting with chapter two, to examine modern Irish history more closely for the remainder of this book.

GEOGRAPHY

Ireland is a small island on the fringes of western Europe, and geography has played a very important role in its history. For centuries, many areas of the island were inhospitable. Excessive rain and rugged terrain prevented much of the soil from becoming fertile. The island was partly made up of mountains, bogs and small hills called drumlins, which were steep and unsuitable for tillage. Roughly half of the rest of the land in the country was good for farming, but not much of it was connected in large unified spaces. Small good patches were separated by stretches of barren land, which acted as barriers to the development of any large-scale agriculture. The poor land had its advantages, however. It provided for some grazing, and the more remote areas were havens from invaders and warring factions. Specifically, there were two geographical features that have been important to the rest of Irish history. First, the north of the country is somewhat different from the south. It is ringed by small mountains in the west, and drumlins and forests along its southern border. Once inside these boundaries, however, the northern land becomes more gentle and accommodating. Its close proximity to Scotland and northern England also made outside settlement more likely than migration from the rest of Ireland. The second major geographical feature is that the east is very different from the west. The east has gentler land, less rain, fewer bogs and mountains and greater potential for communication and trade with the rest of Europe. The west was far more inaccessible, with arable patches of land existing as margins to mountain and bog. Both of these major features proved to be dividing lines for settlement, economic development and communication as different groups started to populate Ireland.

PREHISTORIC IRELAND

As the glaciers from the last European ice age retreated (*c.* 8000 BC), forests grew rapidly, driving out the deer and horses which had grazed on grassy plains during the ice age. This forced early European hunter groups to search further for food, and migration became common. The first inhabitants of Ireland probably came from Scandinavia, through Britain, crossing over to Ireland as it was gradually being cut off by the rising ocean (*c.* 6500 BC). They settled mainly in the north-east of the country, where food was more plentiful. These were hunters, gatherers and scavengers. By about 3000 BC, new settlers began arriving in Ireland, bringing with them Neolithic agricultural inventions, more sophisticated tool making and the domestication of animals. These people founded small settlements and concentrated on diverse living, comprising basic agriculture, clearing of woodland for space and fuel, tool making, hunting and rearing animals. The way these people met the day-to-day requirements of living shows that they were relatively sophisticated. This is also evident from their treatment of the dead, which seems to indicate strong religious beliefs. Huge burial monuments dating from this period (3000–1800 BC) can be found all over Ireland. Long stone burial chambers and 'dolmens' (tripods of stone with a capstone) still exist in many parts of the country. These burial chambers often had highly decorative interiors, which shows how much time was set aside for their planning and construction. By 2000 BC, metalworking technology had reached Ireland. As with other advances, this had come largely from the migration of peoples from the Middle East through Europe. Metalworking had many practical applications, ranging from arms (knives, swords and spearheads) to domestic tools and jewellery. Further improvements in such technology, starting around 800 BC, brought more sophisticated tools, including an early plough. From about 600 BCE, the iron age began to establish itself in Europe, led by iron-using tribes from central Europe. The Greeks called them *keltoi*, from which we get the name Celts [kelts]. Their use of superior iron technology led to their gradual spread west and north through much of Europe. The Celts came into Ireland in two movements. The first was to the west, coming directly from the European mainland. The second was from northern Britain, settling in the north-east of Ireland. By 150 BC, the Celts were well established in Ireland.

EARLY IRISH SOCIETY

Much of early Irish society was concentrated in Ulster and Connacht, and many of the sites of Irish myths and legends have corresponding ancient Celtic settlements. Most of the pre-Celtic groups in Ireland survived the Celtic migration, but were thoroughly Celticized by AD 450, with a common language and culture. There was much movement between the Celtic peoples of Ireland and those of Britain, as well as raiding and warring. By AD 600–700, however, Ireland was becoming a settled agricultural country, with many small kingdoms called 'tuath' [too-ah]. This was a very rural society, with no cities or towns. People lived on small farms. The wealthy and the rulers surrounded their farms with earthen banks for defence, and many of these still survive. The king of each small kingdom was expected to lead the people in war, if necessary, and to preside over regular assemblies and festivals. It was a simple, agrarian life, with no coined money, most of the business conducted in bartering, and the value of things related to agricultural products or livestock.

These were law-based societies, centred around the tuath and the 'fine' [finna], the extended family. Most of the laws in this culture were based on the family and its relations with other families. There was a great deal of mutual responsibility between fine, and the legal system rarely required the intervention of the chief of the tuath. Although the law tracts surviving from this time do not identify a king of all Ireland, by the fifth century the Uí Néill dynasty from Ulster claimed to be high kings of Tara, the ancient fort near Navan in County Meath. To what extent this family had true power over the rest of the country is open to debate, but the significant thing was that they claimed they did, and a new political phenomenon appeared in Ireland – the idea of a high king. This is not to say, however, that the country was completely united under one ruler. Each successive Uí Néill king had to continue difficult and often divisive negotiations with other kings in order to retain his prominence. Although the island was politically diverse, it was culturally quite unified. The language was more or less the same, and many cultural practices were held in common across the country.

EARLY CHRISTIAN IRELAND

During this period (AD 400–500), Irish trade with Britain and Europe was fairly extensive, and it was through these links that Christianity probably came to Ireland. There were, therefore, Christians in Ireland before the arrival of St Patrick, the most significant Christian missionary in Irish history. Most of these early Christians came from Roman Britain and Gaul (France), and there were enough of them in Ireland for Rome to appoint a bishop, Palladius, in 431. Patrick succeeded him, but there are different theories about when he arrived in Ireland (tradition says 432, but 456 has also been argued). Much of what is known about Patrick comes from his own writings. He was a Roman Briton who was captured by Irish raiders when he was sixteen years old. Like other such captives, Patrick was put to work tending sheep for six years. While he was in Ireland, Patrick became very religious, and after he escaped back to Britain he had a vision that he was being asked by the Irish to return to them. He returned to Ireland via France (where he had probably received his seminary training). Most of his missionary work was done in the northern half of Ireland. Despite the uncertainty over the dating of Patrick's time in Ireland (432–61, or 456–90), it is clear that he introduced two important religious structures into Ireland – the episcopal system of dividing the country into areas controlled by bishops, and the system of church monasteries. The monasteries flourished, especially after Patrick's death. They were austere places. Few of them had stone buildings; most had wooden structures built like a camp or small fort. The monks spent their time working to maintain the monastery, and in studying religious texts and making copies. Students from Britain and the continent came to study in Irish monasteries, and Irish monks went abroad to study and to live in other monasteries. Customs and practices were interchanged in this way.

Alongside the monasteries, there was a parallel education system in early Ireland. It was based not on reading and writing, but on memorization of tales and stories. This was the system that educated lawyers and poets. But during the seventh and eighth centuries (600–800), the two educational systems, the Latin system of the monasteries and the Irish system of oral teaching, began to communicate more and more with each other, and to borrow ideas and methods. The Irish system gradually started training students to read and write, and the Irish oral tradition began to be written down. The Latin system was influenced by secular Irish law, and clergymen began to be able to accept roles in noble society. Further, the church did not suppress Irish stories. Indeed, much surviving Irish literature was preserved in monasteries. During this period, many monasteries grew in wealth and power, and consequently built more permanent structures. The sites at Clonmacnoise, Armagh, Kildare and Glendalough are among these. Monasteries also diversified their roles. They became places of learning and refuge, as well as religious centres. Books were brought in from other countries, such as Spain, and Irish books were being sent to the continent. There was also a flowering of Irish art and carving, and this was the period of illuminated texts such as the Book of Kells (*c.* 800).

THE AGE OF THE VIKINGS

During the first forty years of the ninth century, Viking (or Norse) ships raided islands off the coast of Ireland, coastal Irish towns, and river towns further inland. This was part of a larger movement of men out of Scandinavia, raiding and settling all over northern Europe, and eventually as far as the Mediterranean. The Viking invaders of Ireland came mostly from western Norway, via the Orkney Islands off the northern Scottish coast. These Vikings had developed great 'long ships'. Single ship raids to Britain started in 795, and by 837 Viking fleets were landing in Ireland. During the late 830s, the Vikings were also trying to settle in Ireland. In 841 they established a foothold at the mouth of the Liffey, which eventually became Dublin city. Irish kings were too divided to put up a common defence, and the Vikings made significant inroads to the interior of the island while the native kings fought each other. From 850 onwards, it was common for treaties and alliances to be made between a Norse band and an Irish king in order to defeat another Irish king. By the end of the ninth century, the Norse settlement-making largely stopped, and raids, although still happening, were less frequent. The Vikings in Ireland settled more or less permanently in Ireland, and began to intermarry with native Irish groups.

One effect of the Viking raids and wars was that the kings of Tara gradually gained more power. Just as the Viking threat was beginning to wane, the king of Tara defeated the king of Cashel in an important battle which was to bolster Tara's power. But early in the tenth century, a new wave of Viking invasions came. In 914, the Viking town of Waterford was established, and much of the south and south-west of the island was raided from this base. A small native kingdom in the west of Ireland began to expand, however, and repel the Norsemen. They captured the Viking town of Limerick, and then all of Munster by 980. Under their leader, Brian Boru, they began building a powerbase in Cashel. Meanwhile, the king of Tara defeated the Norse in Dublin in 981. But Brian Boru wanted to expand his kingship and he defeated both the king of Tara and his subordinate Dublin Norsemen in 999. After defeating another important Irish king in 1002, Brian declared himself king of Ireland. He spent the next decade defeating various other Irish kings in Ulster and Leinster. In his final battle to overcome a resistant king in Leinster (who was allied with some Viking tribes), Brian was slain in the battle of Clontarf in 1014, even though his armies were victorious. Dynastic wars amongst the Irish kings followed soon after Brian's death.

There were many other effects of the age of the Vikings. Trade increased dramatically between Ireland and Scandinavia. Metal-working and craft skills were traded extensively. Irish sailing was perfected. Town settlements became more common and Ireland ceased to be a completely rural society. One of the most significant effects of the age of the Vikings was that the centre of power and commerce in Ireland moved from the midlands to the east coast. Further, many monks and scholars removed books and other valuables from the country to prevent them falling into pagan hands. They brought many texts to the continent for safe-keeping. This helped to found a long tradition of Irish scholarship and teaching. This was also the period of much stone building in Ireland, and some monasteries built tall 'roundtowers' in order to protect themselves and their valuable manuscripts from plunder. There are still many of these towers surviving. Great stone carving also flourished in these years, and many of the famous stone crosses that survive in Ireland today date from this period.

After the disruption of the age of the Vikings, Ireland experienced a religious flowering in the tenth and eleventh centuries. Monastic expansion and increased sophistication in stone carving were all part of a period of strong growth in Irish culture and the arts that lasted through the eleventh and twelfth centuries. It was a high point of Celtic Ireland, before the invasion of the Normans in the late twelfth century. Perhaps one of the most significant changes to take place during this period was, however, reform in the church. The monasteries changed from being based solely on Latin and producing Latin manu-scripts, to recording Irish traditions, epics and other learning. Since the church was largely monastic, there was a general lack of priests to work with the people. Also, some church offices were hereditary, which led to problems. In 1152, a church synod was held at Kells (county Meath), and Ireland was divided into thirty-six sees (bishoprics) with four archbishoprics. This reform completely changed the nature of Irish Christianity because it started the process of connecting clergy more directly with local people. By the time the Normans arrived in Ireland, therefore, the political and religious culture of the island was diverse and sophisticated. Although not strongly unified geographically, Irish culture at this time was strong enough to make it almost impossible to overturn. This is perhaps one important reason why the Normans, and subsequent settlers, did not attempt its eradication.

NORMAN IRELAND (1169–1300)

The Normans were a dynastic group from Normandy in France, with their origins in the Viking bands that had settled there and ruled since the early 900s. In 1066, under their leader William, they invaded and conquered England. The Norman arrival and settlement of Ireland a hundred years later was one of the most significant events in the history of the island. It established the effective control of the crown of England over Ireland. But the Normans did not 'invade' Ireland in the same sense that they invaded England with a plan of attack and massive armies in 1066. In Ireland, it all began in a bitter dispute between Dermot MacMurrough of Leinster and Tiernán O'Rourke of Breifne (modern County Leitrim). Between 1156 and 1166, two kings fought for control of Ireland (Murtough MacLochlainn in the north and Rory O'Connor from Connacht). Dermot MacMurrough supported MacLochlainn and Tiernán O'Rourke supported O'Connor. The battle engulfed the whole country. O'Connor eventually won, but O'Rourke did not want to make peace and continued to fight MacMurrough. MacMurrough fled to seek the help of English king, Henry II, in defeating O'Rourke and gaining back his lands.

In 1155, Pope Adrian IV had given Henry permission to go to Ireland and bring about religious reform. Henry had been too preoccupied with other affairs of state to bother with an Irish religious expedition even though he had papal permission. But when Dermot MacMurrough asked for his help in early 1167, Henry saw an opportunity to conquer Ireland without having to commit himself personally, so he told MacMurrough he would allow him to recruit armies in England and Wales. In return,

MacMurrough swore fealty to Henry and promised to rule in Ireland under the English king's control. In Wales, MacMurrough found men who were willing to fight with him, and gained the important help of Richard FitzGilbert de Clare, also known as Strongbow. In return for helping to conquer Ireland, Strongbow demanded MacMurrough's daughter in marriage as well as the kingship of Leinster. MacMurrough went back to Ireland with a small force in August 1167, but was defeated by O'Rourke. He then sent messages back to Wales promising great riches and lands for Strongbow and his other allies if they would invade. The first force (without Strongbow) came in May of 1169 and captured Wexford. O'Connor and O'Rourke settled terms with MacMurrough and offered him the kingship of Leinster if there were no further invasions. He agreed but sent word back to Strongbow in Wales that it was obvious that all of Ireland could be taken. Strongbow came and captured Waterford in August 1170. He married MacMurrough's daughter immediately and became king of Leinster. His forces then captured Dublin in September 1170. In May 1171, MacMurrough died and Strongbow took over the kingdom. Under Strongbow, the Normans were in a very solid position in Ireland. But Henry II worried that perhaps Strongbow was getting too powerful, and might eventually prove a threat. So he went to Ireland himself in 1171, landing in Waterford and proceeding up to Dublin. Strongbow and the Normans, the Irish and the remaining Vikings all submitted to Henry in November 1171. Rory O'Connor recognized Henry as king of Ireland in exchange for O'Connor becoming High King of the unconquered areas of the country. Henry directly controlled Dublin and some of the surrounding areas. Strongbow retained most of Leinster as a vassal to Henry. The rest of the settled part of the country was given to various Normans.

The Norman conquest of Ireland was only half-done, however. It was not centrally organized, nor was it complete. Many of the more remote parts of the country were left untouched, and the different Norman lords ruled differently. By 1250, roughly seventy-five per cent of the country was controlled by the Normans. Norman superiority in weaponry, battle strategy and tactics made them very difficult to defeat. Eventually, under King John (1199–1216), the Normans built some sort of centralized administration and brought a measure of peace in Ireland. They held the first Irish parliament in 1297, with representatives coming from various parts of the country. Despite border wars with some native Irish chiefs, this period was one of relative calm. In fact, the Normans usually restored order amongst warring Irish tribes in most areas. Most native Irish retained their land under the Normans, even though many of the old Irish nobility lost land to them. They established many towns, and built monasteries, abbeys and cathedrals. By the mid-thirteenth century, however, Norman influence in Ireland began to decline. This was largely because there had been no comprehensive plan to conquer the country. Also, the English wars in Scotland and Wales were drawing away many great Norman fighters, and there was an increase in native Irish opposition to Norman rule. Throughout the thirteenth century, there were several battles between native Irish and Norman Irish, and the native forces won many of them, wresting back control of many counties. Also important was the fact that several victorious native kings agreed to name Brian O'Neill king of Ireland in 1258. But he was killed in the battle of Downpatrick in 1260. A few chiefs had failed to recognize him, so the idea of a unified kingship died with O'Neill.

Many historians argue that the problem with the Norman rule of Ireland was that it was only half a conquest. English kings never paid full attention to Ireland, and consequently, for their own interests, they left native Irish chiefs in possession of too much of the country. By 1300, therefore, there was a sort of stalemate between the natives and the settlers, but it was a stalemate which could have erupted into violence at any time.

THIRTEENTH- AND FOURTEENTH-CENTURY IRELAND

Thirteenth- and fourteenth-century Ireland has often been described as a peaceful time. It was also the period of the beginning of the Irish legal and monetary systems, based largely on English models. But like the rest of Europe, Ireland suffered from the bubonic plague, which arrived in the winter of 1348–49 and killed about a third of the people. This period also saw a flowering of native Irish (or Gaelic) art and culture. A great many important Irish books were written in this period, including poetry, stories and legal tracts and commentaries. Many scholars were patronized by Anglo-Irish nobles, so there was a good deal of cultural communication between the descendants of the Normans (the Anglo-Irish) and the native Irish. Indeed, some Anglo-Irish wrote poems and stories in the Irish language. There was also much intermarriage, so the connections between the two groups became stronger. But this intermingling began to worry the English government, and they attempted to prevent the Anglo-Irish from marrying the native Irish. This proved impossible to enforce, but the revival of Gaelic customs also became a military concern. Financial resources and men were sent over from England, but never in sufficient numbers to quell the Gaelic chieftains. England was involved in the Hundred Years War with France and could ill afford to send precious resources to Ireland. King Richard II (1367–1400), however, finally led his own force to Ireland. He forced all the Irish leaders to submit to him in 1394. Richard went back to England, but the Gaelic chiefs rose again, and he was forced to return to Ireland in 1399. While he was fighting in Leinster, the Lancastrian Henry Bolingbroke (1367–1413, later Henry IV) seized the English throne. Richard returned to England to defend his crown but was defeated. After his victory over Richard, Henry IV had too many domestic problems to concern himself with Ireland, even though the Anglo-Irish appealed for help in fighting Irish chiefs who were regaining land. The Anglo-Irish were pushed back to the area around Dublin known as 'the Pale'.

FIFTEENTH- AND SIXTEETH-CENTURY IRELAND (1400–1534)

Generally speaking, Irish chiefs had supported the Yorkist side during the English Wars of the Roses (1455–85). They also supported the Yorkist pretenders to the throne after the House of Lancaster had won. The Anglo-Irish in Ireland (generally loyal to the House of Lancaster) either bribed Gaelic chieftains not to attack their land, or raised taxes on their populations to fund small armies. In 1449, Richard, Duke of York (1411–60), came to Ireland to be lieutenant of the country. He was an efficient administrator and became quite popular. Many Gaelic chieftains swore fealty to him. When it became clear that the Lancastrian king, Henry VI (1421–71), was weak, many looked to Richard as a potential king. Richard fought in the Wars of the Roses, but he was defeated and returned to Ireland in 1459. The Irish parliament made him chief governor and declared in 1460 that only laws passed by the Irish parliament were valid in Ireland (English laws were not necessarily valid until they were subsequently passed by the Irish parliament). With the support of Irish chiefs, Richard went back to England but was defeated at the battle of Wakefield in 1460. But the York cause eventually won, and Richard's son, Edward IV, became king of England in 1461.

In subsequent years, Irish support for various Yorkist pretenders to the English Crown continued. Edward IV made the Earl of Desmond, a somewhat gaelicized Anglo-Irish lord, the chief governor of Ireland. But Desmond became too independent and too Gaelic for Edward's tastes, and the king sent the Earl of Worcester to bring Desmond to heel. Worcester arrived in Ireland in 1467; he charged Desmond with treason and had him beheaded in February 1468. But the reaction to Desmond's execution was swift and strong from both the Gaelic chieftains and many Anglo-Irish. Worcester fled back to England, and Desmond's brother-in-law, the Earl of Kildare, took over. The Kildare earls ruled for a long time, wisely intermarrying their daughters and sons into Anglo-Irish families and into those of Gaelic chieftains. So, when Henry VII (1457–1509) came to the English throne in 1485, the earls of Kildare presented a potential threat. In May 1478 the Yorkist pretender, Lambert Simnel (1475–1535), had himself crowned as Edward VI of England at a ceremony in Dublin, and the 'Great Earl of Kildare', Gerald More Fitzgerald (1456–1513), sent a force to invade England. It was defeated in 1487, and Simnel was captured. Again, in 1491, a Yorkist pretender came to Ireland to enlist the support of the Earls of Kildare. Clearly Henry VII could not let these threats continue, so he sent Sir Edward Poynings to Ireland in 1494 to bring the country into 'whole and perfect obedience'.

Poynings summoned the Irish parliament and passed a number of acts in 1494. These created a formal boundary between the Pale and the rest of the country, proscribed the use of Irish customs and laws, and tried to discourage Irish dress and manners. The most significant legislation became known as 'Poynings' Law', which essentially said that the Irish parliament was subordinate to the British one, could only meet when given permission by the King, and could only pass laws that had already been approved by the King. Poynings' Law was an attempt to prevent another strong Irish earl from using the Irish parliament to gain too much power and threaten England. Poynings had the Great Earl of Kildare arrested on treason, but King Henry VII released him in 1496, and he again controlled most of the country. Kildare changed his sympathies to the Lancastrian House (the Tudors) and was in control of Ireland, although not its official governor or king, until his death in 1513. In 1491, the new English king, Henry VIII (1491–1547), sent the Earl of Surrey to Ireland in an attempt to quell disturbances. But the earl could not accomplish this without a massive force, and told Henry that control of Ireland would require a complete conquest.

THE TUDOR CONQUEST

The main impact on Ireland during Tudor times (1534–1603) was its more or less complete conquest by the English crown. There were several reasons why the Tudor monarchs wanted to control Ireland, but the most important was the desire to prevent the country from being used by someone trying to usurp their power. They also needed Ireland to be able to expand English trade overseas, and as a base to challenge the power of the Spanish, who were building a maritime empire. Henry VIII took the first step in this direction by ending the policy of separation between the Anglo-Irish and the Gaelic Irish. He forcefully put down both the independent Anglo-Irish and Gaelic Irish chiefs, and he sought to end the distinction between the Anglo-Irish and the Gaelic Irish groups. What the Tudors wanted was a more homogeneous Irish population, based on English customs, manners and dress. Henry ruthlessly quelled a rebellion by Thomas Fitzgerald, the Anglo-Irish son of the ninth Earl of Kildare, which broke the last remaining Irish claim on self-governance in this period. He then installed a governing council in Ireland, led by a viceroy answerable directly to him. This policy was largely successful, though it had to be brought about by a combination of persuasion and force. In 1541, the Irish parliament officially declared Henry

King of Ireland. Many of the major Gaelic chiefs swore fealty to the English crown, and much of the old Gaelic world disappeared.

The other major change that Henry brought to Ireland was religious reformation. Beginning in 1529, Henry forced a split with the Catholic Church in Rome and declared himself supreme head of the Church of England in 1534. English monasteries were dissolved in 1536, and an attempt to anglicize Ireland soon followed, culminating in Henry being declared head of the (Anglican) Church of Ireland in the same year. But Henry died in 1547, with most of Ireland outside the Pale untouched by his religious reforms. His son, Edward VI (1537–53), also failed to anglicize the country. At Edward's death, Henry's daughter, Mary I (1516–58, sometimes called 'Bloody Mary' for her execution of Protestants), became queen. Mary was a Catholic and officially restored the religion to England and Ireland. She also introduced the practice of 'plantation' into Ireland, whereby recalcitrant Anglo-Irish and Gaelic groups were dispossessed of their land, and English settlers established in their places. Alliances with Catholic Spain and war with France, however, plagued her reign. She died childless and was succeeded by her Protestant sister, Elizabeth I (1533–1603). Elizabeth tried to establish Protestantism throughout her kingdoms, but met a great deal of resistance in Ireland. As during the reign of her father, Henry VIII, the Irish Pale largely conformed, but the rest of the country balked, and the desire to retain Catholicism became a uniting force between the Anglo-Irish and Gaelic Irish. Under Elizabeth, plantation continued wherever English power was strong enough to enforce it. She found the most difficulty in subduing Ulster, especially since Hugh O'Neill, the Earl of Tyrone, had enlisted the help of the Spanish and tried to inflame all of Ireland in a war against the English crown. From 1595 until 1603, he and other chieftains waged a sort of guerrilla war against Elizabeth. A Spanish force landed at Kinsale in County Cork in September of 1601, and O'Neill went to join them. The combined forces were routed by the English, led by Lord Mountjoy. In January 1602, the Spanish withdrew and O'Neill accepted defeat later at the battle of Mellifont on 30 March 1603.

STUART IRELAND 1603-60

A major effect of Stuart rule was that land ownership changed dramatically. At the time of Elizabeth's death in 1603, most of the land in the country was owned by Catholics (whether they were Irish or Old English). Sixty years later, however, Catholics could only hold land west of the river Shannon. There were new landowners to replace them. These, generally, were the 'New English' and Scots settlers who were given land by the government. At this point there needs to be an explanation of a change in terms. Up until now, the two main political groups in Ireland have been called the Anglo-Irish (descendants of the Normans) and the Gaelic Irish (descendants of the 'native' Irish). From this point onwards, however, the terms for these groups change to 'Old English' (for the Anglo-Irish) and 'Irish' (for the Gaelic Irish). English settlers who arrived during the reign of Elizabeth and the Stuart monarchs (that is, from 1558 to 1714) tend to be called 'New English'. These, however, are scholars' terms, invented in an attempt to understand and explain the different groups in Ireland during this period. They were not necessarily used by the people at the time. But the different names are important because this was a period of plantation and civil war, and saw the different groups playing different roles in the political events that were so important to future Irish history.

Hugh O'Neill and his followers had been allowed back to their land after their defeat at the battle of Mellifont (1603), but problems remained. O'Neill was not content with the new situation in Ulster and elsewhere, with a whole new set of elites with whom he had to share status. Seeing that no redress of this situation was forthcoming from the crown, O'Neill and more than ninety other leaders left Ulster in September 1609 and sailed to France, and then to Rome. This has become known as the 'flight of the earls', and it left a power vacuum amongst the Irish and Old English in Ulster. It also left Ulster perfectly open to settlement because many of the largest landowners had left. This presented an ideal opportunity for James I of England (1566–1625), the first English monarch from the House of Stuart (who had come to the throne in 1603 at the death of Elizabeth). He saw it as a chance to solve the problem of having a rebellious Ulster so close to Britain.

'Plantation', granting land to English and Scottish settlers in Ireland, provided a potential solution to many problems in Ulster. The new landowning class would be Protestant, thereby weakening Catholicism in the closest province to Britain. Plantation under the Tudors had been unsystematic, but under the Stuarts it was more organized. From 1609 onwards, Catholics (both Irish and Old English) were moved to areas within strictly defined boundaries. Land was confiscated throughout Ulster and given to New English and Scots in plots ranging from one to two thousand acres. In return, the settlers had to agree to bring in Protestant tenants to work the land. The settlers were mainly from the lowlands of Scotland, but some came from England. They preferred a more settled type of agriculture, based on arable (or tillage) farming, and disposed of pastoral native farming where they found it. They brought in a more settled way of life, with planned towns containing markets, churches and schools. More than their religion, this is what set them apart from the Irish and Old English. Native Irish remained in Ulster, however, as tenants and labourers, because there were not enough settlers to provide for the economy. This embittered many of the native Irish, and some of them remained in contact with the enemies of England in France and Spain.

After James I died in 1625, his son Charles came to the throne. One of the major problems that Charles I (1600–49) had in Ireland during this period was the position of the Old English. Although loyal to the English crown, they had remained Catholic. They saw themselves as having rights as Englishmen living in Ireland, and thought of the Irish parliament as the guarantor of those rights. Viscount Wentworth, the King's Lord Deputy in Ireland, however, changed the structure and practice of the Irish parliament so that opposition to government plans was effectively ruled out. This meant that, although there was a parliament in Ireland, local concerns and local opinion were not a priority. The crown and the crown's needs, through its administration in Ireland, came first. But this did not satisfy any of the groups in Ireland. Wentworth was called back to England as clouds of civil war between the crown and parliament started to gather there. The Ulster plantation settlers, the Old English and other Protestants soon brought down the system Wentworth had created, and joined forces with the English parliament to have him executed in 1641. The Old English were eventually given promises by Charles that he would not try to control domestic Irish affairs to the degree he had under Wentworth, but they were only hastily agreed to because of the pressure Charles was under from the English parliament.

As it became clearer, however, that the English parliament was getting stronger (and might usurp power from Charles), many in Ireland worried that it might suppress Catholics even further and open up more areas for plantation. A rising amongst native Irish was planned for October 1641, but the plans for an attack on Dublin were found out and the rebellion fizzled out in Leinster. Local risings in Ulster took place as planned, however, and were quite successful. The native Irish established control of Ulster fairly quickly, and began to march south towards Dublin. They laid siege to Drogheda in November and joined forces with local Old English to form a 'Catholic Army' to defend themselves against the English parliament. In early 1642, the rebellion began to spread to the rest of the country, but stronger forces from England arrived and pushed the Catholic Army back into Ulster. Although many of the rebels sued for peace, the English forces saw this as their chance to subdue Ireland completely. It looked as if it was going to be a total war that could only end in the elimination of the Catholic Army. But then the English civil wars (1642–49) intervened, and a seven-year period of confused squabbling and fighting amongst the various groups in Ireland began. At the end of the civil wars, with the parliamentary forces under Oliver Cromwell (1599–1658) victorious and King Charles executed in 1649, Ireland stood open to complete control from the English parliament, a situation which very few in Ireland wanted. When Cromwell landed in Ireland in 1649, he and his army exacted revenge on what they saw as a Catholic religious rebellion, not one over political control of the country. There were massacres at Drogheda (which had been loyal to Charles), Wexford and other places. But many of the rebels were allowed to leave the country unharmed, and over thirty thousand emigrated to the continent. The majority of the Irish poor felt none of Cromwell's wrath, and he issued a general pardon to those rebels who remained alive and in Ireland. Still, the image of Cromwell as a butcher of Catholics was set into Irish folk memory.

Ultimately, Cromwell was interested in Irish land and the potential for wealth that it contained. And it was in the 'Cromwellian Settlement' that he had his most lasting impact on the country. Catholic landowners who had taken part in the rebellion were stripped of their existing land and of the right to own land. Those Catholic landowners who had not taken part in the rebellion were given a proportion of the amount of land they had held before. Their new land, however, was not to be where they had held it before. Ireland was divided in two. The non-rebel Catholics were given their land parcels in Connacht and in County Clare (amongst the least arable places in Ireland). This policy went into legend as giving Catholic landowners the choice of going 'to hell or Connacht'. The rest of the country was either confiscated to pay the government's debts, or given to soldiers and officers in Cromwell's army. The Cromwellian Settlement was different from the settlements and plantations under the early Stuarts, however. Most of the soldiers who were given land sold it to existing Protestant landowners and returned to England. There was no plan for building towns or planting Protestant communities where they had not previously existed. What had changed, significantly, was land ownership, and with it, the nature of the upper classes in Ireland.

IRELAND DURING THE RESTORATION AND THE JACOBITE WAR (1660–91)

The end of Cromwell's Commonwealth and the restoration of Charles II (1630–85, the son of Charles I) to the English throne seemed to indicate that the Cromwellian Settlement in Ireland might be overthrown. But Charles II had difficulties satisfying those Catholics who had been loyal to him in Ireland, as well as the demands of the Protestant English parliament and the Cromwellian settlers. An uneasy compromise was reached whereby the Catholics who had been loyal to Charles but had not taken part in the rebellion were to be given back a portion of their land. The Cromwellians were to be compensated for any land they had to return. In practice, this proved very difficult. Many Catholics did not recover any land, and some Cromwellians resisted giving back any land. Some displaced Catholics 'turned tory' (became outlaws) and camped in the woods and hills, from where they raided the settlements. Before the civil war, Catholics had owned roughly sixty per cent of the land in Ireland. After the dust had settled over Charles II's restoration and the land agreements (called the Acts of Settlement), Catholics were left about twenty per cent of the land in the country. This naturally caused deep bitterness and resentment amongst those Catholics who felt they were being ultimately dispossessed of their full landholdings when they had been loyal to the English crown during the civil war.

The Catholic religion was tolerated to some degree during Charles II's reign, although Catholics had to agree to recognize the Protestant king. In other ways, however, this period was one of peace and economic progress. There were restrictions on Irish trade in cattle and wool, but in other products, such as meat and butter, strong trade links with England and Europe were developed. The population grew, and while Protestants remained in control of most of the land, the government and commercial activity, there was a small but significant group of Catholic gentry, professionals (mainly lawyers), and merchants who made up a functioning Catholic upper and middle class. When Charles II died in 1685 and was succeeded by his Catholic brother James II (1633–1701), these Catholics saw some hope of having their land restored and their religion fully recognized. At first it seemed as if James would bow to Protestant pressure, and he promised to retain the Acts of Settlement. Soon, however, he appointed a Catholic viceroy, who reorganized the Irish army by dismissing many Protestants and replacing them with Catholics. Catholics were also named as judges and government officials. Plans were also laid to revise the Acts of Settlement in favour of Catholics. These changes (and similar ones in England) caused many Protestants to think of James as a political despot, and to fear for the security of their religion. In 1688 a group of English nobles invited the Dutch prince William of Orange (1650–1702) to invade England and re-establish a Protestant monarchy. James fled to France in December 1688, and sought the protection of Louis XIV. William and his wife, Mary (the daughter of James II), were crowned as joint monarchs of England in February 1689. In March, James attempted to regain his throne through an invasion of Ireland, which he hoped to use as a springboard for an invasion of England.

James summoned the Irish parliament and came to a series of agreements which reversed the Acts of Settlement, and offered religious equality whereby Catholics would pay tithes to their church and Protestants to theirs. James decreed, however, that the Irish parliament would remain subservient to the English parliament and crown. The war that was fought between James and William in 1689 was to settle the question of the English crown, the future of Ireland and relations between the major powers of Europe. European leaders took sides, but did not always follow their religion. The Holy Roman Emperor, the Catholic King of Spain and the Pope sided with Protestant William. Louis XIV of France sided with James. Both James and William had armies made up of soldiers from many nations. The war began in Ulster, but went badly for James there. His siege of Derry was famously broken in July 1689, and James's army withdrew to the south. In July 1690, William himself led an army to Ireland and met James at the River Boyne near Drogheda on 1 July. William's troops outnumbered James's significantly and though William himself was wounded in the battle, he won. James fled again to France on 4 July. The war continued well into 1691 as James's remaining forces in Ireland fought rearguard actions, notably at Limerick. As the rest of the country came to terms with William, James's forces eventually signed the Treaty of Limerick with William's commander, the Dutch general Ginkel, on 3 October 1691. Under the treaty, many of James's soldiers were allowed to go in exile to France (they became known as the 'wild geese'). The treaty also granted some lost property and professional rights to Catholics, but the largely Protestant Irish parliament refused to ratify it, and all the agreements that had been reached were lost. This caused a great deal of bitterness amongst Catholics, as well as almost complete mistrust of English promises or treaties.

IRELAND UNDER THE PENAL LAWS (1691–1778)

After the Treaty of Limerick debacle, Protestant Ireland was bolstered in its dominant position. The Irish parliament became completely Protestant. Although some prominent members of the dominant Protestant order desired greater domestic freedom for Ireland, most felt themselves in need of English protection from a potentially hostile Catholic majority. Also, England had entered the War of the League of Augsburg (1689–97, also called the War of the Grand Alliance) against France. Many Irishmen were in the French army under Louis XIV. These were the famous 'wild geese' who had left Ireland after the Treaty of Limerick. Protestants in Ireland were, therefore, afraid of a French invasion which might be bolstered by native Irish Catholic support. This was the background to the Penal Laws.

Between 1695 and 1728, a series of measures was passed to restrict Catholic worship, bar Catholics from the Irish parliament and government office and to prevent them from voting or becoming lawyers or officers in the army and navy. The laws of exclusion were enforced by the creation of an oath for all government and professional positions which denied 'the transubstantiation of the elements of bread and wine into the body and blood of Christ' at the last supper, and declared that the 'adoration of the virgin Mary, or any other saint, and the sacrifice of the mass, as they are now used in the church of Rome, are superstitious and idolatrous'. These things were central to Catholic beliefs. They could never swear to such an oath if they wished to remain true to their faith, and therefore could not hold these offices or professions. The Penal Laws never really worked, however, because they were not universally applied. The restrictions on Catholic worship were gradually ignored from the 1720s onwards, but the political and professional bans continued until 1829. The Penal Laws did not prevent Catholics from entering trade and industry, but Catholic progress in these areas was stunted by restrictions on their ownership of land. Acts were passed in 1704 and 1709 which prevented Catholics from buying any land and from taking leases longer than thirty-one years. These restrictions eventually meant that, by 1778, Catholics only owned five per cent of the land in Ireland. Many prominent Catholic landowners converted to the Anglican Church of Ireland in order to retain their land and positions.

Social conditions were also not very good for the majority of the people. A rising population and a stagnant economy made pressure on the land intense, and trade restrictions imposed by the crown meant that there was little opportunity for employment in the non-agricultural economy. There was a terrible famine in

1741, and rural life consisted of living on the margins of survival, although local artistic and musical culture seems to have flourished during this period. The Catholic Church survived the banishment act of 1697, which sent many hundreds of clergy into exile in Europe, although about a thousand were allowed to stay in Ireland. By the early decades of the 1700s, however, it was clear that the Penal Laws against religious practice were never going to destroy the Catholic Church, and it was allowed to reorganize and reform itself. For most of the eighteenth century, the Catholic religion was practised openly and without much attention from the government. When England was at war with France, however, fears of an Irish-French Catholic connection forced some cautious priests to hold mass in private or to suspend regular worship. The government's toleration of Catholic practices was based on their insistence that the church preach respect for private property and English rule. The entire Irish population, regardless of religious affiliation, however, had to continue to pay tithes to the Anglican Church of Ireland until 1833.

Meanwhile, a small group of Catholics sought to re-establish a sense of Catholic and Gaelic identity in Ireland. They founded the Catholic Committee in 1760. In their books and pamphlets, they tried to counter the then popular idea that Gaelic Ireland had been a barbaric place and that Irish Catholics were constantly plotting to overthrow English rule in Ireland. They tried to act as a go-between for Catholics and the government, to convince the latter that Catholics were loyal to the English crown and that their Catholicism did not prevent this. Many Catholics throughout the country professed loyalty to the crown during the Seven Years' War (1756–63) between England and a Catholic alliance of France, Austria and Spain. A radical group of discontented rural Catholics, called the Whiteboys, led an outbreak of agricultural violence in Munster which lasted until 1765 and flared up again in Leinster between 1769 and 1795. The government reacted by passing a series of acts that made violent protest a capital offence. These did not work very well, and only engendered bitterness amongst many Catholics. After Whiteboy violence had died down, and there seemed less need for coercion, a group of members of the Irish parliament began to call for a relaxation in the Penal Laws and a reduction in the influence of the British government in Irish affairs. They were not able to get these proposals passed, but the coming of the American War of Independence (1775–83) changed the situation greatly. This time, some relief for Catholics came directly from the British government, bypassing the Irish parliament. As an ally of the American colonists, France had declared war on Britain in 1778. The government feared that a suppressed Catholic majority in Ireland would welcome and aid a French invading force, and so passed the Catholic Relief Acts between 1774 and 1793. These allowed some freedom in buying and inheriting land and granted some political rights.

IRELAND 1775–1800

One of the other effects of the coming of the American War of Independence and the potential of French invasion was the rising of a massive volunteer movement to defend the country. These Volunteers were mainly middle- and upper-class Protestants, and between 1778 and 1779 they formed into corps based on their locality or professional connections. They armed themselves, gave themselves uniforms and held parades and reviews of troops. This organized middle- and upper-class Ireland as never before. For the first time, there was an armed force that was not directly under government control, and for the first time politically minded people were able to use the common bond of volunteering to discuss other pressing matters. Gradually, as the immediate threat of French invasion passed, the Volunteers began to discuss the economic and political problems facing the country. The most serious of these was the effect of the war on the Irish economy. Already hampered by trade restrictions imposed by Britain, the war cut off most of Ireland's trade with the European continent. This caused much discontent, and the Volunteers began to demand free trade, and demonstrated for it while displaying their weaponry and cannons. The government decided eventually to repeal trade restrictions on Ireland in 1779, but by then the Volunteers had moved on to the broader issue of the degree of control that the British government had over the Irish parliament. They agitated for the repeal of Poynings' Law, which had limited the powers of the Irish parliament, and against the Declaratory Act of 1720 which had given the British parliament the right to legislate for Ireland. The leader of this movement was Henry Grattan (1746–1820), a member of the Irish parliament, who was an eloquent orator. Grattan demanded independence for Ireland, but the retention of the British monarch as monarch of Ireland as well. In response to this agitation, the Declaratory Act was repealed in 1782 and Poynings' Law severely watered down. The British parliament now only had the right of veto over the Irish parliament.

The economy improved somewhat during this period, and some Irish industries, such as the linen industry in Belfast, expanded. But there was still a problem. British power in Ireland was retained through the office of the lord lieutenant, the king's representative in Dublin. Through the lord lieutenant, the British government controlled the Irish executive and distributed government patronage, which heavily influenced many members of the Irish parliament (who sought government jobs for themselves and others). So the British government was still largely in control of Irish politics. The only way to solve this problem, reformers argued, was to change the nature of the Irish parliament so that it more adequately reflected the Irish population and Irish opinion. The Volunteers held a national convention in November 1783, and presented their ideas for reform to the Irish parliament. It rejected them immediately. The Volunteers had thought that the obvious force of public opinion would mean that the Parliament would agree to reform itself, but they had not realized how strongly the members of the Irish parliament wished to retain their positions under the existing system. Apart from one further attempt at a reform convention, this movement started to fade during the rest of the 1780s. But events in France would revive it.

The political excitement surrounding the French Revolution (1789–99) was felt in Ireland as well as in Britain. The long-standing links with France meant that the events of the Revolution were heavily reported in Ireland. But another crisis occupied politics in Britain and Ireland. The English king, George III (1738–1820), became mentally incapacitated in November 1788. The British parliament debated making his son, the Prince of Wales (1762–1830, the future George IV), regent of Britain and Ireland. There was fierce controversy in the Irish parliament over the regency issue. Grattan and other reformers thought that the prince should not become regent of Ireland automatically. George III recovered in March 1789 and the regency debate was put on hold, The issue symbolized the question of who should rule Ireland. It united the Irish reformers, and they began to turn their attention to what they called the 'purification' of Irish government. They wanted the number of crown-appointed members of the Irish parliament reduced in an attempt to clean up what they saw as deep-seated corruption between the Irish executive and the Irish parliament.

In the meantime (June–July 1789), there was tension between England and Spain over an attack on British fishing vessels off the western Canadian coast. In Ireland, Grattan and his party pledged support for the king, saying that, in most external affairs, English and Irish interests were the same. Other reformers outside parliament, including a young Protestant lawyer in Dublin named Theobald Wolfe Tone (1763–98), argued that Ireland had no quarrel with Spain and no responsibility to aid the British Empire. In his pamphlet, *An Argument on Behalf of the Catholics of Ireland* (1791), Tone said that the Irish parliament must be reformed to rid itself of British control, and that the only way this could be achieved was for Protestants and Catholics to agree on their common political interests and fight for reform. The pamphlet was widely read, and a number of reformers founded the United Irishmen in Belfast and Dublin in late 1791 to push for political changes. The United Irishmen were initially a debating society, but their ideas caught the attention of a few Volunteers and other reform-minded people. Also, in December 1791, a group of militant Catholics took over the Catholic Committee and pressed for changes in the few laws that still restricted Catholics from participation in politics, especially the right to vote in parliamentary elections. They enlisted Tone as their secretary and held a convention in December 1792. They sent Tone with a delegation to London to appeal for these reforms. Desperate to avoid any potential problems in Ireland, especially given that a war with revolutionary France loomed, the British government agreed to a limited number of political reforms in April 1793. These included granting Catholics the right to vote, but still preventing them from sitting in the Irish parliament, from the judiciary and from the offices of state. The government also wished to strengthen its control in Ireland, so formed a state militia (and suppressed the

Volunteers at the same time). In August the government also passed the Convention Act, which said that no groups could assemble in Ireland except for the Irish parliament. This meant that political organizations like the United Irishmen could not meet.

In Ulster, the relaxation of many of the Penal Laws, and an increase in Catholic employment in the linen trade, caused a group of discontented Protestants called the Peep O'Day Boys to attack Catholics in County Armagh, starting in 1784. A Catholic group called the Defenders tried to counteract the Peep O'Day Boys, and violent confrontations lasted until 1795. An offshoot of the Peep O'Day Boys, called the Orange Boys (after the Protestant William of Orange, later William III, who defeated the Catholic James II), defeated the Defenders at the battle of the Diamond on 21 September 1795. This led to the founding of the Orange Order, a Protestant defence society which would continue to play an important role in Irish history.

In London, the British government briefly toyed with the idea of further concessions to Catholics, including the right to sit in parliament (which came to be known as Catholic Emancipation). But they ultimately rejected it as too dangerous. This caused Irish reformers such as Tone to consider the option of alliance with France as a way to gain further political rights in Ireland. The British government soon found out about these plans. Rather than execute Tone for treason, they allowed him to emigrate to America in June 1795 because the legal evidence they had against him was slender. Early the next year, Tone left America for Paris and began negotiations for a French invasion of Ireland. He made a convincing case and in December 1796, a French fleet of forty-three ships sailed for Ireland. The British defensive fleet was somewhat disorganized and the French expedition might have succeeded except for a bad storm. Thirty-six French ships eventually arrived at Bantry Bay in County Cork, but did not attempt to land there, and returned to France.

The British government reacted to this stalled invasion by forming its own corps of volunteers in Ireland, imposing a curfew in many places, and trying to disarm the United Irishmen and other militant reformers. The United Irishmen went underground and formed an extensive network of secret societies dedicated to securing Catholic emancipation and reform of the Irish parliament and executive in Dublin. But the British government started to infiltrate them in early 1797. In March 1798, a meeting of the Leinster United Irishmen was raided and its members arrested. This led to a general rising by the United Irishmen, with flashpoints in the counties around Dublin, and in Wexford and Waterford. Initially, the Wexford and Waterford United Irishmen were successful, but when they tried to push north and west they were defeated at Vinegar Hill near Enniscorty in County Wexford in June 1798. The United Irishmen rebellion in Ulster was also swiftly put down. In August, a small French force landed at Killala in County Mayo and defeated the militia at Castlebar, but they were surrounded by Lord Cornwallis and his troops at Ballinamuck in County Longford and were forced to surrender on 8 September 1798. Another French force carrying Tone then sailed for Ireland and engaged the British fleet off Lough Swilly in County Donegal in mid-October. The superior British fleet was victorious. Tone was captured, court martialled in Dublin, found guilty of treason and sentenced to be executed. Rather than face death at British hands, Tone cut his own throat and died on 19 November 1798.

Although the rebellion of 1798 was not successful, the persistence of the rebels and the constant threat of French assistance made the new British Prime Minister, William Pitt (1759–1806), realize that Irish discontent and Irish problems must be solved. Pitt thought that a union of the Irish and British parliaments would both please Irish reformers and reassure nervous British politicians. Such a union would wipe away the corruption of the Irish parliament (which would please Irish reformers), and would bring Ireland under more direct control from London (which would satisfy British politicians). He also thought that a United Kingdom of Great Britain and Ireland would encourage the modernization of Irish trade and commercial life. British investors would be more willing to set up industries in a more placid Ireland, and rising living standards would make calls for Irish independence seem irrelevant amongst the majority population in Ireland. Many Catholics supported the idea of union because it brought the hope of Catholic Emancipation (Pitt had implied that this was the next logical step after union). Pitt thought that Catholic Emancipation could be granted more safely under the Union because, within the entire United Kingdom, Catholics would be in a minority and could not threaten the existence of a Protestant state. Within Ireland, alone, however, Catholics were the majority of the population. As long as they had no chance of any political power, they would always be disgruntled, he thought. An unhappy majority ultimately makes for an ungovernable country, and so Pitt's solution to a powerless Catholic majority in Ireland was to change it to a Catholic minority (with increased political rights) within the United Kingdom. Many members of the Irish parliament opposed the Union, however. These included reformers and radicals who wanted an independent Irish parliament (but an improved one), Protestants who feared Catholic Emancipation, commercial interests who thought they would be swamped by more powerful British firms and people who benefited from the status quo. Pitt's proposals were initially rejected in the Irish parliament by a majority of five on 24 January 1799. The British government was, however, able to persuade and use their powers of patronage (which were commonly accepted at the time) to get enough members of the Irish parliament to vote for union on 6 February 1800. Under the Union, the Irish Parliament was dissolved, and a number of Irish MPs would now sit in the British House of Commons. Economic restrictions between the two countries were to be eliminated gradually, and free trade was to operate between the two countries. On 1 January 1801, the United Kingdom of Great Britain and Ireland was officially proclaimed. Some Irish rebels, led by Robert Emmet (1778–1803), tried to raise a rebellion against the union with French help. None was forthcoming, and Emmet's rising proved little more than an isolated scuffle in Dublin on 23 July 1803. Emmet was captured and executed on 20 September.

INTERPRETATIONS

It would be impossible to discuss the interpretations of nearly two thousand years of Irish history in a short space, but there are some important questions in the interpretations of the century before the Act of Union that address issues that have lasted ever since, in both scholarly and popular minds. These are mainly grouped around the broad question of what kind of place Ireland was in this period. Did it comprise a nation on its own, with its own politics, culture and social structures? Was it a colony of Britain, having been settled and half-conquered over a number of centuries? The question of whether Ireland was a nation or colony has had a great deal of significance for Irish history up to the present day.

The traditional interpretation of the hundred or so years before the Act of Union was that Ireland was a colony of Britain. It was under its political control through the subordination of the Irish parliament to the British one, and British interests in Ireland were always considered more important than native Irish ones. Economically, Ireland was also under British control, and since British political interests were dominant, it followed logically that British economic interests were also paramount. This kept Ireland poor, and the poorest members of Irish society were those who were the least likely to be able to interact with the ruling Protestant class – the Catholics. Irish trade was restricted when it suited British economic needs, landholding relationships were skewed heavily in favour of landlords (largely, in this interpretation, English or Anglo-Irish), and, consequently, peasant agriculture was primitive and mired in backwardness. Finally, Irish society was completely divided between the Protestant and English-speaking landed classes (who in many ways mirrored landed English society) and a Catholic and Irish-speaking peasantry (which, although it had its own rich and distinct culture, could never gain dominance). Although these two groups were geographically and physically very close, they were worlds apart in all other aspects. This interpretation has largely been the work of Irish and British historians of the period before the 1950s and 1960s. Representative examples of this include George O'Brien's *Economic History of Ireland in the Eighteenth Century* (1918) and Daniel Corkery's *Hidden Ireland* (1924), which concentrates on Munster in the eighteenth century.

In part, this interpretation was a holdover from the view of Irish history held by nineteenth-century Irish politicians and nationalists. From Daniel O'Connell in the early part of the century (see chapter 2) to Charles Stewart Parnell and other Home Rulers at the end of the century (see chapter 5), ideas of Irish independence were largely based on what they saw as the national and economic success of the country during the brief independence of the Irish parliament under Henry Grattan. This, they argued, showed that Irish problems were solved under Irish rule, and that it was only the unhelpful presence of Britain that kept Ireland impoverished and nationally frustrated. Priests also remembered the discrimination that Catholics endured under the Penal Laws, and passed those memories on to generations of their congregations. And throughout the nineteenth century, landlord-tenant relations were generally strained, and it was not too difficult to see these problems as having their historic roots in plantation and Anglo-Irish estate building. This was not only the view of nationalists in the nineteenth and twentieth centuries, however. Two important British historians, W.E.H. Lecky (*History of Ireland in the Eighteenth Century*, 1892) and J.A. Froude (*The English in Ireland in the Eighteenth Century*, 1874), saw eighteenth-century Ireland in similar ways. But they were supporters of the Union, and argued that the mis-governing of Ireland during this period meant that it had been impossible to bring Ireland into the British fold, and that the subsequent problems with the Union and the agitation against it can be traced to the politics and economics of this period. In short, they argued, the British government was its own worst enemy by its mismanagement and suppression of Ireland. Better governing practices would have brought the benefits of British rule to Ireland, and there would have been little cause for native Irish opposition to it.

The first area of the traditional interpretation to come under revision was religion, specifically the Penal Laws, which had been seen as the legal manifestation of the suppression of Catholics and Catholicism. Maureen Wall, in her *Penal Laws 1691–1760* (1961), and J.G. Sims, in his *Williamite Confiscation of Ireland 1690–1703* (1956), argued that the Penal Laws and their enforcement were much more complex than previously understood. The complexity they showed manifested itself within the English government (where there was much uneasiness about whether the laws were just and feasible), and in the patchy way in which they were enforced, both regionally and over the decades of the eighteenth century. In most instances, this school of thought argued, there was only a token enforcement of the laws. On the whole, although officially restricted, Catholics were allowed to practise without much difficulty. Further, Maureen Wall argued, the Penal Laws could not be blamed for the poverty of the Catholic population. While taking land away from many Catholics and giving it to Protestants had done a great deal to damage the Catholic landed class, she argued, the Penal Laws did not affect the economic circumstances of the Catholic poor (neither did the lifting of the Laws improve their economic standing).

Similarly, political life underwent a reinterpretation. R.B. McDowell, in his 1944 *Irish Public Opinion*, and E.M. Johnston's later *Great Britain and Ireland 1760–1800* (1963), revised the traditional interpretation by examining previously unknown sources and sketching out the broadness and complexity of the politics of the period. Further reinterpretations questioned the previous belief in both the independence of the Irish parliament, and the benefits that it supposedly brought for the population. J.C. Beckett argued in 1964 that, prior to the 'independence' of Grattan's parliament, the London government had only rarely used its powers to overrule Irish legislation coming out of Dublin, and also that the Irish parliament was not as independent during the Grattan period as the traditionalists had maintained. London retained a great deal of control, while allowing only a veneer of Irish distinctiveness and independence (see J.C. Beckett, 'Anglo-Irish Constitutional Relations in the Later Eighteenth Century', *Irish Historical Studies*, vol. 14, 1964). Joseph Lee took this even further in the 1970s, when he argued that, far from the independent Irish parliament being a beacon for a tolerant and progressive Irish nation, it served mainly to support the Protestant elite and their economic interests (see his article, 'Grattan's Parliament' in Brian Farrell (ed.), *The Irish Parliamentary Tradition*, 1973). In his *Irish Politics and Social Conflict in the Age of the American Revolution* (1965), Maurice O'Connell also argued that the traditional interpretation had been too quick to attribute radicalism and tolerance to the patriotic movements of the late eighteenth century (such as the Volunteers). A more accurate impression of their motives, he argued, came from their middle-class backgrounds and preoccupations and tolerance of Catholics (and agitation for Catholic rights) that can at best be called tepid.

Other revisions of the traditional interpretation began in the 1960s. L.M. Cullen argued that the Irish economy was far more diverse and had more healthy periods than the research of Corkery and O'Brien had allowed for. Cullen argued in a series of articles and books that not only did the Irish economy expand from the 1740s onward, but also that Gaelic society was more diverse than the traditional interpretation allowed. Previous studies, he argued, had partly relied on the evidence presented in Irish poems, which reflected a lament for a more traditional way of life that may have been fading as much due to economic modernization as to English cultural dominance. Further, he argued, there was a large class of Gaelic lesser gentry and moderately wealthy farmers. There were also great differences in the Irish peasantry, which had previously been seen as one group sharing poor economic circumstances. Cullen argued that peasant economics depended greatly on regional differences, which manifested themselves in the quality of land used, the commercialization of agriculture and the existence of local industry.

The interpretation of landlord–tenant relations also underwent a revision during the mid-twentieth century. Several economic historians (including W.H. Crawford, Peter Roebuck and David Dickson) argued that such relations were more complex, and indeed were more contractual, than the traditional interpretation allowed. Dickson showed that, in Munster, landlords had much less freedom to dispose of their land than previously thought. Through careful and exhaustive work in the records of landed estates, these historians were able to show that tenants were somewhat sophisticated in negotiating the terms of their leases and rentals. This certainly complicated the traditional picture of land questions during this period. Another aspect of this, of course, was rural violence such as the Whiteboys' risings of the 1700s. Maureen Wall and J.S. Donnelly both did important work to argue that rural violence was not so much an expression of proto-nationalism as an aspect of local and regional discontent over the economic questions of tithes and the enclosure of land. Indeed, some Whiteboys had sworn loyalty to George III, which makes them seem less anti-English than the traditional interpretation of this period has implied.

In more recent years, however, there have been further reinterpretations of this general revision of the traditional interpretation. This is partly due to a renewed emphasis on the rebellions of the 1790s. Mainly, this newer work has shown that the level of sectarian differences and mistrust between different groups of Protestants and Catholics was higher than the revisionist argument would imply. While the complexities of the situation and the different social and political aspirations of the various groups played a part, Thomas Bartlett, among others, has shown how important the partisan violence was once it broke out. His *The Fall and Rise of the Irish Nation* (1992) argues this strongly.

By 1800, therefore, Ireland was already a very diverse place, with many different people and forces affecting its political and social history. The varying historical interpretations discussed here mirrored the contested situation in Ireland during the period before the Act of Union. Chapter 2 will examine an equally contested period, a time when further political rights for Catholics were sought and a new type of nationalism appeared. Reactions against both of these events were also strong, and the theme of complexity in Irish history continues.

T W O

O'Connell, Religion and Politics, 1800–48

Political power in Ireland had been transferred to London after the passage of the Act of Union. While on the one hand this meant that the inefficiency and exclusiveness of the Irish parliament no longer had an impact on Irish affairs, on the other it meant that there was effectively no native control of the country. Although representative of the Irish population within the United Kingdom, the fact that the new Irish MPs only made up one-fifth of the total in the House of Commons meant that any Irish issue was ultimately in British hands. Throughout the nineteenth century, the British parliament wrestled with Irish problems, but it was always done with British preoccupations paramount in the minds of most members of parliament. This was not necessarily a case of wilful misgovernment of Ireland or ignorance of the concerns of the different groups who lived there. For most British MPs, the Union was thought to be a worthy and noble arrangement because it would bring benefits and better government to the Irish people. At best it was a sort of proto-internationalism based on what they saw as the real benefits of British government and British ideals. At worst, it was simply an attempt to subjugate another people and protect Britain's western flank from invaders. 'The Union', therefore, became an important and contested issue for most of the nineteenth century. It had an impact on religion and politics.

Pitt had implied that Catholic Emancipation (the right of Catholics to sit in parliament) would be the natural next step after the Act of Union. When Emancipation took nearly thirty years and much political agitation to become reality, many Irish people called into question both the justice of direct British rule in Ireland, as well as the benefits that Union was supposed to bring. Emancipation, therefore, was related directly to the question of the Union. Both of these concerns became the life's work of Daniel O'Connell (1775–1847), the most prominent Irishman of his time, and the man who would come to symbolize a certain type of restrained and constitutional Irish nationalism. His failure to get the Act of Union repealed in the 1840s would help bring about another type of nationalism, that of Young Ireland – a separatist movement that created its own issues through its own propaganda, and that eventually turned to violence. While O'Connell had a direct and immediate impact during his lifetime but was nearly forgotten a few decades after his death, Young Ireland would provide a model for militant Irish nationalism for generations.

O'CONNELL AND CATHOLIC EMANCIPATION

Daniel O'Connell was born in County Kerry, the son of a local Catholic landowner. He studied to become a lawyer and was admitted to the bar in 1798. He was one of the first Catholics allowed to become a lawyer after the Penal Law preventing this was removed in 1792. O'Connell became very successful very quickly, and he rose in prominence amongst Catholics after joining the Catholic Committee in 1804. The Committee was suppressed in 1811, and O'Connell and many others began to agitate for Catholic Emancipation and other reforms by writing pamphlets and holding public meetings on the subject. The country, however, was generally preoccupied with other matters. Catholics in Ireland had shown their loyalty strongly during the Napoleonic Wars (1800–15), and during those wars the British goverment had made a few informal proposals for Emancipation. But after the wars (that is, after 1815), the government became less interested in making serious Emancipation proposals, and the difficulties of the post-war economy meant that Catholics across Ireland turned to more pressing matters than Emancipation. A rising population and the lack of sufficient good farming land was forcing up rents, which hit the poor hardest. Farming methods were outdated and desperately needed to be improved to make the land more productive. Unfortunately, land concerns did not trouble the government until the famine of 1845–52 (see chapter 3) made them ominous. Other problems seemed to get more attention than Catholic Emancipation. Local government was generally corrupt and in the control of exclusive small groups. There was no official relief for the poor, and many Irish industries were suffering from direct competition from more powerful British companies. There was also resentment over the fact that Catholics and Presbyterians had to pay tithes to the Anglican Church of Ireland.

O'Connell and his allies thought that none of these problems could be solved until Catholics (the vast majority of the population of Ireland) participated in government at parliamentary level. This meant agitating for the right to sit in parliament, and O'Connell's great success during his early career was in convincing people, even poor tenant farmers, that this was relevant to their everyday lives. Until about 1820, the campaign for Emancipation was largely a Catholic upper-middle-class concern, headed by landlords, business-men and professionals. The early Emancipation movement was also hampered by disagreements within its ranks over how best to proceed, and what powers the British government might be allowed to retain, including a right of royal veto over the appointments of Catholic bishops in Ireland. O'Connell tried to keep up popular interest in Emancipation by founding a Catholic pressure group, which lasted from 1815 to 1817, and by his work on the Catholic Board (a sort of successor to the Catholic Committee) until 1818. There was very little practical result of the early Emancipation agitation, which consisted largely in discussing the issue in newspapers and journals. The British government saw no real reason to listen to this group because they could not claim to speak even for the majority of Catholics. O'Connell changed all that.

THE CATHOLIC ASSOCIATION AND THE CATHOLIC RENT

Although he had been active in the debates about Catholic Emancipation in Dublin circles, O'Connell had been largely dissatisfied that the issue was not discussed beyond certain urban, middle-class circles. In 1823, he founded the Catholic Association, a pressure group to agitate for Emancipation. There were two important aspects of the Association that made it different from previous Irish pressure groups. O'Connell realized that getting the Catholic clergy involved in the Association was vital to its success. Previously, Catholic clergy had not been overtly political. But O'Connell realized that their distribution across the country, their standing within local Catholic communities and their captive congregations made them the perfect people to enlist as lieutenants in the agitation for Emancipation. In its early days, the Association agitated on a number of Catholic issues (not just Emancipation), and opposed the Orange Order demonstrations and gatherings that were increasingly evident, mainly in Ulster. The Association gained a good deal of publicity because of this activity. The Catholic Association cost one guinea per year to join, which was too expensive for the vast majority of Catholics. O'Connell wanted to have the Association open to all Catholics, whatever their economic circumstances. In order to do this, but at the same time raise enough money for pay for organizational activities, he set a subscription charge of one penny per month (less than one-twentieth of the full membership cost) to become an associate member. This was low enough for even the poorest to pay. The 'Catholic Rent', as it came to be called, raised much more money than getting large subscriptions from a few wealthy donors. Between 1824 and 1829, it raised £52,000. Collecting the Catholic Rent also meant creating a network of local agents, which provided a sophisticated national infrastructure for the Association. Finally, the Catholic Rent had a strong psychological effect on the people who paid it. Paying made people feel they belonged, and that they were part of a larger movement to bring about the reforms they sought. This completely changed the nature of the Catholic Association and O'Connell's power within Catholic Ireland. Before 1824 and the associate membership scheme, O'Connell was not the obvious leader of Catholic Ireland. He was one of many prominent Catholics (although he was probably the best known). After the associate membership plan took off, O'Connell became the most important Catholic in Ireland. The Catholic Association and its agitation now also made the Emancipation question paramount in Ireland and the question of the accommodation of Catholics the most important Irish issue in the British parliament.

There were some indications in the mid-1820s that the British government was willing to grant important concessions to Catholic Ireland. The Orange Order was outlawed in 1825 (so was the Catholic Association, but it was relaunched as the New Catholic Association). Also in 1825, a backbench MP proposed Catholic Emancipation, along with a reduction in the Irish franchise and the state payment of Catholic priests. O'Connell was pleased that the bill passed the House of Commons, but it was defeated in the House of Lords. O'Connell now thought that he had convinced enough members of the Commons that Catholic claims were justified, and that the only thing he needed to do was to force the issue a little more, which, he thought, would overcome the opposition of the House of Lords and the king. This was the immediate prelude to the election of 1826, which was the first time that the Catholic Association had an opportunity to act as a real pressure group. Catholics had been given the vote in 1793. This was limited, however, to people who owned or occupied property over a certain value, as it was in the rest of the United Kingdom in this period. In most Irish counties, Catholics formed the majority of electors, but most of them were tenants and many voted along with their landlords' wishes (which was not uncommon in Britain either). One of the first things that the Catholic Association did was to try to reduce this landlord influence. They convinced Catholic electors to vote for candidates who favoured Catholic Emancipation, even against their landlords' wishes. In return, the Association promised to give financial support to tenants who were turned out by their landlords for voting against their candidates. The Association's next priority was to get an electoral organization going. They had priests persuade Catholic voters to support pro-Emancipation candidates, even if they were Protestants. The Association also provided transport so that electors could get to the polls. This was done in groups, often led by the local priest. The Catholic Rent provided all the money for these activities. The result of the 1826 general election was that MPs who had opposed Emancipation were defeated in Counties Louth, Monaghan, Waterford and Westmeath. Pro-Emancipation Protestants were elected in their places. These results were not enough, of course, to overturn the ban on Catholics sitting in parliament, but another opportunity came quickly.

POLITICAL PRESSURE AND THE GRANTING OF EMANCIPATION

In 1828, the MP for Clare, Vesey Fitzgerald, was appointed to the British cabinet. In accordance with electoral law, this meant that he had to stand for election again. This was intended to give voters a chance to reaffirm their commitment to their MP who was about to accept higher government office. Vesey Fitzgerald was a relatively popular MP, even amongst Catholics. He was in favour of Catholic Emancipation. The cabinet he was about to join was opposed to Emancipation, however, so the Catholic Association decided to contest his re-election. After failing to get a more strongly pro-Emancipation Protestant interested in fighting the election, the Association decided to have O'Connell himself stand against Fitzgerald. Although O'Connell could not sit in the House of Commons because he was a Catholic, there was no specific law preventing him from becoming a candidate for a parliamentary seat. The Catholic Association put the full weight of its organization and its money behind O'Connell's bid. On 24 June 1828, he defeated Vesey Fitzgerald 2,057 to 982. O'Connell had won the election, but he could not take his seat.

Many Catholics in Ireland became very excited by the victory, and began to press more strongly for Emancipation. O'Connell stressed the application of peaceful means only, but there was too much excitement to contain some over-enthusiastic Catholics. After O'Connell's victory in the Clare election of 1828, a number of new political clubs were formed in Ireland, with the intention of spreading Catholic Emancipation propaganda and support. These 'Liberal Clubs' were opposed by new 'Brunswick Clubs', designed to foster resistance to Catholic concessions and to promote Protestant interests in Ireland. This raised the possibility that organized and opposing political groups in Ireland would raise the tone of sectarianism in Ireland, and might, indeed, arm themselves as the Volunteers had done in the late eighteenth century. The British government saw this as further reason to grant Catholic Emancipation. The government, under the Prime Minister, the Duke of Wellington (1769–1852), and the Home Secretary, Sir Robert Peel (1788–1850), had been opposed to Emancipation, but feared that there might be a general rebellion in Ireland. Further, although the government was opposed to Emancipation, there was a slight majority of MPs in the House of Commons in favour of it. So, not only did Wellington and Peel have a potentially hostile Ireland on their hands, if the issue of Emancipation came up in the House of Commons, it might be passed. They decided, therefore, to present their own Catholic Emancipation bill in early 1829. It had taken a few months of behind-the-scenes negotiations to ensure that the bill would pass the Commons and the Lords (where opposition to it was strong), but Wellington and Peel were able to get it through, and it became law on 13 April 1829. Catholics were then allowed to sit in parliament, to hold all military ranks and to hold all but the highest government offices. As a way of reassuring nervous Protestant voters in Ireland that their influence would not be greatly diminished, however, the government also raised the property qualification for voting in Ireland, effectively taking away the vote from many lower-middle-class Catholics. Even with this compromise, Emancipation was received as a great victory for O'Connell in Catholic Ireland. He was hailed as the 'Liberator', and he and a number of his followers became members of the House of Commons. He and his Irish party generally co-operated with the Liberals, who were in office after 1830. O'Connell was successful in gaining a number of significant reforms from them in the 1830s (including increasing the number of people who could vote, reforming corrupt municipal government and abolishing the tax that Catholics and Presbyterians had to pay to the Anglican Church of Ireland).

Emancipation was a clear victory for Catholics, especially since it was partly brought about by a new type of Catholic leadership and Catholic political organization. Just as significant, however, was the fact that the government passed Emancipation partly as a result of Protestant fears of a Catholic uprising, rather than solely on ideas of equal justice. This meant that any idea that Emancipation would reduce sectarianism was unfounded. There is also some evidence that the campaign for Emancipation and the long build-up of Catholic rights and prosperity since the mid-eighteenth century created a stronger idea of a 'Catholic past', which would more easily form part of future ideas of an Irish national past based largely on Catholic experience. It is possible, therefore, that O'Connell and his movement raised the political consciousness of Catholics to an extent that Catholicism and Irish nationalism came to be seen as the same thing in later decades. This, of course, had an equally strong reaction from Protestants, particularly Protestant activists, and it is not surprising that the linking of Orangeism with the idea of Union (which Orangemen had originally opposed) may have been in reaction to this rise of Catholic political power.

REPEAL

O'Connell's next goal was to get the Act of Union repealed, and get a new parliament for Ireland. He had been opposed to the Act of Union when he was a rising lawyer in Dublin. O'Connell's ideas for repeal, and the sort of government Ireland would have after it, were vague. He wanted a parliament with domestic control, but beyond that, he was non-committal. O'Connell spent most of the 1830s trying to get further reforms for Ireland, rather than fighting for repeal. This is not to say that he ignored the repeal question, but that these other questions seemed to be more open to quick solution than did repeal. In fact, O'Connell did a good deal of agitating for repeal in the 1830s and early 1840s, but it was mostly through speeches rather than direct political action. He founded the Repeal Association in 1840, which worked along the same lines as the Catholic Association. It collected a 'Repeal Rent' in the same way as the Catholic Rent had been organized. The Repeal Rent gathered even more money than the Catholic Rent had (at its height in May 1843, the Repeal Rent was bringing in £2,000 per week). As with the Emancipation agitation, O'Connell realized early on that gaining the good favour of the Catholic priesthood was essential to securing popular opinion and activism. One of the first things he did was to try to convince priests to join the Repeal movement. But British politics changed in 1841. The Liberals were out of office, and the Conservatives, under Sir Robert Peel, were back in power. Also, the Repeal movement was not a success in eastern and north-eastern Ulster. O'Connell seems to have ignored Ulster opposition to Repeal, where unionism was already very strong. In fact, his trip to Belfast in 1841 was met with hostility from Orangemen and other unionists. O'Connell thought that it was a waste of time waiting for the Liberals to return to power and try to get Repeal of the Union from them. He thought that Peel would give way to public pressure over Repeal in the same way that he had over Catholic Emancipation in 1829. Therefore, O'Connell added a new tactic to the Repeal Association – the 'monster meetings', huge gatherings many times larger than any held over Catholic Emancipation. Best estimates put them at hundreds of thousands of people at each Repeal meeting. The sites of these monster meetings were often chosen for their historical significance and connections with past Irish military victories or similar romantic settings. The height of the Repeal movement was August 1843, when there was a massive Repeal meeting at Tara. O'Connell did all this because he thought that an overwhelming display of public opinion would make the case for Repeal too strong to resist. He wanted a peaceful revolution, as had happened with Emancipation. But there were big differences between 1829 and 1843, and O'Connell misjudged their importance. The most important of these was that, however much support Repeal had in Ireland, it had almost no support in the British House of Commons. While there had been many MPs opposed to restrictions on Catholics in 1828 and 1829, Liberals and Conservatives in 1843 genuinely thought that the Union brought benefits to all Irish people. Many had thought that the Irish parliament had been corrupt and that both the Catholic majority and the Protestant minority in Ireland were better protected and had better living conditions under the Union. O'Connell simply could not get the same support for Repeal in the House of Commons that he got for Emancipation. In May 1843, Peel told the House of Commons that not only did the government reject the idea of Repeal, it would use all its powers, including that of the military, to maintain the Union. Even so, Peel pushed some Irish reforms through the House of Commons in the early 1840s, including religious and educational reforms, as well as strict coercion laws to try to contain political agitation. In many ways, Peel was motivated by a desire to prevent the Repeal agitation from getting out of control. He thought that a policy of the gradual amelioration of Irish concerns would lessen the appetite for Repeal of the Union. But, in order to keep a lid on the possibility of militant agitation, and in order to keep the Protestant ascendancy secure, he also had to impose some force, which meant that his policy was one of 'coercion and conciliation', a policy which would be used by British governments, of both Liberal and Conservative parties, until 1920.

Even faced with this stern opposition, the Repeal movement continued its agitation, and planned a climactic meeting at Clontarf for 8 October 1843. Clontarf was symbolic because of Brian Boru's victory over the Vikings there in 1014. The government, however, banned the Clontarf meeting a few hours before it was due to start. O'Connell, who always insisted that political movements should be law-abiding, acceded to the government's demands and called off the meeting. O'Connell and some of his followers were arrested for conspiracy the next week. They were convicted and imprisoned from May to September 1844. This proved to be a depressing anti-climax to the Repeal movement. Meetings were still held, but they were poorly attended and the momentum was lost. O'Connell was in increasingly poor health after an operation in 1845, and the Repeal movement had faded away by the time he died in May 1847. O'Connell's failing health mirrored the full horror of the famine as it reached its peak in 1847 (see chapter three). With a barely audible voice, he made a desperate plea in the House of Commons for more government action to halt the starvation. 'Ireland is in your hands, in your power. If you do not save her, she cannot save herself.'

The history of this period is not only the story of O'Connell, reforms for Catholics, and the building of Irish nationalism through the Repeal movement. The history of the political opponents of these movements is also important. These opponents were largely the ascendancy class, and their political manifestation was Irish Toryism (linked to British Conservatism). O'Connell labelled them 'the Orange Party', and thought that his work for emancipation would destroy Irish Toryism. In fact, Irish Toryism became very successful, and there were more MPs of this political ideology than Irish nationalists in the British House of Commons by 1860. Alvin Jackson argues that, rather than destroy Irish Toryism, O'Connell helped it to thrive by showing the value of electoral organization and holding mass meetings to get the attention of the government. The Brunswick Clubs, organized in 1827–28 after the banning of the Orange Order, were very successful, and were instrumental in Irish Tory electoral victories at both the national and municipal level. The man who came to be the leader of Irish Protestantism in this period was the Reverend Henry Cooke (1788–1868). He held mass meetings to counteract what he saw as O'Connell's broad threat to Protestantism in Ireland, and he tried to ally Irish Protestant groups to the British Conservative party, in the same way that O'Connell had agreed to co-operate with the Liberals after 1835. He also opposed O'Connell's Repeal campaign and pointed to the economic success of Ulster (and Belfast in particular) as proof that Irish life was better under the Union. All this laid the groundwork for the success of unionism later in the nineteenth century and early twentieth century.

YOUNG IRELAND

Although the Repeal movement failed completely, it was to prove significant for Irish history because of its effects on succeeding generations of Irish nationalists. The first of these were a group called Young Ireland, who were active between 1842 and 1848. The early leaders were Thomas Davis (1814–45), Charles Gavan Duffy (1816–1903), and John Blake Dillon (1814–66). In 1842, they founded a newspaper called *The Nation*, in order to promote O'Connell's Repeal movement. Their ideas were to become very important in shaping future ideas of Irish nationalism. Davis, a Protestant Dublin lawyer, believed strongly that the backbone to nationhood was a strong national identity. This should include everyone who lived in Ireland, Catholic and Protestant, tenant and landlord. He was a fierce opponent of the sectarianism that had been witnessed amongst Repeal extremists. Charles Gavan Duffy was a Catholic journalist, who edited *The Nation* and was a political organizer. His main idea was that the Irish party in the British House of Commons should act independently of the British parties, and not form an alliance with any party that did not support Repeal of the Union. John Blake Dillon believed that nationalists of different opinions should work together and (at least initially) that they should use exclusively non-violent means. John Mitchel (1815–75), a Protestant lawyer from County Down, joined the group in 1844. He argued that complete independence from Britain was required in order for Ireland's problems to be solved. He was also the only Young Irelander to advocate the use of physical force from the beginning. James Fintan Lalor

(1807–49) contributed articles to *The Nation*, arguing that the major problem in Ireland concerned land and landholding. The question of nationalism had to be linked with the problems of high rents and the lack of security of tenure which plagued tenant farmers, Lalor argued, in order for common people to be able to agitate for independence without losing their economic base. These ideas were to be taken up by later nationalists such as Davitt and Parnell (see chapters 4 and 5).

Although Davis died of scarlet fever in 1845, Young Ireland continued agitating, and split with O'Connell over the question of the use of force in July 1846. Another important figure at this time was William Smith O'Brien (1803–64), a Cambridge-educated former conservative MP from Limerick, who had acted as head of the Repeal Association during O'Connell's imprisonment and had briefly joined Young Ireland from 1843 to 1846. In early 1848, there was a revolution in France, and the Young Irelanders sought to capture some of that spirit and apply it to a rebellion in Ireland. The government found out about their planned rising, and swept into Dublin to capture the rebels. They fled south and convinced O'Brien to lead them in a larger rising. They tried to organize local people into armed bands, but this largely failed in the face of clergy opposition and general disorganization. O'Brien led a skirmish in Ballingary, County Tipperary, on 29 July 1848. His group encountered police and two rebels were killed. Military reinforcements dispersed the rebels, and the rising fizzled out without further incident. For his part in the rising, Duffy was imprisoned until 1849. After his release, he revived *The Nation* and agitated for land reform in the early 1850s. He emigrated to Australia in 1855, became active in politics there, and was knighted in 1873. Although he did not take an active part in the rising because of physical incapacity, James Fintan Lalor was imprisoned for five months in 1848. He tried to revive and promote some of his ideas, but died in 1849. William Smith O'Brien was convicted of treason and transported to Tasmania. He was pardoned in 1854 and returned to Ireland in 1856, but was no longer active in politics. John Mitchel was convicted of treason in 1848 and transported to Tasmania. He escaped in 1853 and made his way to America, where he was involved in Irish-American politics. He returned to Ireland in 1875 and died in the same year.

The Young Ireland rebellion was considered pathetic by many, including *The Times*, which called it 'a cabbage-garden revolution'. What the Young Irelanders did accomplish, however, was the provision of a succinct propaganda for future nationalists. Not only did their journalism argue an easily understood nationalism, they produced a 'Library of Ireland', a series of biographies and histories which became a sort of extensive textbook for nationalists. It was the Library of Ireland series which did serious damage to O'Connell's reputation, together with the fact that Charles Gavan Duffy lived until 1903, and was able to influence opinion through his retrospective writings about the 1840s and 1850s.

ECONOMY, SOCIETY AND RELIGION

Politics, however, was not everything during this period. Important social, religious and economic changes took place that greatly affected subsequent Irish history, particularly the Famine of 1845–52 and the land issue later in the century. While most of Europe (and certainly England) was industrializing between 1750 and 1850, Ireland remained remarkably rural and agricultural, with nearly seventy-five per cent of the male workforce engaged primarily in farming. Less than twenty per cent of Irish people lived in towns, and since the population reached nearly eight and a half million by the early 1840s, this meant that the Irish countryside was the main place for employment and living.

Population growth in this period was staggering. Ireland outstripped all other European countries in growth rate before the Great Famine of 1845–52. There have been many explanations for this rapid increase in population. An increasing reliance on the potato was among the first. Since the potato was easy to cultivate and had great nutritional value, small farmers were able to have larger families (partly to work the fields), and people married younger and started their own families. But the evidence for this view is not conclusive, and an increased reliance on the potato may have been a result of growing population rather than the cause of it. Alternatively, the rapid growth in population may have been due to a fall in mortality rates and general improvements in health, but even this theory is difficult to prove. One of the few remaining ideas that has been generally accepted is that one important reason for population growth was high marital fertility. This implies that, although people may not have married at younger and younger ages (which would have increased population through a larger number of families in total), but that, once married (at any age), fertility was very high (that is, married couples had many more children than elsewhere in Europe). Economic historians argue all these points, but it is undoubted that an increasing (and largely rural) population was the main feature of Irish society before the Famine.

This society was generally made up of three main economic classes – landlords, farmers and labourers. Landlords owned the land, farmers (generally) rented parcels from them, and labourers worked for both classes. But these distinctions are too broadly drawn. Within each category (especially those of landlord and farmer), there were tremendous differences in wealth and power. There were a few very wealthy landlords who owned vast estates, but there were also those who only owned tiny estates. Farmers ranged from those who rented large tracts of land, and who had many labourers, to those who scratched out a living on small parcels of land and did all the work themselves. Labourers were also a diverse group, with some of them able to rent (or even buy) small plots of land near their dwellings, and others being completely landless and only working the land of others (farmers or landlords). Labourers made up the great majority of the rural population. Land sales and renting were very complicated affairs, and, generally speaking, labourers fared the worst. Contemporary commentators were often shocked at the conditions in which the poorest of the labourers had to live. But this may have been due to the complexities of the system rather than to excessive rents, and there were also great regional variations across the country.

The end of the Napoleonic Wars also had a great effect on the Irish economy, especially agriculture. The wars had raised agricultural prices, and led to an increase in prosperity. But their end brought about a price collapse to about two-thirds the wartime level. Prices grew only very gradually for the next three decades; economic hardship touched most levels of society, but hit the labourers worst. Still, agricultural production was fairly equivalent with that of most other European countries at this time, and a measure of agricultural success was that much of the potato crop was being sold for cash, rather than being used for subsistence (although this remained the practice for most poor labourers). Although agricultural production was good, the lives of many poor labourers were very difficult, and they often lived on the margins of survival. When local crop failure struck, those at this subsistence level often had to resort to begging and charity. Irish industries were also affected by larger economic changes in Europe. The Irish textile industry suffered along with the British textile industry during recessions in the 1820s. The woollen and cotton industries also declined during the 1830s. Further, linen production moved from individual workers in cottages to centralized factories (largely in Ulster), and many cottage workers lost their means of living. This contributed to the first big wave of nineteenth-century emigration from the poorer parts of the country from 1815 onwards.

All of these changes served to increase the differences in conditions between the regions in Ireland. The south and west were generally harder hit because their economies were less diverse and flexible than in the east and north. During periods of economic distress, rural violence and unrest flared up in various parts of the country. As in other aspects of Irish history, however, it is very difficult to find patterns for explanation. For the most part, rural unrest seems to have been highly localized and short term. Those forced to the economic margins often disrupted rural life by agitating against those farmers who were more economically affluent, by demanding lower rents, or higher wages, or even resorting to violence to meet the needs of subsistence. But even this is perhaps too much of a generalization, because much rural discontent was manifested in the poor stealing from the poor in order to survive. What is perhaps most certain is that the picture of rural Ireland portrayed by many novelists at the time as a place of bitter inhabitants and danger for the 'respectable' classes and the traveller was certainly exaggerated. While this image has fed on romanticized visions of rural Ireland as a place of wild beauty, in terms of presenting the country to foreigners (mainly the English), it provided for much misunderstanding and prejudice that was to last for generations.

It is very difficult, however, to make firm generalizations about the Irish economy during this period. It is fairly clear that it was a poor country in relation to the rest of Europe. It is also clear, however, that between 1800 and 1845, those who held land above a moderate amount witnessed increasing prosperity. Those without such holdings were in a gradually worsening condition in this period. And, perhaps most importantly, the difference between the prosperity of Great Britain and that of Ireland was increasing.

Urban life was similarly complicated. As British factories started to produce cheap manufactured goods, artisans who had made such things in the past started to suffer from the competition. Yet merchants were often quite successful, and industrialization in Dublin and Belfast became a permanent fixture. Unskilled labourers, however, were left to the fluctuations of the economy, and they were almost universally poor. One main feature of urban economics in this period was the general division between Catholic and Protestant merchants and businessmen. Although they were fairly evenly balanced in terms of wealth and often worked together to mutual advantage in big projects such as railways, in other respects they were kept apart. Local charities, political organizations and clubs were usually divided along Catholic–Protestant lines. This division would also frequently appear when businessmen supported political movements. Not surprisingly, O'Connell's movement attracted support from Catholic merchants and businessmen, and Irish Toryism received equal support from Protestant merchants and businessmen. Even so, political support was not universal amongst religious groups, and O'Connell, for instance, found it difficult to understand the economic arguments of labourers and artisans who said that Emancipation had done nothing to improve their economic conditions. One of the most important ways in which Irish urban life was similar to rural life during this period was in the numbers of urban poor, and the conditions in which they lived (which may, indeed, have been worse than those in the country). There was a good deal of unemployment, and many families lived on the verge of starvation and were constantly harried by sickness and disease.

Another important area of change in Ireland during this period was in religious life, especially in the expansion of the Catholic Church through the training of more priests and the building of more churches and cathedrals. While the Catholic religion had survived under the Penal Laws, there were not enough priests to cope with the rising population. Maynooth College had been founded by the government in 1795 to provide for the native training of priests (who had previously gone to continental Europe, particularly France, for seminary training). Although this increased the number of priests being trained, it could not keep up with the numbers of new parishioners. In 1800, there were roughly 2,675 parishioners per priest, but in 1835 there were nearly 3,000, and the geographical distribution of clergy was uneven. Throughout the early part of the nineteenth century, new churches were built and old ones expanded to allow for increasing numbers.

Furthermore, the Catholic Church attempted to dictate a more regular set of religious practices to its flock. In much of the country, folk celebrations and superstitions were very popular, and Christian observance of important events (like marriage and death) was often accompanied by other rites which echoed what was thought of as a pre-Christian, Celtic Irish past. These observances and celebrations, however, were not usually held in opposition to church practices, nor would the participants have seen themselves as being anti-Christian or anti-Catholic. They were simply the customs of each region or locality, and they did not affect the degree of Catholic devotion. The church tried to rein in these practices, without complete success. Many people were opposed to losing what they saw as part of their local tradition, and some of the more tolerant local priests did not actively seek to impose restrictions on their parishes. These attempted reforms were more successful in towns and in areas where more prosperous farmers were dominant, and where folk practices had been less pervasive anyway. But these reforms were partially complete, and the 'devotional revolution' which has been traditionally described as a pious reaction to God's wrath during the Famine can more properly be dated to the few decades before 1845.

Protestant religions underwent similar changes in Ireland during the first half of the nineteenth century. Along with their sister churches in Britain, Episcopalians (members of the Anglican Church of Ireland) and Presbyterians saw an increase in the power of central church authorities, as well as an increase in devotional practice. Evangelicalism also came over from England, and the Methodists became a distinct and growing denomination in

Ireland. Perhaps most importantly, however, was a growing consciousness of Protestantism and an increased desire to emphasize differences from Catholicism. This paralleled the rise in Protestant political consciousness (partly in response to O'Connell). The most striking theological aspect of Irish Protestantism during this period, however, was the impact of evangelicalism, not only in its own right, but in its effects on the existing denominations. Several important Church of Ireland ministers were 'converted', and adopted an evangelical tone in their work. The rise of evangelicalism and the increased organization of the Catholic Church eventually led to an increase of sectarian misunderstanding and mistrust. While there were still many examples of ecumenical co-operation as the first half of the nineteenth century continued, the divisions between all religions hardened.

INTERPRETATIONS

O'Connell did what many other Irish politicians were unable to do. Most nationalists tried to educate the populace to somewhat complex political ideas. O'Connell, on the other hand, used religion to motivate the people politically, which made it easier for most people to understand. In the immediate years after his death, O'Connell was treated as a hero in Ireland. A change in interpretation began in the 1860s, when some of the Young Irelanders, notably John Mitchel and Charles Gavan Duffy, started to critique O'Connell in print. They argued that O'Connell was not forceful enough, that he was too willing to co-operate with British politicians, and that his own financial and personal problems affected his ability to gain reforms for Ireland. Mitchel was particularly fierce in his condemnation of O'Connell's policy of applying moral rather than physical force since it allowed the government to ignore the worsening famine of 1845–52. In addition to these charges, there were a few important political and religious changes that made the memory of O'Connell seem less relevant to Irish Catholics and tenants. In 1869, the government disestablished the Anglican Church of Ireland, so that it no longer held privileged status over the Catholic majority. Land reforms in the 1870s and 1880s eased poor tenants' concerns somewhat, and it seemed as if some of the more important aims that O'Connell desired were achieved without him. O'Connell's reputation was dealt a blow by these interpretations and events, and he remained unpopular in nationalist interpretations until after the Second World War in the twentieth century. Indeed, an attempt to preserve and restore O'Connell's family home in 1947 (the centenary of his death) had to rely on publicizing his work on Catholic Emancipation and suppress the failed attempts at Repeal of the Union in order to gain financial support. The state of O'Connell's reputation at this time is also shown by the fact that, in 1945, the centenary of Thomas Davis's death, the Irish government published a commemorative volume, *Thomas Davis and Young Ireland*, while O'Connell's centenary passed without official commemoration in 1947.

Things started to change very slowly after the Second World War. In 1956, Thomas P. O'Neill argued in an important chapter in T.D. Williams and R.D. Edwards' *The Great Famine: Studies in Irish History* (1956) that the Famine was a disaster quite beyond the scope of any one person to affect, and, by implication, that O'Connell's policy of non-violence could not be blamed for government inaction. In 1963, Kevin Nowlan argued that the Young Irelanders had gone too far in their condemnation of both O'Connell's tactics and his personality. Angus Macintyre wrote in 1965 that it was virtually impossible to find enough serious scholarship dealing with O'Connell. His book, *The Liberator*, showed in detail not only how O'Connell acted as a politician within the House of Commons, but how his party set the organizational and ideological tone for Irish parties in the House of Commons for the rest of the century. Textbooks in the later 1960s and early 1970s, including those by Beckett, McCaffrey and MacDonagh (all listed in the Further Reading section at the end of this book), went a long way towards rehabilitating O'Connell and placing him at the centre of Irish history during this period. J.C. Beckett's *The Making of Modern Ireland 1603–1923* (1966), contains one of the strongest interpretations of O'Connell's contribution to the organization of public opinion and Irish national identity, what Roy Foster has called 'the mobilization of popular politics'. Beckett wrote,

O'Connell's great contribution to the development of modern Ireland was that he called into being, and organized for political action, the force of mass opinion; he taught the Roman Catholic majority to regard itself as the Irish nation; and all succeeding nationalist leaders ... have had to build upon the foundations that he laid ... [Despite his failings] ... he remains a man of transcendent genius, which he devoted to the service of his native land: no other single person has left such an unmistakable mark on the history of Ireland.

This emphasis on creating a sense of strong national identity mainly for Catholics raises the question of O'Connell's attitudes towards other religions. Here there is less scholarly work available. Maurice O'Connell argued that O'Connell's speeches and private correspondence indicate that he was one of the first European statesmen to argue for both freedom of religion and the separation of church and state. In this sense, O'Connell shares his ideology with other European liberal Catholics of the period, and he often expressed such opinions concerning the state of religions in France, Spain and Italy. Oliver MacDonagh's two-volume biography of O'Connell appeared in 1988 and 1989, and attempted to remove many of the myths and misunderstandings of O'Connell's complex career and personality, as well as provide an analysis of why he has been unfavourably compared to that other great nationalist at the end of the nineteenth century, Charles Stewart Parnell (see chapter 5).

THREE

The Famine, 1845–52

Few episodes in modern Irish history have become as important as the Great Famine. A mysterious potato blight attacked the country in 1845, and a general food shortage led to massive loss of life and equally massive emigration to other countries over the next seven years. Not only was the Famine a calamitous and deadly event in its own right, it has come to be seen as a defining point in Irish history. It has raised questions about the over-population of the country in the early nineteenth century, the ways in which Ireland was governed and treated within the United Kingdom and the increased emigration to North America and the antipodes. It established bitterness and deep resentment towards Britain, which has also had long-standing consequences. Any event of this significance attracts controversy, and the Famine has certainly seen its share. Folk tales, political rhetoric and novels have all kept the history of the Famine alive, but they have also been responsible for the continuation of many of its myths and misunderstandings. This is somewhat ironic because the Famine is one of the best recorded events in modern world history. Extensive government reports, written eyewitness accounts and the records of voluntary organizations provide us with a very clear picture of what happened during the Famine. What is not so clear is why it happened, and whether anything more could have been done to prevent the death and emigration. It is generally agreed that roughly one million people perished as a result of starvation and disease, and that a further million or so emigrated in desperation to find a better life. Everything else about the Famine is subject to differing interpretations, and historians have been arguing about it for decades.

PRECONDITIONS

There were several preconditions which limited the potential and flexibility of the Irish economy in the late eighteenth and early nineteenth centuries. Compared with Britain, Ireland did not possess large stores of mineral resources, such as coal. Nor was it at the centre of international trading routes. And the climate and history of landownership in the country lent itself to a type of agriculture that provided limited employment. During the eighteenth century, many landowners preferred to rent their land to middlemen tenants on long-term leases. These middlemen then sub-let their farms to smaller farmers, and the land continued to be sub-divided among sons. Further, from the 1750s, there had been a shift from pastoral farming (where a farmer had a relatively diverse system of farming with a few types of crops and livestock of various kinds), to tillage (or arable) farming (which meant concentrating on one type of crop, usually the potato). There had been a rising demand for grain in Britain (owing to a rising population fuelled by the Industrial Revolution), and tillage farming seemed best suited to meeting that demand. The British wars against Napoleon (1800–15) increased this demand further, and the Irish agricultural economy was temporarily and artificially buoyed by the wars. So, although there is some disagreement amongst historians about the efficiency of pre-Famine agriculture in Ireland, it was certainly true that the country was heavily dependent on agriculture by the early nineteenth century.

This overwhelmingly agricultural economy led to three important preconditions which made the Famine worse when it came: overpopulation, poverty and dependence on the potato as the main crop and food source. Population, boosted by the labour-intensive tillage farming system, continued to grow rapidly in the early nineteenth century. Compared with other European countries, Ireland's population grew dramatically between 1750 and 1845. In 1800, there were 5 million people in Ireland, in 1821 6.5 million, and by 1841 over 8 million, which was around 700 people per square mile. There were significant regional variations, however, as western and southern counties (where the effects of the Famine would be more dire) saw more growth than the north and east. Overall, the rate of population growth had started to slow down after 1821, but it still left Ireland overcrowded. This overpopulation caused severe unemployment, and emigration to Britain and North America started. For many of those left in Ireland, the 1820s and 1830s were bleak decades, and many travellers to the country commented on the worsening conditions of the Irish poor. There were bad harvests in 1816–17 and 1821–22, and famine conditions hit some areas. But these famines were highly localized and short-lived, and did not cause people to think there was the possibility of a widespread famine. After 1815, many of the landlords who had leased their land through middlemen took back possession, and the smaller tenants were placed on yearly, and less secure, leases. In the non-agricultural parts of the economy, the 1820s and 1830s were also times of struggle. Irish manufacturing and business suffered during this period. The Irish linen and cotton trades collapsed under the pressure of competition from Britain. The mechanization of the linen industry put many cottage labourers out of work, and they often turned to small plots of land and grew potatoes in order to survive. By 1845, the living standards for the Irish poor (estimated at half the population) had declined significantly, and there is little doubt that the potato blight that arrived in that year would have had less of an impact if the economy had been more flexible, and if the poor had had a greater margin of economic security.

Each of these preconditions, overpopulation, poverty and dependence on the potato, made the Irish situation more vulnerable. Perhaps the most tragic was the dependence on the potato, because it provided an essential and nutritious diet for the poor, yet dependence on it kept them poor. The rising Irish population became dependent on the potato because it could be tilled easily, it yielded more crop per acre than any grain, it was a good subsistence food and could provide the nutritional value of grain at one-third the cost. The Irish ate more potatoes than any other people in the world. Adult males ate over six kilos per day, women and children over ten years old ate nearly five kilos, and young children ate over two. Potatoes were also used as a cash crop, and labourers were sometimes paid in land to grow their own crop. The problem with the potato was that it was perishable and could not be stored like grain. This meant that if anything happened to the crop in any one year, there would be a general food shortage. So, had there been any other crop or livestock crisis in the 1840s, the reliance of the poor on the potato would probably have seen them through. With cruel efficiency, however, nature struck at the very foundation of Irish agriculture.

THE BLIGHT

The summer of 1845 was wet. Ordinarily, farmers would have been concerned that the excessive damp would damage the potato crop. Early reports, however, seemed to indicate a promising harvest for the year. In August a potato disease, called a blight, arrived in the south of England. It had first been seen on the east coast of the United States in the summer of 1843, and had made its way to Europe by 1845. By September it was in Ireland. Although it was not identified until much later, the blight was a fungus called *phytophthora infestans*, which lived in mild and damp conditions and spread by spores. It attacked potato plants through the leaves and the stalk, working its way down to the potato itself and rotting it. Although local reports of the first Irish potato harvest in September were optimistic, the blight was found to have destroyed many crops in counties Wexford and Waterford in the south-east. Even this was little cause for alarm, as the blight seemed localized, and there had been potato crop failures in the past that did not affect the whole country.

The late harvest in mid-October was found to be diseased in many places, however. This late harvest was traditionally the main harvest of the year, and the loss of much of the crop caused considerable alarm. The east was hit very badly, and as the months went by, the blight moved west. One-third of the late harvest was lost by mid-November, and even stored potatoes were found to be affected. This was the worst crop failure in over a hundred years, and the very real possibility of famine loomed. In November 1845, the British Prime Minister, the Conservative Sir Robert Peel (1788–1850), immediately established a scientific commission to determine what the blight was and what was needed to counteract it. This commission thought the blight was a disease of the potato plant itself, and disregarded the hypothesis of a specialist who said that it was a fungus (the cure for which was not discovered until the 1880s). Many months were spent in ultimately fruitless examination of the blight. At the same time as he established the commission, Peel bought £100,000 worth of maize from the United States. He did this partly to stave off hunger, but also to stabilize food prices in Ireland. But it was never Peel's plan for the government to feed all the people directly. This was not generally thought to be the proper role of the state in the nineteenth century. Instead, Peel set up a relief commission to deal with hunger and unemployment. Local voluntary efforts were given funding (sometimes as much as two-thirds of their expenditure). Relief works were also set up to ease unemployment. Peel also wanted a system whereby Irish landowners took responsibility for relief. Nearly 650 local committees were founded, with local landowners in control, to distribute cheap food to the poor.

In early 1846, Peel began a public works project to provide temporary work for the poor and unemployed so that they would be able to buy food. A second goal of the works was to make permanent improvements to the country. These relief efforts, combined with the ability of the country to survive one season's blight, meant that very few people died of hunger or disease in the winter of December 1845 to February 1846. And the spring and early summer of 1846 looked promising, so much so that many farmers felt confident enough to plant potato seeds again. But other troubling signs of famine continued. The corn meal from the United States was less palatable than potatoes, and needed to be cooked for a long time. Hungry people were unwilling to wait, and often ate the grain partially cooked, which caused serious digestive problems. In June 1846, Peel decided to repeal the corn laws, a series of acts which protected British agriculture from an influx of cheap grain from abroad. Irish MPs in the House of Commons had asked that Peel halt grain exports from Ireland, but he refused, thinking that such a ban on exports would ruin the economy and make conditions in Ireland much worse. It was better, he argued, to allow free trade in grain between Britain, Ireland and other countries. This would provide cheaper grain for both the British and Irish poor. The repeal of the corn laws, however, angered many members of the Conservative party who thought the laws protected the British (and Irish) farmer. This split the party, and Peel's government fell in June 1846.

Lord John Russell (1792–1878), leader of the Liberals, formed a government, and was initially reluctant to follow Peel's course. When Russell came into office, he faced several Famine problems. The first was the expectations that had been raised by Peel's reaction in 1845–46. The second was that the general European food supply situation in 1846 was much worse than it had been the year before. Further, and perhaps most significantly, Russell and the Liberals were more attached to the policy of *laissez-faire* in terms of government involvement in the economy. *Laissez-faire* (literally, 'let do') generally meant that government interference in the economy was not only unwise, but unnatural, and would possibly make food shortages much worse. Rather than plan for another potato failure in the harvest of 1846, the new government thought that the better course was to end the direct purchase of food, and to reform basic elements of the Irish economy (which they thought was backward and unnatural) so that the country would be able to survive food shortages. These reforms could be brought about by more locally based relief and public works projects (which Russell hoped would set the Irish economy on a modern footing). Strong *laissez-faire* men in the government, particularly Sir Charles Wood (1800–85) in the cabinet and the civil servant Sir Charles Trevelyan (1807–86) at the treasury department, thought that the problem in Ireland was not overpopulation but underdevelopment. They thought that Ireland possessed the necessary resources to become economically stable, though not to become an economic power. What was needed was the will and entrepreneurship to make the best of the country's resources. Relief was to be limited to public projects, but they were to be paid for out of local taxes. Russell's government wanted to place the responsibility for relieving Irish distress on Irish landlords, whom they blamed for creating the conditions that made the Famine possible. 'Irish property must support Irish poverty', was how Trevelyan put it. This policy of local relief and reform might well have worked had the only real problem been a slow recovery from the 1845 blight without any further shortages. The assumption that this was the case was shown when the government closed the public works in August so that workers could attend to the harvest.

THE COMING OF FAMINE

The harvest of 1846 was black. The failure of the potato crop was complete. Farmers dug up fields of rotten potatoes, and the true disaster of the Famine had begun. Starvation began in earnest and people flooded into the local relief works. The number employed in the relief works went from 30,000 in September 1846, when they re-opened, to nearly 500,000 in December. But the public relief works did little to solve either the problem of employment or hunger. Workers were paid below market rates, and increasingly pointless 'make work' projects were begun. By the end of 1846, it was clear that the works were failing. Even some of those employed were falling over from hunger and dying next to their work. The harsh winter of December 1846 to February 1847 was no help, and food supplies became dangerously low. The government realized that the mounting death toll had to be met with new policies. They centralized the administration of the relief works (although they were still largely paid for from local taxation), and by March 1847, roughly 750,000 people were employed (still at wages below subsistence levels). During 1846, some grain was held back from export and overall export levels dropped dramatically. The amount exported was still large, equivalent to nearly 1 million tons of potatoes, but that was less that ten per cent of what was destroyed by the fungus. A total prohibition on exports, therefore, would have saved a small proportion of people, but would not have stopped massive starvation and death in the winter of 1846–47.

'Black 47', as that year has come to be known in Famine folklore, was the worst year yet in terms of mortality and emigration. By now, the news of the condition of Ireland had spread to many parts of the world, and voluntary relief funds came from Britain, the United States and Australia, and from Irish soldiers serving in the British Army. Scotland was suffering from its own famine (which turned out to be limited in comparison with Ireland's). Most of the voluntary relief came from Britain, with the Quakers taking an early lead. They visited Ireland, wrote reports on the Famine and its effects, and set up their own local relief committees distributing food. The British Association for the Relief of Extreme Distress in Ireland and Scotland raised nearly

£500,000, with Queen Victoria making an early and example-setting personal donation of £2,000. Relief committees in the United States sent over $500,000, and Irish immigrants there sent money to family members to encourage emigration. 1846–7 was also a bleak period for Britain, which led to an unwillingness, perhaps even an inability, from the government to increase Irish Famine relief. Bad harvests in Britain in 1846 led to a huge trade deficit and a drain on gold reserves in the Bank of England. Credit was nearly impossible to obtain, and some industries, such as cotton, suffered severely. Although short, this financial crisis was one of the worst in modern times, and had come at a particularly bad time for the relief of Irish distress.

THE SOUP

In January 1847, many Irish peers, members of parliament and landlords met in Dublin and appealed to the government for direct aid to ease mass mortality. Russell and his government finally realized that their policies were not working. They ended the public works projects and extended direct relief in late January. 'The pressing matter at present,' Russell said, 'is to keep the people alive.' This was a major change in the basic thinking of statesmen at the time, and did not find universal agreement in government circles. Although there were disagreements in the cabinet and the treasury, the government set up soup kitchens throughout the spring and summer of 1847. Compared with the public works projects, the soup kitchens were more successful. During the summer of 1847, three million people per day were being fed at a cost of two pence per person. The total cost of the soup kitchens in 1847 was around £1,700,000, a fraction of what the public works had cost. The soup kitchens had done more with less, but they were a mixed success. In some areas, they began too late, and in most places demand outstripped supply. The food quality was low and the quantities were small. The number of deaths fell during the summer of 1847, but historians have debated whether this was due to the soup or the effect of a mild summer. The soup kitchens, however, were always intended to be temporary, and were shut down (amid much protest) in September 1847, just as they appeared to be having a beneficial effect. Parliament had put pressure on the government to put the burden for Irish relief back on local landlords and taxpayers.

The soup kitchens have also been remembered in Famine folklore as the places where relief from starvation and death were given at the cost of religious conversion. A few private soup kitchens were guilty of demanding or convincing people to convert to Protestantism before giving them any food aid. Although the number of soup kitchens where this occurred was actually very small, word soon spread that 'taking the soup' meant a necessary rejection of the Catholic faith, and 'souperism' has had a hold in the popular Irish historical mind ever since. Catholics who did convert at these few places were called 'jumpers', which remained a family insult for their descendants well into the twentieth century. Like so much else about the Famine, however, souperism mythology has been difficult to displace. Government soup kitchens were banned from conversion or requiring religious pledges, and the Quakers (who had perhaps the largest number of private food depots) never employed the practice. Further, the image of souperism has unfairly tainted the relief work done by many Church of Ireland and Presbyterian clergy, who often worked in conjunction with the local Catholic priest to bring relief to their parishes. But perhaps the greatest shame of souperism is that the rumour of it may have prevented many people from travelling to the soup kitchens in search of relief. We will never know how many died of starvation for fear of losing their faith.

HUNGER, DISEASE AND EMIGRATION

As the terrible winter of early 1847 continued, various illnesses related to hunger and poverty began to spread. By the spring of 1847, people were not only starving to death, but hunger left them open to diseases that their bodies simply could not fight. Compared to the numbers dying from disease, relatively few people died of starvation. Hunger lowered the body's natural resistance, and many otherwise non-fatal diseases became fatal. Since most of these conditions had a weakening and wasting effect on the body, sufferers could not work and many could not travel to relief stations. They simply declined and died, in their cottages or by the side of the road. Even Ireland's relatively good network of hospitals and medical facilities could not handle the massive need for medical care. Temporary fever hospitals were set up and staff were recruited, but it was all inadequate, and there were no known cures for famine fever or dysentery, two of the most common diseases.

It was these conditions which drove many of the desperate to emigrate, and 1847 saw the first real wave of Famine emigrants. Emigration as a solution soon began to move down the economic scale to the poorest levels. This shows the desperation to leave, since this class found it very difficult to find money for the passage. Most of those who left in early 1847 went to Liverpool or Glasgow. In many cases, British ports were the place to catch trans-Atlantic ships to North America. But demand to leave the country was so great that direct sailings from Irish ports soon began. More than 100,000 people sailed for Canada in the spring of 1847, and roughly twenty per cent died before they got there. Many of these deaths were caused by passage on ill-fitted or unseaworthy 'coffin ships'. By the time that direct sailings from Irish ports began, the government ship inspection system was overwhelmed, and many ships slipped out without being examined. Passengers with Famine-related diseases were often allowed on board, and overcrowding and lack of food and medical care compounded the problem.

THE EXTENSION OF THE POOR LAW

The potato crop did not fail in the summer of 1847. This led some people, notably Trevelyan and other government officials, to declare that the Famine was ending. There were other reasons to think this. There were reports of a good grain harvest in Ireland, and grain imports from America were beginning to stem the tide of starvation. The harvest reports were greatly exaggerated, however. The good grain harvests were largely limited to the north and east, and the rest of the country, which relied on a potato economy, saw no easing of conditions. But in London the belief that the worst was over won the day. In June, the government passed the Poor Law Extension Act, which put the burden of paying for Famine relief on local Irish taxes, in an attempt to get the landlords to pay for what the government thought was ultimately their responsibility. This 'extension' of the Poor Law meant that paupers could get 'outdoor relief', that is, relief without working for it 'inside' the workhouses. It was difficult, however, to convince a sceptical parliament that these poor deserved outdoor relief. The government was forced, therefore, to agree to include a 'quarter acre clause' in the bill, which said that any tenant who held more than a quarter acre of land was ineligible for relief. This meant that many of the working poor could not get relief, and many quarter-acre owners willingly gave up their holdings in order to qualify for help. This Poor Law affected many landlords as well. The depressed economy had whittled away their financial reserves, and they found themselves staring at bankruptcy. Evictions of those who could not pay rents rose, which threw even more people on to poverty relief. By the winter of 1847, the Poor Law Guardians (the committee who set and collected the taxes that funded the workhouses and the outdoor relief) found it almost impossible to do their jobs. The taxes were often ignored or proved difficult to collect, and the amount of money they raised was insufficient to ease the problems of unemployment and suffering. So the Poor Law system was not working well. The workhouses had been generally overcrowded by October 1846, and the strain of 'Black 47' was almost unbearable for them. Poor Law officials in the regions and in Dublin begged the London government to do more. Lord Clarendon, the new governor of Ireland, pleaded with the government not to 'allow above a certain number' to starve. In response, Trevelyan at the treasury decided that much of the west of Ireland deserved more relief funding, but even that proved to be inadequate.

Although 'Black 47' has often been characterized as the height of the Famine, 1848 was just as bad, perhaps worse. The potato blight returned in full force in that year. The official estimated loss was half the crop, but again it was worse in the west of the country. The 1848 blight and Famine showed how overwhelmed the Poor Law system and its workhouses were. Over three-quarters of a million people were on outdoor relief by July 1849. Even more people tried to cram into the workhouses but were turned away. By this time, it was not just the poor tenants who were clamouring for relief; it was also the small farmers who collapsed under the crop failure and, ironically, the burden of the

Poor Law taxes. The death toll in the workhouses rose; roughly 2,500 people were dying each week in the workhouses. This was only partly due to conditions in the workhouses themselves, and mainly due to diseases outside. By the time many of these people got to the door of the workhouse, they were already dying. By 1848, it was also clear that some of the Boards of Guardians who ran the workhouses were corrupt. Government rules for running workhouses were ignored. Irish merchants often acted as Poor Law Guardians so they could get the relatively lucrative government contracts for food and provisions, and they often did not deliver on those contracts. The government was too overwhelmed with other relief work to prosecute them. Another tragedy of 1848 was that private charity had reached its financial limit. The Quakers, amongst the most generous of private relief organizations, were stretched to the limit. The winter of 1848–9, therefore, proved to be a particularly terrible one in terms of deaths from starvation and disease.

NEW RELIEF POLICIES

In early 1849, Russell tried other avenues of relief. He first introduced the 'rate in aid' plan, in which the relatively more prosperous north and east of Ireland would pay higher taxes to support the ravaged west and south. This was not well received in the north and east, and many landlords refused to pay the extra taxes. The government then tried another tack, aimed at correcting what they saw as one of the underlying problems leading to the Famine. This was a 'free trade in land' policy. The idea was to open up landownership to the general market, making it more likely that the middle and lower middle classes (from England as well as Ireland) would be able to buy land, and break the dependency on large landlords for both land and employment. But the plan did not have the desired effect. Most of the land sold simply changed hands between the existing landowning class. These two efforts at solving underlying problems showed that the government had hardened in its *laissez-faire* policy towards direct food aid. Perhaps the only positive thing to happen in 1849 was that Queen Victoria visited Ireland, in order to solidify the perception that the Famine was coming to an end, and to try to help the free trade in land policy. The Queen visited Dublin, Cork, Belfast and some of the Kildare countryside. She was enthusiastically received by huge crowds wherever she went, but she only saw a limited amount of the country, and none of the ravaged west. In some important ways, the Queen's visit gave a psychological boost to many Irish people, but the marking of the end of the Famine was, sadly, two or three years too soon.

In 1850, Russell persuaded the treasury to give £300,000 pounds for Irish relief, and to rearrange Irish Famine debts so that they would be easier to repay. But the terrible cycle of blight, starvation and disease continued. The workhouses were increasingly besieged, and voluntary efforts had completely collapsed. The Quakers, out of money, had given up their work in June 1849, believing that 'the Government alone could raise the funds and carry out the measures necessary . . . to save the lives of the people.' This, of course, meant that the under-funded and over-worked government relief systems were burdened even further. But little direct aid was forthcoming from London, and 1850 and 1851 saw many of the same scenes as 1847 and 1848. The potato crop was healthy in 1852, however, and the beginning of the end was in sight. The harvests of that year were not affected by the blight, although the high potato yields of pre-Famine years were not reached. Slowly, Irish agriculture and the economy began to rebuild themselves, and the pressure on poor relief eased (although emigration continued at a high rate, no doubt due to fears of a return of the blight or the hopelessness of a ravaged economy).

Ireland was not free of the potato blight, however. It returned in 1860, 1879, 1890 and 1897, but for much shorter periods each time. These blights did not create famines like that of 1845–52, although there was a good deal of food shortage and some starvation. By the later Victorian period, attitudes to the relief of suffering had changed considerably, strict *laissez-faire* policies had been seen to be failures, and the Famine had forced people to realize that dependency on the potato was potentially dangerous. These other blights were less devastating, then, and government responses more humane. Finally, a cure for the blight of *phytophthora infestans*, using a treatment of copper sulphate, was discovered in 1882. Tragically, however, a similar treatment using copper was found to have worked to some extent in south

Wales in 1846, but it failed to attract the notice of the government commission looking into the problem. It is not clear how well this copper treatment would have worked during the Irish Famine of 1845–52, or whether it could have been applied quickly enough to prevent massive crop losses, but it may be seen as symbolic of the larger tragedy of the Famine, and of the inadequate measures taken to relieve it.

EFFECTS

Like most major historical events, the effects of the Famine are disputed, and it is clear from this section and the 'Interpretations' section that they will be discussed and debated for a long time. The most immediate effect, of course, was the number of people who died. Economic historians use the phrase 'excessive mortality' to describe the number of deaths in a given situation that are above the natural death rate at the time. In this sense, the Famine and its attendant diseases killed roughly a million people. The worst affected counties were Mayo and Sligo, in the far west, with 50,000–60,000 deaths per year during the Famine. The rest of the western counties (Galway, Roscommon and Leitrim) lost 40,000–50,000 per year. Cork and Clare in the south-west lost 30,000–40,000 per year. The north and the east suffered less. Dublin lost under 10,000 per year, as did many other eastern counties. Other counties, particularly those in the north-east, lost between 10,000 and 30,000 per year.

Agriculture and the agricultural economy were heavily affected by the Famine. Although some historians have pointed out that many agricultural changes and much modernization was taking place before 1845, it is clear that the Famine changed the way people thought about Irish agriculture. The post-Famine Irish family farm mixed tillage and livestock, with an emphasis on the livestock for cash income. Land was no longer subdivided amongst sons. There was less need for a large family to run these farms, so the pattern of early marriage ended. But perhaps most significantly, the Famine placed the possibility of emigration permanently in the Irish rural mind. Younger sons often left the country rather than trying their hand at other Irish industries. This strengthened the image of Ireland as a land of no opportunity. But

the new agriculture did not reach all areas, particularly the poorer regions in the west. There, poor farmers returned to their small holdings, and a heavy reliance on the potato. Large landowners and farmers with more land were the least affected by the Famine. As a result of evictions, clearances and depopulation, many were able to consolidate and even enlarge their holdings. They were also able to use government reforms for agricultural modernization.

The political effects of the Famine were also significant. Resentment against the English deepened and spread, although no effective political force or movement was able to use this resentment to agitate for meaningful change. The resentment was directed first at the landlords, which flared up in the agricultural aggression of later decades (see chapter 5). It also provided strong folk memories, which were used by Fenian radicals to demand independence in the 1860s. And, of course, those forced to emigrate to North America and Australia brought with them a bitterness that was eventually turned into political action and, more importantly, political fund-raising, as the Famine immigrants in those countries gradually rose in economic and political prominence. Again, this was to have major effects in the late nineteenth and early twentieth centuries. Back in Ireland, however, the Famine's impact on the structure of Irish politics was less inflamed, but potentially more devastating. Localism and local issues, rather than ideas of repealing the Union, came to dominate Irish politics from the end of the Famine until well into the late 1860s. Some of the most troubling effects of the Famine were psychological. These, of course, are difficult to measure, but show themselves in post-Famine literature, political speeches and folk customs. In the late nineteenth century, songs and ballads bemoaned the coming of the blight. Some of these songs gave the impression that Ireland was a permanently tragic country, while others were clearly more political, blaming landlords and the British government for the deaths and emigration. Some historians have noted that market fairs and traditional gatherings went into a period of decline in the immediate post-Famine decades, and those that were held were far more sober and orderly affairs than they had been in the past.

The Famine has also been seen as causing the decline of the Irish language. Not only had the Famine hit predominantly Irish-speaking areas (and therefore many Irish speakers died or emigrated to English-speaking countries), it also seemed to symbolize that Ireland was a backward country. Many people thought that the Famine was the result of backward agricultural practices and fatalist Irish thinking. The gradual loss of Irish seemed to reinforce this. Like most historical trends, however, the decline in Irish speaking is more complicated than this. The Famine did kill or send away a disproportionately large number of Irish speakers. In 1845, there were over three million Irish speakers in Ireland and about half a million elsewhere (mainly in Britain). By 1851, the total number of Irish speakers had fallen to below two million. But Irish speaking had been declining rapidly before the Famine, and fewer and fewer young people were learning it as their mother tongue in the 1830s and early 1840s. This was partly the effect of the Act of Union of 1800, which meant that ties with Britain were even closer than they had been before. It was also because there had not been a conscious effort to keep the language alive. Daniel O'Connell and other nationalist leaders had not linked the Irish language with demands for Irish sovereignty, and it was not until the end of the nineteenth century (when the language was nearly dead) that a new generation of nationalists tried to revive it (see chapter 6).

The Famine also had a strong effect on religion. With its overtones of moral punishment and curse from God, the Famine helped accelerate the 'devotional revolution' that had been slowly taking place in previous decades. This was especially true of the Catholic religion, which became increasingly formal in the mid-nineteenth century. Cardinal Cullen, an authoritarian and reforming leader, helped revitalize the Catholic Church in the post-Famine decades. Protestant churches also saw increases in attendance and devotional worship. But some Catholics and Protestants saw the Famine as largely a Catholic problem. That is, many Catholics thought they were the victims of British Protestant indifference and souperism because they were Catholics, and many Protestants felt that providence had spared them from hunger and disease precisely because they were not Catholic. So sectarian distrust began to solidify, especially in Belfast and other parts of the north-east, where many Protestants and Catholics had fled to avoid starvation and disease.

INTERPRETATIONS

As stated at the beginning of this chapter, interpretations of the Famine have been under contention almost since it ended in 1852. Folk memories have preserved vivid images of the Famine. Some, such as those of food being taken out of the country, universally callous landlords and the uncaring British, are half-truths. Others, such as stories of brutal evictions, are true. These stories are still told in Ireland, and in countries where descendants of Irish immigrants have made their homes, so they are very important in their own right. They are also important because they provide the basis for popular ideas about the Famine and its importance for Irish history. Some of these folk memories were, no doubt, fed by the first major interpretation of the Famine, which dates from the decades immediately following it. In 1848, Charles Gavan Duffy, the Young Ireland nationalist (see chapter 2), wrote that the Famine all around him was 'a fearful murder committed on the mass of the people'. Later, in 1860, the Irish nationalist John Mitchel (see chapter 5), wrote *The Last Conquest of Ireland (Perhaps)*, in which he argued that the Famine was murder on a huge scale, and that the British government used the natural disaster of the potato blight to get rid of a troublesome population. 'A million and a half men, women, and children', he wrote, 'were carefully, prudently, and peacefully *slain* by the English government. They died of hunger in the midst of abundance, which their own hands created.' To Mitchel and those who agreed with him, the government's reaction to the Famine was the inevitable outcome of centuries of mis-rule and disregard for the Irish as equals. This interpretation, sometimes called the 'nationalist' or 'Mitchelite' interpretation, had a great impact on the Irish consciousness. Generations of nationalists after Mitchel, including Arthur Griffith (see chapters 6 and 7) used it as part of the justification of their cause. Since much of the popular literature of the late nineteenth and early twentieth centuries was politically motivated, this is the only interpretation that many Irish people heard.

In the middle of the twentieth century, however, there was a reaction against the Mitchelite interpretation. The overblown and over-dramatic language of many nationalists sat uneasily with

Irish professional historians, and many of them began to do the first scholarly research into the subject of the Famine. Since there was no evidence of a conscious attempt by the British government to implement a policy of genocide during the Famine, this revisionist interpretation tried to provide cool historical detachment from the Mitchelite interpretation. This was partly a natural reaction against so strong a traditional way of thinking. But it was also an attempt by Irish historians of the mid-twentieth century to cast off the nationalist tint that had coloured previous Famine interpretations. Such interpretations were not considered scholarly. The revisionist interpretation attempted to go beyond 'the political commentator, the ballad singer and the unknown maker of folk-tales' to research a more historically accurate picture of the Famine. In this, they argued that nationalism was a poor schoolmaster for history, and that the British governors of the time were simply acting as men of their time, and should not be held up to anachronistic blame. The two main revisionist historians were R. Dudley Edwards and T. Desmond Williams, who edited a collection of essays entitled *The Great Famine: Studies in Irish History 1845–52*, published in 1956. The contributors to this volume questioned long-standing assumptions about the Famine, including the number of deaths, and concentrated on revising the assessment of the responsibility of landlords and the British government. In the introduction (ghost-written by Kevin Nowlan), revisionist ideas about British responsibility for the Famine were made clear.

> If man, the prisoner of time, acts in conformity with the conventions of society into which he is born, it is difficult to judge him with an irrevocable harshness. So it is with the men of the Famine era. Human limitations and timidity dominate the story of the Great Famine, but of great and deliberately imposed evil in high positions of responsibility there is little evidence.

It was this interpretative tradition, which held sway until the late 1970s and early 1980s, that dismissed Cecil Woodham-Smith's popular history *The Great Hunger* (1962) as 'a great novel'. F.S.L. Lyons, the major figure in academic Irish history of the post-war generation, argued that Woodham-Smith's book was naive and that it pandered to the nationalist ideas of government responsibility without taking the contemporary context into account. According to the revisionists, then, the British government was caught in the grip of the politics and ideology of its time, and could not have acted in any other way than it did. It was, rather, the larger system which was at fault, and the words of the great Irish socialist James Connolly sum up the revisionist ideas about government responsibility neatly – 'No man who accepts capitalist society and the laws thereof can logically find fault with the statesmen of England for their acts in that awful period.'

While this interpretation undoubtedly provided a necessary corrective for the anachronistic expectations of how the government could have reacted during this period, it has been criticized for presenting a sanitized version of events, and one that focuses too much on the administrative side of the story. Critics claim that it avoided using non-governmental sources, and that it all but ignored the real suffering of the Famine. Such critics may be grouped together into a 'counter-revisionist' school of thought (although their ideas about the Famine differ at various points). This school draws on the massive amount of Famine research done in recent decades on economic history, anthropology and historical demographics. It criticizes the Mitchelite nationalist account for being ahistorical, but understands the reasons why it was so. It also criticizes the revisionist interpretation for inadequately addressing the depths of starvation and sickness. One of the most important historians of this new tradition is Cormac Ó Gráda. His study of the Famine over a number of years has led him to conclude that 'food availability was a problem; *nobody* wanted the extirpation [destruction] of the Irish as a race'.

In her recent book, *This Great Calamity* (1994), Christine Kinealy agrees generally with the counter-revisionist interpretation. She has done a close analysis of the government relief structures, particularly the workings of the Poor Law, and has come to the conclusion that much more could have been done to relieve suffering, if the political will had existed. One of her strongest arguments is that the fact that over three million people were fed by the government in 1847 shows that similar levels of relief could have been reached in the other Famine years. Clearly the structure was there, but the ideology was not. Most modern historians would agree with this. Kinealy takes her analysis further, however, to argue that the government, by placing the burden of relief on the localities, had a hidden agenda, that of attempting to use government resources for longer-term economic reform in Ireland. Government policy was, she argues, 'inadequate in terms of humanitarian criteria, and increasingly after 1847, systematically and deliberately so'. Again, she stops well short of untenable claims of genocide, but amongst contemporary historians condemns the British government most strongly for its inadequate relief of hunger and disease.

Perhaps the most interesting and challenging of recent interpretations of the Famine has arisen from the work of Peter Gray on the ideology of providentialism. As we have seen, many people in England and Ireland saw the Famine as the work of God, and thought that interference with such providence was immediately dangerous and ultimately disastrous. Gray has shown how this thinking operated in Ireland during the Famine. He argues that the strict *laissez-faire* ideas of Trevelyan at the treasury department were far more widely shared than has been previously argued. Before Gray, many historians (and certainly many popular commentators) saw Sir Robert Peel as more humane and pragmatic in his reaction to the Famine than the dogmatic Lord John Russell. Gray has argued, however, that Peel faced a much milder Famine in late 1845 and early 1846 than Russell did later, and that it was easier to convince parliament to grant direct food aid in such a circumstance. Once the Famine became total devastation, it would have been unlikely that Peel would have continued direct aid because he was nearly as much in the grip of providentialism as were the stricter *laissez-faire* men of Russell's government. Gray also argues that providentialist thinking was so widespread in parliament that a mild course of relief was the only one Peel or Russell could have followed for any length of time. Again, we return to the question of ideology and the degree to which it controlled the actions of those in the government. While Gray obviously does not agree with the genocide interpretation he does hold these strong religious beliefs to account for Famine suffering. Finally, Cormac Ó Gráda has argued that one of the few positive things to come out of the Famine was that it helped destroy ideas of providentialism and government non-interference in the economy, so that subsequent

British governments responded to crop failures and other social crises in far more humane ways.

The diversity and sophistication of recent scholarship on the Famine has been shown in Cormac Ó Gráda's *Black '47 and Beyond* (1999). This book examines not only questions of economics, demographics and responsibility, but also the importance of the Famine in Irish memory. Using the under-explored material at the Irish Folklore Commission, Ó Gráda shows the extent to which memories lasted well into the twentieth century and how they affected Irish social and political thought.

FOUR

Fenianism and the Land, 1848–81

The Famine did much more than depopulate the country through death and emigration. Its severity raised important underlying issues about the structure of the Irish economy. The most important of these issues were land use and landownership. Land has always been a central theme in Irish history. Native Irish chieftains fought each other (as well as invaders) over the question of land, and the various settlement plans of English governors were centred on the land. But 'the land' became more than an agricultural and economic question. In the second half of the nineteenth century it became a political issue as well, and became more closely tied to the national question (that is, who should rule in Ireland). Perhaps more importantly, it was *presented* as being tied to the national question and Irish nationalism. And for the first time, tenants formed organized political movements for land reform. The politics of this period are represented by a division between constitutional and parliamentary attempts at reform (much like O'Connell's largely peaceful means) and revolutionary attempts at forcing change (much like the Young Ireland rebellion, but more organized and effective). This chapter will deal mainly with the revolution-aries, and the next chapter will discuss the more moderate agitators. The important thing to note, however, is that these two groups joined forces after 1879, under the leadership of Charles Stewart Parnell (1846–91) and Michael Davitt (1846–1906). This merging was seen as a 'new departure' in Irish nationalism.

One of the most significant aspects of Irish history from the Famine to the end of the twentieth century was the changing relationships between landlords, farmers and labourers. Some of these changes were the result of population devastation from Famine deaths and emigration, and other changes were the result of political and social movements and government legislation. In the first place, the numbers making up each of the three groups changed during this period. Most significantly, the number of agricultural labourers declined by nearly fifteen per cent. There was a gradual change from tillage to more pastoral farming (which in most cases meant fewer potatoes and more livestock), and this reduced the need for labourers. The number of farmers increased by roughly the same amount as the number of labourers decreased. This may be part of the reason that agitation over the land issue centred on the rights of farmers, and that the reforms eventually reached were mainly aimed at the rents they paid and the security they received, as we shall see in this chapter. In fact, this caused bitterness between farmers and labourers, which sometimes sparked into violence.

Although labourers' wages slowly increased during this period, they still lagged behind those in Britain and most of Europe. Labourers and their families, therefore, did not see much improvement in their living conditions. Farmers, on the other hand, did see some increase in their material comforts. Generally speaking (and accepting that there were significant regional variations), the size of farms increased, and nearly a third of all farmers held land over thirty acres in size. Furthermore, prices for agricultural goods rose over this period, but they did so in a very chaotic way. There was not a gradual increase in prices; farmers could not predict which way prices could go, and they had to react to market changes quickly.

Landlords who had survived the Famine without going bankrupt generally found that they could increase their holdings dramatically by purchasing land that other landlords had been forced to vacate. But running and managing estates became more and more expensive, and many landlords found that their incomes did not allow them to live in a manner comparable with their English counterparts. Even though landlords were in a reasonably safe position, and tenant farmers seemed to be benefiting from increased farm size and rising prices, there was a great deal of tension between the two classes. This may not be immediately obvious because most of the statistics about growth of tenant landholdings and rising prices conceal a very important aspect of Irish agricultural life. It was true that, as a result of increased numbers of farmers with more land, agricultural production increased by over twelve per cent between the mid-1850s and the mid-1870s (which would seem to benefit farmers). Further, rents increased by over fifteen per cent (which would seem to benefit landlords). But the fluctuations in prices from year to year and other factors meant that farmers' incomes did not keep up with either production or rents (increasing at roughly seven and a half per cent over this period). Farmers, therefore, were producing more but earning less, in relative terms. Tensions between the agricultural classes were still acute, and a temporary downturn in the economy could result in serious rural unrest.

The immediate post-Famine period also saw a decline in nationalist fervour. Preoccupation with earning a living and a sort of resigned depression set in after O'Connell's failed Repeal bid and Young Ireland's brief rebellion. This kept nationalist feeling low. There was, however, a deeper divide between those who supported the Union (largely Protestant) and those who opposed it (largely Catholic). The Catholic majority of the population were disappointed by the Union. They thought it had not delivered on its promises of a better life for all the people in Ireland. Supporters thought that it had improved things in Ireland and that it must be maintained. These supporters were largely Protestant landowners and the Protestant communities in Ulster.

THE THREE Fs AND THE TENANT LEAGUE

During the period 1800–50, Ulster underwent an industrial revolution, which the rest of the country did not do to any great extent. Belfast in particular was in the early stages of becoming a linen, shipbuilding and engineering centre. Also in Ulster, tenants lived under what was called Ulster Custom, or tenant right. This meant that tenants had a right to what was eventually called the Three Fs – fair rent, fixity of tenure and freedom to sell interest in a holding. The Three Fs were to become the demands of organized tenants elsewhere in the country. The earliest tenant organizations were founded during the Famine, but they stayed local and did not last very long. The first group that provided some sort of permanence, as well as an organizational model for the rest of the country, was the Tenant Protection Society of Callan in County Kilkenny, founded in October 1849. It was the growth of these local organizations that led Young Irelander Charles Gavan Duffy and others to propose a national network of tenant associations. A conference of local organizations was held in August 1850, which resulted in the formation of the Irish Tenant League.

The Tenant League tried to have the Three Fs apply throughout the country (and to have them codified into law in Ulster, where they were only a custom). The Tenant League's proposed method of attaining the Three Fs was to help elect an independent Irish party to the House of Commons. The Irish Parliamentary Party does not owe its origins solely to the Tenant League, however. There were other imporant factors, particularly religious ones. The increase in sectarian mistrust (discussed in the previous chapter) and the controversy over Catholic ecclesiastical titles in 1850 and 1851 (a battle over whether the Pope had the right to create territorial titles for Catholic bishops in England) caused many Irish politicians to think that they must do something to protect Catholic interests in Ireland. In May 1851, therefore, a number of Irish Liberals in the House of Commons decided to band together as 'the Irish Brigade'. The Brigade then sought support outside parliament, so they founded the Catholic Defence Association and made an alliance with the Tenant League. This was the first step towards a uniting of the land movement and Catholic defenders, which would have a profound effect on the way the Home Rule movement was conducted later in the century. In the 1852 election, they were largely successful, returning about forty MPs out of a total of a hundred and three Irish MPs. They became known as the 'Irish Brigade' and the 'Pope's Brass Band'. But the Irish Party soon failed in one of its fundamental aims: to remain independent of other parties in Parliament. Two leaders of the party joined the new government administration in 1853, in an attempt to gain further concessions for Catholics. This caused a bitter split in the Party and in the Tenant League because many of its members wanted to remain loyal to their idea of independence from other parties; they then formed the Independent Opposition Party.

Rising economic prosperity in the mid-1850s also slowed down the Tenant League's momentum, since many people did not have immediate grievances to air. The Tenant League gradually fizzled out and held its last meeting in 1858. The Independent Opposition Party continued its work, but eventually allied with the British Liberals in 1866. The collapse of the League's efforts caused many Irish reformers to question constitutional and parliamentary tactics. Not only would it be difficult to get the British government to accept reform, they argued, it now seemed impossible for Irish politicians to bring effective pressure to bear on the government. The Tenant League cannot be seen as a complete failure, however. Its main success was simply in the fact that it organized itself and gained a good deal of support from the agricultural community. The fact that it could not bring the right pressure to bear on the government to effect significant land reform does not detract from this point. It was as a popularizer of land issues and as a propaganda machine that the Tenant League was a success. The reason that it received so much attention, and was credited with so many other successes, was that Duffy was a very effective propagandist. It also was non-sectarian, and appealed to agricultural workers and farmers of all religions and political opinions. All these things provided models for the more successful Land League of the 1880s.

FENIANISM

With the failure of O'Connell's Repeal movement and now the failure of the Tenant League, many reformers thought that the impetus should be taken out of the hands of constitutional politicians and put into the hands of revolutionaries. These revolutionaries were generally known as 'Fenians', which referred to ancient Irish warrior tribes. The most significant of these revolutionary groups became known as the Irish Republican Brotherhood (IRB), but it was initially simply called 'the organization'. It was founded on 17 March 1858 (St Patrick's Day) in Dublin, and a parallel organization was founded in New York in April 1859. Most of the leading Fenians had played a part in Young Ireland's 1848 rising. James Stephens (1824–1901), from Kilkenny, was the founder of the Dublin Fenians and became the nominal head of the New York Fenians in 1859. He established a Fenian newspaper, the *Irish People*, put down rival revolutionary organizations, and was the chief organizing inspiration behind Fenian activity. John O'Mahoney (1816–77, leader of the American branch), John O'Leary (1830–1907), Thomas Clarke Luby (1821–1901) and Jeremiah O'Donovan Rossa (1831–1915) were other prominent members. There were several reasons for the Fenians to think that they might be successful. Stephens had a good deal of experience with secret societies in Paris, they had financial support from America and Britain's difficult 'victory' in the Crimean War highlighted serious problems with British military effectiveness; there was a mutiny in India in 1857, and British relations with France (a potential ally of Irish radicals) were dangerously close to war. But war with France never came, and the Fenians began to look to the United States as their most likely ally. This impression was further strengthened during the American Civil War (1861–5), when it appeared at several points that Britain might enter the war on the southern side. Although the purpose of Fenianism was to overthrow British rule in Ireland and to found an Irish Republic, it is fairly clear that a number of its more important leaders would have compromised a good deal to obtain control over Ireland's domestic affairs yet retain the formal supremacy of the English crown. Further, connections with Irish constitutional leaders such as the Home Rulers (see chapter 5), though informal, was generally good.

O'Donovan Rossa went to the United States in 1871 and raised funds for a terrorist campaign in Britain between 1881 and 1885. The Fenians' main idea was that Britain would never succumb to constitutional methods for Irish reform. It would never grant Irish independence except when compelled by physical force. Further, they focused solely on the goal of independence. They had no social or economic policies or ideas for governing an independent Ireland. The organization and its methods were designed to be completely secret, and was organized by 'cells', local groups with a local leader. Fenianism was successful in gaining members (roughly 54,000 by 1864, which was a large number for a supposedly 'secret' society). It appealed to the middle classes, as well as to artisans and shopkeepers. Fenianism also offered recreation and entertainment, and this was a very important aspect of its organization and appeal. Some of the games it offered were distinctly military in style (and even included drilling, marching and 'war games'). It organized hiking trips, gymnastics, boxing and social events such as picnics. By 1865 there were thousands of Fenians across the country. The Catholic church banned its members from becoming Fenians, although it is impossible to know how effective this ban was. The Fenians received considerable help from abroad, especially from Fenian groups in Britain (including in the British army) and the US (mostly made up of Irish immigrants). Some Irish officers who had served in the American Civil War came back to Ireland to plan for a rising in 1865. The government realized that Fenian activity was reaching a climax and quickly moved in to arrest many of its prominent members and leaders (including Stephens, O'Leary, and O'Donovan Rossa) in late 1865. Another Fenian rising of 4–6 March 1867 was based mainly in Dublin and Cork. There were less extensive battles in Tipperary and Limerick. Rather than attack well fortified positions or attempt arms raids, the Fenians concentrated on capturing less important areas and institutions, such as railway and coastguard stations. The hoped-for arrival of an American ship with troops and arms did not materialize (indeed, it did not arrive until May, although there were still regional skirmishes taking place then). Three prominent Fenians were executed in Manchester for killing a policeman while rescuing two Fenian leaders on their way to trial in September 1867. The execution of these 'Manchester martyrs' did a great deal to turn Irish public opinion in favour of the Fenians. After their initial hostility to Fenianism, many Catholic clergy held masses of mourning for the Manchester martyrs (many saw the policeman's killing as accidental rather than calculated). This support from much of the Catholic clergy (although it is important to note that the church hierarchy, especially Cardinal Paul Cullen (1803–78), were strongly opposed to Fenianism), helped to ease the hesitation that had prevented many people from supporting Fenianism. It also led to a thaw in relations between militant and constitutional Irish reformers. Isaac Butt (1813–79), the founder of the Home Rule movement, defended Fenian prisoners and argued for a general amnesty (which never came). After the failures of 1867, the Fenians regrouped and reorganized. Fenianism would not emerge again publicly for another generation. But, like Young Ireland, the Fenians and the Fenian ideal still had a great hold on the nationalist psyche.

THE LAND PROBLEM RESURFACES

All this agitation and political stress took its toll on the British government. In the election of 1868, the Liberals were returned to power under their leader William Ewart Gladstone (1809–98). He had won the election with a great deal of Irish support (after promising to disestablish the Anglican Church of Ireland). When told of his victory, Gladstone was reported to have said, 'my mission is to pacify Ireland'. In 1869, Gladstone's government pushed through its disestablishment of the Church of Ireland. This ended the official dominance of the Anglican Church in Ireland, and it had to rely on its own resources from then on. Gladstone had also raised the land issue during the election campaign (and, indeed, had spoken of many Irish landlords in harsh terms). A new Tenant League was founded in September 1869, and a massive Land Conference was held in February 1870 to discuss different ideas for land reform from different groups and to settle on a common strategy. Gladstone's next Irish reform was the 1870 Land Act. It codified the Ulster Custom and brought in some reforms for tenants in other parts of the country, although it fell short of granting the Three Fs the Tenant League had demanded. They also allowed farmers to borrow money more easily to buy more land. With prices fluctuating as they were, a debt burden became a particular economic danger. With this re-emergence of the land question, and the work of constitutional nationalists like Isaac Butt to convince farmers and tenants that a measure of Home Rule would be the solution to their problems, Fenianism seemed to lose much of the attention it had gained in the 1860s. At the Fenian Convention in March 1873, the supreme council declared that another rising would be postponed, and that, until then, Fenians should support any movement which increased Irish independence. At the 1874 election, Isaac Butt's Home Rulers were very successful (winning sixty seats) and the Fenian-sympathizing Irish Liberals nearly eliminated (holding on to ten seats).

At roughly the same time as the Home Rule movement was starting in the early 1870s (see chapter 5), the Fenian movement began further agitation. While the Home Rule movement was becoming a serious parliamentary force, the IRB condemned the Home Rulers and in 1876 demanded that IRB members cease to co-operate with them. This did not work completely because many Fenians saw Home Rule as a potential solution, and they converted to its cause. There was also a split between the supreme council of the Fenians in Ireland and the American branch, who were beginning to see potential in the rising Home Ruler Charles Stewart Parnell. In December 1877, the Irish radical Michael Davitt was released from Dartmoor prison in England. Born at the height of the Famine in 1846, Davitt was the son of an evicted tenant farmer in County Mayo. Davitt had joined the Fenians in 1865, but was arrested for gun-running and sent to prison in 1870. Leading Home Rulers such as Isaac Butt and Parnell pressured the British government to grant amnesty to Fenians, and Davitt was released. His hatred for England had deepened while in prison, although he apparently liked English people, especially the working classes, partly because he had spent much of his boyhood working in a cotton mill in Lancashire in the north of England. After he was released from prison, Davitt failed to get Parnell to join the IRB. In 1878 he went to the United States and met with John Devoy (1842–1928), a Fenian who had gone to New York after being released from a British prison in 1871.

Together they devised a policy called the New Departure in June 1878. The New Departure was based on the idea that the question of national sovereignty was inextricably linked with land issues. Davitt and Devoy argued that the British government would never grant land reform that would benefit tenants. A land reform movement would provide the basis for an eventual national movement, they stressed, once tenants and farmers saw that their land interests could only be addressed by a native Irish government. The supreme council of the IRB and Parnell disagreed with the New Departure and would not endorse it initially. A worldwide agricultural depression hit in the late 1870s, coinciding with a run of bad harvests. This made agricultural workers fear that a severe economic downturn loomed. Crop prices dropped dramatically. Although the bad harvests would normally have prompted a rise in prices for crops, they actually suffered because of cheaper imports from North America. Livestock values also fell. Further, emigration had slackened because of the economic recession in America in the late 1870s, so more people had stayed in Ireland than would normally have been the case. Some of these were young men who became bitter as economic opportunities closed all around them. Overall agricultural output fell, and farmers who were in debt were pushed to the wall. Landlords were asked to reduce rents. The winter of 1878–9 was very harsh, however, and an economic crisis loomed in Ireland. Some Home Rule moderates were beginning to change their minds about the New Departure. Crops failed, and small farmers and their tenants faced the real possibility of ruin, eviction and even starvation. Davitt decided that this crisis demanded the immediate attention of Irish reformers. He called a land meeting at Irishtown in County Mayo for 20 April 1879. It was a big success, and it was followed by a good deal of land agitation in the west. Davitt scheduled another meeting for 8 June 1879 at Westport in County Mayo, and he persuaded Parnell to agree to speak at the meeting.

THE LAND LEAGUE AND THE LAND WAR

By this time, Parnell had begun to see the importance of the land question and its potential in bringing about Home Rule. At Westport, he raised the rallying cry, 'hold a firm grip on your homestead and lands'. This meeting was a tremendous success. On 21 October 1879, Davitt founded the Irish National Land League in Dublin, and Parnell became its president. Parnell provided general leadership and brought in nationalists of differing opinions, and Davitt served as the Land League's organizer. Moderate Home Rulers as well as extreme nationalists joined the league. Money poured in from the United States. Catholic clergy also supported the League.

The main work of the League was to resist landlords who sought to evict tenants. They also agitated to reduce rents, with the ultimate goal of making land cheap enough for poor farmers to buy plots. This was the beginning of the Land War of 1879–82, which many argue was the greatest social and political movement in modern Irish history. It started because tenants demanded rent reductions in response to a fall in agricultural incomes in the late 1870s. When these were not granted, they turned to a campaign against landlords and landlordism (the system of landholding which allowed landlords to have so much power). The Land War started in County Mayo and spread through the west and then throughout the country by 1880. The reason the Land War did not just fizzle out after the first local, and disconnected, agitations is because there was leadership to take up the cause. So the combining of the national question with the land question (the 'new departure'), and providing organization and leadership, made sure that the land agitation could continue. Land War tactics were as follows. Whenever there was an eviction, public demonstrations were held at the property. Sometimes evictions were prevented by Land Leaguers physically blocking bailiffs. Tenants sent in to take over property from those evicted were also often prevented from doing so by masses of Leaguers. Families who were evicted were given financial support and often taken into the homes of Land Leaguers. The League provided legal defence for those accused of agrarian agitation. There were many mass meetings, marching bands and speeches proclaiming the League's message of land reform throughout the country. The most famous method of agitation used by the League, however, was social and economic ostracism of landlords whom the League thought were unjust. In September 1880, Captain Charles Boycott, a land agent for Lord Erne's estate in County Mayo, refused to stop evicting tenants. The League surrounded his lands and cut him off from agricultural labourers who could help him with his harvest. Boycott finally received help from Ulster Orangemen and a thousand army troops, and brought in his harvest (worth about £350). Boycott's name was soon used to describe economic ostracism.

In the election earlier that year, Gladstone's Liberal Party had been brought back to power. Parnell gained many more seats for his Irish Party, and forced the government to pay attention to land concerns. Gladstone appointed W. E. Forster (1819–86) as Chief Secretary in Ireland. Forster tried to pass a bill to protect tenants, but it was rejected by the House of Lords. This meant that the government had to enforce harsh laws against tenants who resisted eviction, and it raised a great deal of bitterness and hatred towards London. The Land War worsened during 1880 and 1881. The League set up its own courts to adjudicate land disputes (particularly in the west), and acted almost as a revolutionary government in many parts of the country. The government adopted a two-pronged strategy to deal with the Land War. First it passed a

Coercion Act, which allowed for arrest without charge. Davitt was arrested on 3 February 1881 under this Act. Gladstone also passed a Land Act in August 1881. It basically granted the Three Fs and set up a special court to fix rents. The League were not satisfied with this Act, and began to demand peasant ownership of property. They continued to agitate and to call for increased agitation across the country. Gladstone then had Parnell and other leaders arrested, and outlawed the League in October 1881. The Ladies' Land League then took up the agitation. It was run by Anna Parnell (1852–1911), Charles's sister. But the Land War ran out of control and much violence attended its activities. Gladstone reached an understanding with Parnell in the 'Kilmainham Treaty' (so called because Parnell was imprisoned in Kilmainham jail in Dublin). Gladstone agreed to implement further reforms to help tenants, and Parnell agreed to end the agitation. The Chief Secretary, Forster, refused to agree to the Kilmainham Treaty and resigned. He was replaced by Lord Frederick Cavendish (1836–82). Soon after they arrived in Ireland, Cavendish and his secretary were murdered in Phoenix Park on 6 May 1882. This raised the spectre of renewed violence and tension was high. The government passed an even stricter Coercion Act, but also passed a number of other reforms for tenants. Gladstone's land reforms went a long way towards the eventual creation of a peasant landowning class in Ireland. Under the terms of his 1881 Act, some land was to be held under dual ownership between landlord and tenant. Many landlords did not want to operate under this system and sold out to their tenants. Gradually, due to the work of the land courts, rents were reduced. Two further important land reforms in 1885 and 1903 eventually helped establish a system of owner-occupiers, which in many cases meant peasant ownership. This pattern of landholding has largely continued in Ireland.

The Land War and land agitation was taken up by people like Parnell because they thought that it would eventually lead to a solution of the national question. In Galway on 14 October 1880, Parnell had said, 'I would not have taken off my coat and gone to this work if I had not known that we were laying the foundation in this movement for the regeneration of our legislative independence.' This was all part of the Home Rule movement which is discussed in the next chapter.

RELIGION

Just as politics was not everything during the years of O'Connell and Young Ireland, so 'the land' was not the only issue during this period. This was also an important period for religion in Ireland, particularly in the area of increased reforms of the Catholic Church. The central figure in all this was Paul Cullen, who became archbishop of Armagh in 1849 and then archbishop of Dublin in 1852. He continued earlier attempts at ending folk celebrations which had become intertwined with religious observations (see chapter two). Because of his training at the Vatican as a young man, he thought it was crucial to the continued strength of Catholicism in Ireland that religious practices be standardized and be brought under the control of local priests (meaning, for instance, that observances of marriages and deaths would be under the control of the local church). His efforts were greatly helped by the fact that the reduction in population due to Famine deaths and emigration (along with a slight increase in the number of priests being trained) meant that there were more parish priests per capita. This no doubt helped local priests gain more control over religious practices (as well as semi-religious and folk practices) in their areas.

Along with this tightening of religious practices came an emphasis on increased purity in relations between the sexes. One effect of the Famine had been that farmers did not divide their land up amongst their children, but settled on one (usually male) who would inherit the whole. This heir would often be matched with an available marriage partner who also had property (usually as part of a dowry). In this way, marriage generally became mainly a question of increasing property holdings in a family. All of this meant that marriages usually happened later in life, and that fewer people married (these were generally those who did not inherit land). Many of those who did not marry emigrated, and for those who stayed behind, the increased influence of the church meant that celibacy was supported and encouraged. This combination of economic necessity and church influence led to the acceptance of a stricter moral life amongst most Irish people, and may have led to the strong influence that the Catholic Church was to have on Irish life for the rest of the century and at least the first half of the twentieth century.

INTERPRETATIONS – FENIANISM

Traditionally, the Fenians have been seen as a strictly nationalist movement without social or economic goals. Although the Catholic Church and much of the O'Connellite Catholic middle class were opposed to Fenianism, it quickly became part of general nationalist history, which merged most specific types of national struggle into one general movement. John O'Leary published his *Recollections of Fenians and Fenianism* in 1896, which tried to establish that his own hostility towards the Catholic clergy was held by Fenians generally. John Devoy published his *Recollections of an Irish Rebel* in 1926, arguing that Fenianism was a serious revolutionary movement with committed members selflessly fighting for its ends. By this time, however, Devoy had become more of a constitutional nationalist, which was reflected in his supporting the Treaty of 1921 (see chapter 6). James Connolly wrote in his *Labour in Irish History* (1910) that Fenianism was part of a wider European movement of working-class agitation. Connolly was a socialist who argued that trade unions and working men's associations were going to take over covert nationalist revolutionary organizations. This socialist emphasis was taken up by Emile Strauss in his *Irish Nationalism and British Democracy* (1951), but the Fenians were given more credit for the social and economic background of their members, who were largely drawn from the working class. Strauss argued that while Fenianism's lack of social and economic militancy for the working class was regrettable, it may be seen as a valid part of a larger tradition of European class struggle. Desmond Ryan argued something similar in his biography of James Stephens (*The Fenian Chief*, 1967). He wrote that Stephens was a proto-left-winger and that Fenianism was a popular movement for democracy. This nationalist tradition with a socialist tint was taken further by Leon Ó Broin, whose history of the 1867 rising, *Fenian Fever* (1971), was a detailed examination of the failed rebellion. This emphasis on violence and rebellion, Ó Broin argued, was central to Fenian ideas. In his *Fenian Movement* (1968), T.W. Moody had argued something similar. Most Irish revolutionaries started out as constitutional moderates and only gradually turned militant. The Fenians, however, decided from the very outset that violence was the best means to secure independence. This was a fundamental change in nationalist thinking that greatly affected future generations.

R.V. Comerford revised this interpretation in 1985 with his publication of *The Fenians in Context* (1985). Comerford argued that nationalism was only part of the Fenian movement. He emphasized the social and recreational aspects of Fenian organizations and tried to show that they were much more broadly based than previously thought. The argument is that the political factors of Fenianism were not enough to attract members in the numbers that it did. The IRB, Comerford argues, provided 'a form for fraternal association and communal self-expression'. Fenianism was 'a voluntary social movement posing as a military organization'. Comerford's work has unearthed new information and insights about the Fenians, but his interpretations have been criticized for a lack of consideration of the primary nationalist purpose of the Fenians. John Newsinger's *Fenianism in Mid-Victorian Britain* (1994) argued this strongly. Newsinger's analysis of the deep revolutionary nature of the Fenians, and their class-based hope of overthrowing the British, is somewhat polemical, however.

In some ways, this argument over the precise purpose of the Fenians mirrors the debate over the scope of nationalism – whether political independence would be enough, or whether cultural aspects were equally important. This question will arise more starkly in chapter 6.

INTERPRETATIONS – LAND WAR

The popular view of landlords as English foreigners controlling Irish land, as absentee owners who did not care about their tenants, who charged them excessive rents and who evicted them heartlessly, was born out of popular folklore and mythology. It was also upheld by J.E. Pemfret's *The Struggle for the Land in Ireland, 1800–1923* (1930). While undoubtedly true in many instances, this view has been criticized in recent years for being too sweeping a condemnation, and for covering over the very real and deep complexities in landlord and tenant relations. One of the most interesting, and controversial, interpretations to be put forward in recent years is W.E. Vaughan's re-assessment of the relations between landlords and tenants during this period. His *Landlords and Tenants in Mid-Victorian Ireland* (1994) argues that, between 1858 and 1876, rents were relatively low, there were few evictions, reasonable agricultural prosperity, and a well-established relationship between landlords and tenants during this period. On the question of absenteeism, he shows that seventy-three per cent of Irish landlords were resident in Ireland. Vaughan also argues that threatened evictions were intended to get tenants to pay their rents rather than clear them from the land in order to create larger holdings. The legal and financial difficulties in obtaining an eviction (partly due to the work of the Land League) made it unlikely that a landlord would press his property rights to the extreme point of eviction. Vaughan also shows that the landlord class itself was most at fault for its social and economic difficulties during this period. They incurred high social expenses in trying to live like their counterparts in England. They did not invest in the land or new agricultural technology to the extent they should have, and they sought to live off their rents alone rather than become agricultural entrepreneurs, which was what English landlords were trying to do.

The Land League has also undergone extensive scrutiny. Patrick O'Farrell argued that

> the Land League was not a movement for land reform, it was a wholesale crusade for the establishment of a peasant Ireland. It was not – despite Davitt's personal advocacy of land nationaliza-tion – a forward-looking socialist solution to the problem of Irish freedom and identity, it was a backward-looking peasant solution. (*Ireland's English Question*, 1971)

Joseph Lee expressed the opposite view. In his *Modernization of Irish Society* (1973), he argued that the Land League did not have a strong vision of a peasant Ireland. League rhetoric was based on political ends, not on romantic ideas of a pastoral society. Such visions, Lee asserts, were actually constructed by landlords. This difference between the establishment of a backward-looking, nostalgic feeling towards peasantry (which lasted well into the twentieth century) and the Land War and land reform as part of Irish modernization, is central to the debate on the Land War. In his *Land and the National Question in Ireland, 1858–82* (1978), Paul Bew argued that, rather than being a defensive organization aimed at helping distressed tenants, the Land League was an 'offensive movement'. The number of evictions was simply not great enough to allow a purely tenant defence league to raise an outcry and mobilize. This is partly based on the argument that the boycott was actually rather limited in its application, and that the more dominant strategy was 'rent at the point of a bayonet'. That is, the League's idea was to force landlords and land agents to collect their rents through the use of the courts or the militia, which would almost instantly cause a confrontation, with all its intended propaganda value. The Land League's most important contribution, according to Bew, was that it paid the legal bills for tenants while the eviction process was grinding along. American dollars were instrumental in funding this aspect of the League's work. Bew also showed the diversity of motives and desires in Land League agitation across the country, as well as among different economic classes of tenants. Some stressed rent reductions, some wanted land redistribution, and some land labourers mainly wanted better wages. Although these various parts of the League seemed to go in different directions, there was a good deal of general anti-landlord feeling among all Leaguers. Bew praised the League for its successes, notably the success in having the Three Fs passed and forcing the land courts to set reasonable rents. Its failure was that many of these reforms did not help the social and economic situations of many poor tenants. In the west, particularly, emigration continued to be seen as the only effective alternative.

In addition to a debate over the Land League itself, historians have argued about how closely the land and the national question were actually linked. There are two main arguments. The first says that the land and the national question were woven together, that, for the Irish peasant, 'the landlord' and 'the English' were the same enemy. This was part of the traditional nationalist argument. There is some truth to this interpretation, and it certainly captures the rhetoric perfectly. As with most of these interpretations, however, it is too strong. It does not take full account of the fact that many of the more constitutional nationalists like Isaac Butt (see chapter 5) did not take a deep interest in land questions. The second line of interpretation is that the Land War grew out of an already established tradition of rural conflict, and that Fenianism or any other national movement would have to join this underlying Irish rural movement. This is Robert Kee's basic argument in *The Green Flag: a History of Irish Nationalism* (1972). Bew counters this by arguing that the Fenians had a stronger political purpose than Kee implies. They thought that the British government would never grant land reform, and therefore the only option left for Ireland was self-rule. Philip Bull has argued more recently (in his *Land, Politics and Nationalism: a Study of the Irish Land Question*, 1996) that the reason that the land and the national question became so closely linked was that there were a series of conflicting assumptions about the land held by landlords and tenants. Further, these were left unresolved for so long that they became the major issues in Irish life. The national question, therefore, was completely influenced by this long-standing problem and had to address it. 'The land' and 'the nation' were not necessarily linked in theory, but they became so in practice.

FIVE

Home Rule, 1870–93

During the period of Fenian activity and increasing land agitation, a constitutional force to gain a form of independence was founded. This was the Home Rule movement, and it was to dominate Irish politics until the First World War. As in the age of O'Connell, Irish politics became hopelessly entangled with British parliamentary and party politics in this period. The Home Rule drama was largely played out in political circles in London. The Independent Irish Party and Fenianism both contributed to the Home Rule movement, though. The Independent Irish Party provided parliamentary models for Home Rulers to follow, and the Fenians provided a popular movement from which Home Rulers could draw strength. Home Rule was almost immediately attractive to many Irish people, especially those who could vote in parliamentary elections. It basically argued that an Irish parliament should be re-established and the Union be repealed, but that the British government should retain control of foreign affairs. This, of course, was reminiscent of O'Connell's repeal movement. There were various reasons why Home Rule was attractive to different sections of Irish society. Catholics (who made up the majority of agricultural workers) had been let down by Gladstone's somewhat weak Land Act of 1870, and Protestants had been unhappy with the disestablishment of the Church of Ireland. This led many from both religions to think that Irish affairs would be better handled from Dublin.

ISAAC BUTT AND THE ORIGINS OF HOME RULE

On 1 September 1870, Isaac Butt, a prominent Protestant lawyer in Dublin, founded the Home Government Association, and began agitating for a type of federalism, or local rule for each country in the United Kingdom. According to this idea, England, Scotland and Ireland would have their own parliaments, and the British parliament at Westminster would handle foreign affairs and imperial questions. While he was a student at Trinity College Dublin, Butt and a few other students founded the *Dublin University Magazine* and an 'Orange Young Ireland' group, the name jokingly applied to Butt and his friends who were strongly Protestant and unionist, but also patriotic nationalists in terms of Irish culture and national identity. Butt's group thought that much of the government of Ireland was badly handled and wrote of the difficulties of ruling Ireland from London. Butt had also defended many of the Young Irelanders at their trials in 1848 and 1865–8. This experience, as well as what he had seen in the Famine, led him to become more active in nationalist politics. This has traditionally been explained as a sort of conversion from unionism to nationalism. More modern historians see no such conversion, but a continuous strand of ideology going back to his Trinity College days. Throughout the period of his political activity, Butt was committed to the British Empire and to Conservative politics. While later supporters of Home Rule thought of it as the best they could obtain from a British government (while, in reality, wanting full independence), Butt thought that Home Rule was the best possible solution to the problem of conflicting national identities within the United Kingdom. Butt founded the Home Government Association with the co-operation of Protestant and Catholic middle-class support, and he hoped it would lessen sectarianism. The hierarchy of the Catholic Church was suspicious of the movement and discouraged people from joining (although this proved difficult, and the church warmed to the movement later on). And conservative Protestants worried that they would be overwhelmed by Catholic participation in the movement. In 1873, the Home Rule Association was replaced by the Home Rule League, and a British counterpart, the Home Rule Confederation, was also set up. Home Rule became a popular idea amongst many farmers, and the fact that many of them were organized into local farmers' clubs meant that spreading the Home Rule message among them was quite easy.

Some Fenians, such as Patrick Egan and John O'Connor Power, came to the conclusion that Home Rule was an acceptable first step towards independence and joined Butt's parliamentary campaign. (Butt had been an MP from 1852 to 1865. He was also elected for Limerick from 1871 until 1879.) At the general election of 1874, Butt's Home Rule party won over half of the seats for Irish members. Between 1871 and 1880, Butt and his party pushed the Home Rule cause in parliament, but neither Prime Minister Benjamin Disraeli's Conservatives nor William Gladstone's Liberals were interested in allying themselves with the Irish Party. Since Butt refused to use anything but constitutional and moderate means, there never seemed to be a sense of urgency about the Home Rule question, and each of the main parties in the House of Commons could afford to ignore it. Butt, however, had difficulties in leading his party. He generally thought of them as independent men who held the idea of Home Rule in common. The idea that he needed to form a well-disciplined party would have seemed radical to him. Butt retained his respect for the British constitution, and his ideas about Ireland retaining a place at the centre of the Empire, even though they were not shared by some of the more radical members of his party. This meant that he was not willing to breach the standards and codes of accepted parliamentary practice. Also, his popular appeal in Ireland was limited to those who shared his mild constitutional views. On the one hand, therefore, he could not put sufficient pressure on the House of Commons to pay attention to Home Rule, and on the other he did not have the depth of support in Ireland to force Home Rule up the British political agenda.

This gradually made a number of Butt's followers very impatient. They thought that moderation had failed and that it was time for more direct action. Two important members of Butt's party, Joseph Gillis Biggar (1828–90) and John O'Connor Power (1848–1919), thought that the best way to get the attention of the other parties in the House of Commons was to obstruct parliamentary business using ancient procedural methods. In 1875, Biggar and Power were joined by Charles Stewart Parnell

(1846–91). Parnell was born into a Protestant landlord family, educated at Cambridge University, and became MP for Meath in 1875. Parnell took quickly to the policy of obstruction, which alienated him from Isaac Butt and other moderate members of the Home Rule Party. There was a struggle for the leadership of the Home Rule Party between 1877 and 1879, partly because of these differing views on tactics, but also because Parnell and many of the younger men in the party were impatient with what they saw as Butt's slow pace. One of the main problems was that Butt was generally opposed to obstruction of parliamentary business, except in extreme cases. There were times, however, when Butt pushed the Home Rule case right to the edge of obstruction, but then did not follow it through. This frustrated Parnell and Biggar and their followers. In early 1877, therefore, Parnell and Biggar started obstructing parliamentary business on their own. While this did not advance the parliamentary cause of Home Rule, it did attract a great deal of attention, and the Irish nationalist press were able to play on the theme of a few heroic Irish MPs battling against the might of the rest of the British House of Commons. Parnell was able to use this popularity to become president of the Home Rule Confederation in late August 1877. The division between Parnell and Butt (and the two strains of Home Rule tactics they represented) helped build Fenian support for the obstructionists. By late 1877, however, it was clear that Parnell and his fellow obstructionists would gain control of the Home Rule Party in the House of Commons as well.

THE RISE OF PARNELL

Butt died in May 1879, and another constitutionalist, William Shaw (1823–95), took over the leadership of the Home Rule League, although there had been much support for the election of Parnell. Parnell, however, formally took over the leadership of the Irish Parliamentary Party at the 1880 election. He built up relations with Clan na Gael [clan nah gale], the Irish-American revolutionary group who were allied with the Fenians. They insisted that the land question and the national question be linked. Parnell had seen that the election in Ireland was fought on the land issue, and so when the new parliament convened in 1880, he was the head of a now more militant Irish Parliamentary Party. During the Land War (see chapter 4), Parnell provided effective leadership, often acting as a go-between for the British government and Land League radicals. After the passage of Gladstone's Land Act of 1881, Parnell tried to steer Irish reformers more strictly towards a Home Rule policy. With the ending of the Land War of 1879–82, Parnell wanted the national movement to concentrate on the question of Home Rule. The Land League was, therefore, replaced by the National League, which became a political organization based on constituency groups and organized other such groups for the purpose of raising money, having candidates elected and supporting MPs in office. This was a tremendous organizing effort, and the party became quite disciplined.

The mid-1880s were the highpoint of support for Home Rule within Ireland. In 1884, the Catholic Church publicly backed the movement (in exchange for the Irish Party's support for Catholic educational reforms). In the election of 1885, Parnell urged Irish voters in Britain to vote against the Liberals, in punishment for dragging their feet on Home Rule. The Liberals gained more seats than any other party, but Parnell's party had enough seats, if they voted with the Conservatives, to eliminate the Liberal majority on any measure. The election of late 1885 was a triumph for Parnell. Home rulers won every seat in Ireland except for those in eastern Ulster and the Dublin University seat. In Great Britain, the Liberals gained power again under Gladstone, who saw the electoral result in Ireland as a clear expression of the people's wish for Home Rule. On 17 December 1885, Gladstone came out in favour of Home Rule. When he formed his government in early 1886, he decided that Home Rule was going to be a central policy. On 8 April 1886, Gladstone presented a Home Rule bill based on Butt's ideas and on the colonial practice followed in Canada. Under the bill's provisions, Dublin was to have its own parliament consisting of two chambers and to be in charge of domestic Irish affairs. The British parliament in London would retain control of imperial affairs, foreign relations, the military, currency and major taxation. Gladstone presented his bill to the House of Commons using the language of historic justice for Ireland and Home Rule as a pragmatic solution to a continuing problem. The details of the bill were criticized, however, by most nationalists because they did not see it as a lasting settlement. Conservatives in the British parliament thought Home Rule would mean the break-up of the Union, and eventually the empire, as well as being a betrayal of the loyal Protestants who wished to remain more directly linked with Britain. They also worried that the Irish MPs who would be retained in the British parliament would have too much say over British affairs. This was because, under Gladstone's plan, Ireland was still to pay imperial taxes, and so would have to be granted Irish MPs to sit in the British parliament. Gladstone replied that the upper chamber of the new Irish parliament would solve the problem of Protestant loyalists. Since that chamber was to be based on property, it would naturally be full of Protestant landowners, and would safeguard their minority rights. He thought that the militant loyalists and Orangemen would see that Home Rule would grant them more direct control over their interests. It was not only the Conservatives who opposed the bill, however. A large number of Liberals were also against it. Many of them were unionists at heart and genuinely believed in the benefits of the Union. These Liberal Unionists were from both the aristocratic section of the party (led by Lord Hartington, 1803–1908) and the radical section (led by Joseph Chamberlain, 1836–1914). With this combined opposition, Gladstone's bill was defeated by 341 to 311 votes in the House of Commons on 8 June 1886, with 93 Liberals voting against Gladstone. Even if it had passed the Commons, it would have certainly been thrown out by the House of Lords.

This defeat put Parnell in a difficult parliamentary position. Until this point, his party could hold the Liberal government to ransom by threatening to vote with the Conservatives. Once a significant section of Liberals had deserted Gladstone over Home Rule, however, Parnell's threat became meaningless. Rebellious liberals posed a greater danger to Gladstone than Parnell's party could. This rejection of such a major part of Liberal government policy meant that Gladstone had to call an election for 1886. It was fought on the issue of Home Rule, but was a massive defeat for Gladstone, and Lord Salisbury's Conservatives came to power. The Home Rule movement, however, retained much support in Britain and intensified in Ireland. There was a change in attitude amongst many nationalists, who were increasingly willing to try constitutional methods in the House of Commons. This gradually meant that the Irish Parliamentary Party became more closely allied with the Home Rule Liberals. Gladstone continued to campaign for Home Rule, and gathered many supporters during the late 1880s.

All this raised more opposition to Home Rule, and the issue captured broad national attention in Britain as well as Ireland. *The Times* newspaper, a generally establishment, Conservative and Unionist paper, tried to tar the Home Rule movement with the brush of crime. With nationalist demonstrations going on in Ireland, and in the wake of the Phoenix Park murders (see chapter 4), *The Times* ran a series of stories entitled 'Parnellism and Crime' from March to December 1887. These stories were based on a series of letters which *The Times* claimed Parnell had written, linking him to the Phoenix Park murders and terrorism generally. In an editorial, *The Times* claimed that Gladstone was unwittingly allied with 'the worst of criminals, with agents and instruments of murder-conspiracies'. Parnell denounced the letters, refuted their authorship in the House of Commons and demanded an investigation by the government. Salisbury's government, however, decided to investigate the charges against Parnell rather than the authenticity of the letters. This had the effect of implying that the Irish Parliamentary Party was linked to terrorists. The investigation backfired, however, and it was proved that the letters were forged by a disaffected Irish nationalist. This revelation was a tremendous boost to Parnell and to Gladstone's efforts to make Home Rule acceptable to the British public. It helped Home Rulers appear as forward-thinking reformers rather than as a front for terrorism. Opinion in favour of Parnell and the Liberals improved, and *The Times*'s credibility was seriously damaged.

PARNELL'S FALL

Parnell's credibility was restored by 1889, but his personal life was soon to be his undoing, and would seriously damage his Irish Parliamentary Party. Parnell had been having an affair with the wife of a member of his party, Captain O'Shea (1840–1905), and had been living with her in south-east London since 1886. This meant that he spent less time in the House of Commons, and even less time in Ireland. Parnell's period of lax attendance to the Home Rule cause meant that he did not take an active part in the second phase of the Land War, the 'Plan of Campaign'. Although the 1881 Land Act had granted the Three Fs, agricultural depression continued to plague Irish farmers, particularly in the south and west. William O'Brien implemented the Plan, which basically said that distressed farmers would offer landlords what they thought was a reasonable rent. If a higher rent was demanded and eviction threatened, the amount that the farmers had offered would be placed in a fund to help all farmers who might be thrown off the land. The National League bolstered the funds when needed. This worked initially, but the Plan could not hold up under the pressure of landlord resistance and of the new Irish chief secretary Arthur Balfour's support for landlords on the one hand and small concessions to farmers on the other. Balfour was trying to 'kill Home Rule with kindness'. Although the Plan of Campaign was largely a failure, it did signal to many landowners that the landlord system could not survive much longer. Parnell, though preoccupied, gave the Plan a minor degree of support, but not so much that its failure could be blamed on him. Meanwhile, the affair with Katherine O'Shea (1945–1921) had been going on since 1880, largely with Captain O'Shea's knowledge. The Captain probably used the affair as a way to become close to Parnell and further his own political career. He was also important as a political intermediary in getting Parnell out of jail during the Land War. But he did not vote for Home Rule in 1886 and resigned his seat. O'Shea did not wish to divorce his wife because he hoped to profit from the will of one of her aunts. When this proved in 1889 to be a false hope, O'Shea started divorce proceedings against his wife, and named Parnell as her lover in the case on 24 December 1889. Initially it looked as if the case would fail or that Parnell could successfully defend himself. But since the affair had been so well known in political circles, the divorce case soon became a public scandal when it came to trial in November 1890. O'Shea won his case and there was an outcry against Parnell amongst British nonconformists (non-Anglican Protestants), who had been strong supporters of Gladstone.

Reaction in Ireland was also one of shock, particularly amongst Catholics. Parnell was re-elected leader of his party on 25 November 1890, but there was a fairly quick backlash against him, even amongst some of his parliamentary supporters. At a party meeting during the first week in December, forty-five Irish MPs withdrew their support for Parnell, leaving him with twenty-eight followers. The split in his party became permanent, and an anti-Parnellite candidate won a by-election in late December 1890, symbolizing the ability of the Home Rule movement to win without him. Throughout 1891, the Irish Parliamentary Party struggled against itself. Parnellites and anti-Parnellites both claimed to be the true Home Rulers. Parnell married Katherine O'Shea in June 1891, but died on 6 October, after campaigning in another by-election. He was buried in Glasnevin cemetery in Dublin on 11 October. Although his fall is often described as tragic, many Irish people saw Parnell as continuing a nationalist tradition which began with O'Connell, progressed through Butt, and was symbolized in Parnell himself. But the split in his parliamentary party continued and made it difficult for further Irish reforms to be enacted.

Gladstone continued his Home Rule efforts, and in the election of 1892 his Liberals won a majority and he returned to power. He presented another Home Rule bill in 1893, which passed the House of Commons on 2 September but was defeated in the House of Lords a week later. Home Rule would continue as an issue until the First World War, but this will be discussed in the next chapter.

CONSERVATIVE AND UNIONIST OPPOSITION TO HOME RULE

The Home Rule period saw an increasingly strong line being drawn between the north-east and the rest of the country. This was caused by several important factors. One of the most important was that the British government opened up the electoral franchise in the whole of the United Kingdom in 1884 and 1885 to include much of the working class. In Ireland this meant that a far greater percentage of Catholics could vote than before, and that electoral power was slipping away from the propertied and merchant classes (which were mainly Protestant). This further meant that those unionists who opposed Home Rule were now generally in a majority only where the overall electoral majority was Protestant (which usually also meant it was unionist). The north-east was the only area that had such an electoral make-up. Although there were a great many unionists in the south of Ireland, they no longer had enough electoral power to make their votes count in electing members of parliament. Unionism, therefore, became a political force confined to Ulster in the north-east. Further, the fear of 'Rome Rule' meant that many Irish Conservatives and Protestants (such as Orangemen, Protestant landowners, and Ulster indus- trialists) found themselves bound together in opposition to Home Rule as they had never been before. There had been disagreements between these groups in the past, but they now realized that they needed to form a more united opposition to Home Rule.

Groups such as the Ulster Loyalist Anti-Repeal Union were formed in 1886 when Gladstone proposed his first Home Rule bill. Lord Randolph Churchill (1849–95), a leading British Conserva- tive, took up the case of Ulster refusal of Home Rule. He did this at least partly to advance his own career, but he did spend a good deal of time in Ulster giving rousing speeches in defence of the Union. The Irish Unionist Party was founded in 1886, under the leadership of Colonel Edward Saunderson (1837–1906) who organized military drilling and even acquired uniforms for unionists to display as defiance to any potential Home Rule proposal. But organized unionism only prospered while Home Rule bills were being pushed in the Commons. In 1886 and 1893, unionists presented a united, and impressive, opposition to Gladstone's Home Rule bills. But when these failed and the split in the Liberal Party became obviously serious and permanent, that unity fell apart, and most unionists returned to concentrating on local affairs and renewing old quarrels, such as that between landlord and farmer. To most nationalists in the south of Ireland, political unionism in the north- east seemed to be a strange, and transient, expression of Protestant insecurity. Although Parnell paid some attention to the growing organization of unionists, most of the other members of his party either ignored it or dismissed it as being run by reactionaries who could not sustain popular support. This misunderstanding of the depth of attachment to the Union would have serious effects on the next two decades of Irish history.

INTERPRETATIONS

There are four main strains of interpretation of Home Rule: unionist, liberal, nationalist and revisionist. They differ on the background of the Home Rule movement, the motives of its main supporters, the reasons why it failed and whether it would have been a feasible solution to the main problems in Ireland.

The unionist interpretation was quite extensive between the fall of Gladstone's 1886 government and the start of World War I. The basic argument was that there were too many instances in Irish history when it could be shown that the country was not able to govern itself for a Home Rule scheme to work. The unionist A.V. Dicey's main argument as put forward in *England's Case Against Home Rule* (1886) was that the specific plans for Home Rule were flawed, and that no matter how much they might be seen as the first step towards full independence, they were not. 'Any plan of Home Rule whatever implies that there are spheres of national life in which Ireland is not to act with the freedom of an independent State', Dicey argued. This unionist interpretation of the potential damage of Home Rule was certainly the dominant one in British public opinion until the early years of the twentieth century.

The unionist interpretation of Home Rule was countered by liberal and nationalist interpretations. And these interpretations have been the dominant ones until very recently. The liberal interpretation was generally the work of the British historians and began with John Morley's biography of British Prime Minister Gladstone, published in 1903. Morley had been a contemporary of Gladstone, and a strong believer in his liberalism. For Morley, Gladstone's taking up of the Home Rule cause was symbolic of the liberal idea that justice was to be based on humanitarianism and humanitarian motives. Not only were Gladstone's efforts morally just, according to Morley, they were heroic. 'Few are the heroic moments in our parliamentary politics,' he wrote, 'but this was one'. Morley's interpretation was very influential throughout the middle decades of the twentieth century. The corollary to Morley's view of Gladstone as the morally righteous politician pursuing a just cause was that it was the unionists who wrecked Home Rule and that this wrecking was the cause of the partition of Ireland and the subsequent Troubles in the North. This view was held by four important historians, whose works have been very influential and were found on university reading lists for decades. George Dangerfield wrote that the unionists who killed Home Rule were also responsible for the end of liberal values and liberal progress in

England by the time of the First World War. His *Strange Death of Liberal England* (1935) and *The Damnable Question* (1977), argued that unionists and the Conservatives who supported them were responsible for not only the lack of a solution to the Irish question and the subsequent violence in Northern Ireland, but for the end of the liberal century and liberal progress. R.C.K. Ensor was the second liberal historian to have a large impact on Home Rule. He had been a correspondent for the *Manchester Guardian* during the Anglo-Irish war (see chapter 6), and had been horrified by the brutality of it, especially the atrocities committed by the British. His textbook, *England 1870–1914* (1936), which was to become standard reading for students, made the argument that Gladstone's Home Rule plans would have solved the Irish problem and prevented this bloodshed. J.L. Hammond's *Gladstone and the Irish Nation* (1938), argued that Home Rule was the greatest tragedy in modern British history, and that the fact that 'more than half the nation' supported Gladstone's Home Rule Bill of 1893, yet the government was unable to pass it due to unionist pressure, would haunt the British people 'on the day of Judgement'. In other words, the defeat of Home Rule was the biggest missed opportunity in modern British history. Nicholas Mansergh continued with this interpretation. He argued in *Ireland in the Age of Reform and Revolution* (1940) that only the Famine was a greater tragedy than Home Rule's lost opportunity.

The nationalist interpretation of Home Rule is somewhat similar to the liberal interpretation, in that it has argued that Home Rule was to be the first step towards independence, and was a tragic missed opportunity. The first major exponent of this interpretation was R. Barry O'Brien, who was very close to a major figure in the Home Rule movement – Parnell. He was with Parnell during 1890–1 and wrote first-hand accounts of the politics of the period. He published a two-volume biography of Parnell in 1898. According to O'Brien, Parnell was the key figure in the Home Rule struggle; he had 'brought Ireland within sight of the Promised Land', and had laid the groundwork for independence – 'the triumph of the national cause awaits other times, and another man'. O'Brien's argument and his emphasis on Parnell shows the major difference between the liberal interpretation and the nationalist interpretation. To liberal historians, Home Rule was in Gladstone's hands and its failure not only affected Ireland, but British politics also. In the nationalist interpretation, Parnell was the central figure, and it was his imagination and political power that drove Home Rule as far as it went. Gladstone was not forgotten in the nationalist interpretation, it is just that the focus of attention is on Irish Home Rule efforts.

After 1922 and the founding of the Irish Free State (see chapter 6), the nationalist interpretation of Home Rule underwent a slight change. While Home Rule may have seemed the best possible avenue for self-determination to contemporaries at the time, the post-1922 generation of nationalist historians argued that, even if it had been granted, it would not have fulfilled Ireland's national needs and aspirations. T.A. Jackson was the most prominent exponent of this idea. In his *Ireland Her Own* (1947), he argued that Parnell was the only one who could have transformed Home Rule eventually into a meaningful movement for independence. Later Irish Home Rulers, such as John Redmond (see chapter 6) were categorized as being willing stooges of the British, who were mainly interested in quelling disturbance, not granting Irish independence.

Along with other aspects of Irish history, Home Rule history underwent a revision during the mid-twentieth century. F.S.L. Lyons argued in his *Ireland Since the Famine* (1971) that the nationalist view of Home Rule as a movement for a completely separate (and Catholic) Ireland is too simple. Home Rule ideas and the agitations for it were more diverse and complex than that, Lyons argued, and it was not at all clear that Home Rule would have formed the type of Ireland that twentieth-century nationalists desired. Roy Foster took this argument further, both in his 1976 biography of Parnell and in his *Modern Ireland* (1989). Foster showed the detail of differing Home Rule opinions and the background of Home Rulers, as well as the difficulties in reaching a consensus on Home Rule.

Some British historians, notably Michael Hurst, David Hamer, A.B. Cooke and John Vincent, began to broaden the interpretation of Home Rule, calling into question the motivations of leading British politicians at the time. Their main argument was that both the British politicians such as Gladstone who fought for Home Rule, and those who opposed it, such as Joseph Chamberlain (the liberal unionist) were more concerned with their own positions within British politics than they were with Irish affairs. Cooke and Vincent, in their *Governing Passion* (1974), argued that Gladstone and his cabinet were more interested in Home Rule as a party problem and as a way to gain support and remain in power than they were in Irish reform. They claimed that Gladstone used Home Rule as a way to thwart the increasing popularity of Chamberlain (who was younger and a potential rival for the Liberal leadership). Hamer made similar arguments in his biography of John Morley (1968). Hamer argued that although Gladstone believed that Home Rule was the solution to the Irish problem, his motivation came primarily from a desire, ironically, to keep the Liberal party together. The party had been suffering from other, unrelated internal problems, and Gladstone thought that Home Rule was enough of a liberal justice issue to unite the party and forestall a split. Michael Hurst, in his *Joseph Chamberlain and the Liberal Reunion* (1967), argued that Chamberlain had similar ideas in mind, and that he never wanted to heal any split in the Liberal party, but used his opposition to Home Rule to bolster his own political position. Much of the most current work on Home Rule has also concentrated on its impact on British rather than on Irish politics. Terry Jenkins and Colin Matthew have revived the British liberal interpretation, focusing on Gladstone and what they see as his genuine belief in Home Rule as a viable solution. (See T.A. Jenkins, *Gladstone, Whiggery, and the Liberal Party 1874–1885*, 1987; and H.C.G. Matthew, *Gladstone 1875–1898*, 1995.) William Lubenow has also written a careful and detailed analysis of parliamentary behaviour on Home Rule, in *Parliamentary Politics and the Home Rule Crisis: the British House of Commons in 1886* (1988).

This recent trend has finally been changed with the appearance of Alan O'Day's excellent, *Irish Home Rule 1867–1921* (1998). It provides the first truly detailed analysis of the different Home Rule proposals, but, more importantly, contains a fresh interpretation. O'Day's main argument is that the old idea that Home Rulers comprised a spectrum from constitutionalists (like Butt) to revolutionaries (such as Davitt) misses the stronger conclusion that within the nationalist movement there were two distinct groups – those who sought Home Rule on moral justice grounds, and those who sought it on material grounds (that is, thought that Ireland's economic future required Home Rule). Finally, like some of the nationalist interpretations, O'Day argues that the failure of Home Rule showed 'the limitations of parliamentarianism, the shortcoming of British responses and a fossilised Irish party'. This would become very important in the minds of the nationalist revolutionaries who appear in the next chapter.

SIX

Nationalism, Unionism and Irish Identity, 1891–1922

This chapter is about conflicting ideas of who should govern Ireland, how it should be governed and what it meant to be Irish in the years between the death of Parnell in 1891 and the partition of Ireland in 1921, which created the Irish Free State and a separate Northern Ireland retained under British control. There are political and revolutionary aspects to this period, but also social and cultural ones, with an attempt to assert certain types of Irishness during what has been called the 'Gaelic Revival'. Social and economic change was also important during this period, and many of the political and cultural events discussed here were affected by them. There were further government land reforms, but emigration regained its former rapid pace. Rural and urban life also changed. In short, fewer people on the land and a greater percentage in towns allowed for a degree of modernization (although Ireland lagged behind most of Europe in living standards).

LAND REFORMS CONTINUE

1891 saw the founding of the Congested Districts Board, which attempted to solve the long-running economic problems in western counties, specifically with powers to divide or combine farms in an effort to reduce overcrowding on individual plots. In 1898, local government was reformed and placed on a fully elected basis. In 1899, the Department of Agriculture was established to help farmers learn about advanced agricultural techniques and

113

improvements. The land reforms that the British government had implemented between 1870 and 1900 had allowed over sixty thousand tenants to purchase the land they worked. The 1903 Wyndham Land Act went even further, and by the beginning of the First World War, over sixty per cent of farms were being worked by their owners, and between 1903 and 1922, eleven million acres of land had been sold to tenants under the provisions of the Land Acts. Between 1881 and 1915, the British goverment paid out £86.1 million in order for the Land Acts to accomplish their goals. Farmers benefited most, and some labourers saw an increased standard of living (though by no means a great improvement). In the north-east, land reforms worked a little differently because landlords there did not have the same burdens of overcrowding and other land problems as existed in other parts of the country. This meant that the landlord class in the north-east held on to much of its land, and since many landlords were strong unionists, unionism began the twentieth century with a very solid landed base there.

This is not to say, however, that all agricultural workers benefited equally from the Land Acts. Since they were designed mainly to allow farmers to buy the land they had previously rented, agricultural labourers did not gain many benefits from the Acts. There was a good deal of bitterness about this, which flared up in violence between 1906 and 1909, when some labourers (mainly in Meath, Westmeath, Galway, Roscommon and Clare) attacked the livestock of 'graziers' (farmers who rented large tracts of land to graze cattle). They scattered herds, boycotted graziers and caused damage to property. This 'Ranch War' highlighted the fact that the divisions within Irish agricultural life were not just between the landlords and those who rented or worked the land. But the agitation petered out when it became obvious that no effective support would come from the Irish Parliamentary Party, and the United Irish League (founded in 1898 by William O'Brien to demand the redistribution of ranch lands to small farmers) proved ineffective because it had become dominated by politicians and, ironically, graziers themselves.

RURAL AND URBAN LIFE

Social conditions in rural and urban areas also underwent great change in the second half of the nineteenth century and the early twentieth century. About four million people emigrated between 1850 and 1914, three million to the United States and one million to Britain. This was largely due to the lure of more work and higher wages in these other countries, rather than the more desperate flight from over-population, starvation and disease that stimulated Famine emigration. Not surprisingly, emigration was highest in those counties which depended heavily on agriculture, and where there were very few alternatives to farm work. Unlike previous emigrations, however, this period saw nearly as many women leave Ireland as men. On farms, there was an increasing tendency for one child to inherit the land, rather than it being divided amongst all the family's children. Along with emigration depleting the number of eligible partners, this inheritance practice helped create an increase in the number of people who never married. If he had not inherited land, it was difficult for a man to support a wife and children (as well as not appearing an attractive prospect in a growing system of arranged marriages, called 'matches'). In 1841, ten per cent of men between ages 45 and 54 had never married. This increased to twenty-seven per cent by 1911.

There were other important social changes in rural areas during this period. Education was on the increase, with more children attending school. Literacy rates rose as a consequence. News-papers and other literature were gradually finding a wider distribution. Rural people could control their finances better when banks began to build more branches in rural towns. The number of retail shops increased, and a greater amount of clothing and household goods came from shops rather than being made at home. The railway network was extended. Work roles in rural areas also changed from the 1860s onwards, especially for women. Women began to be less directly involved in physical farm work. This was partly because the nature of farmwork had changed (and so required fewer hands), but also because the financial conditions of many farmers had improved to the point where they were eager to see their wives adopt more fitting (i.e. genteel) work inside the home. This was part of a growing sense of the differences in prosperity between farmers, as well as ideas of social improvement. Moderate farmers tried to become like richer farmers not only in income but in manners and family work habits.

Ireland was still mainly a rural country in this period, but there were important changes in towns and cities as well. In the first place, the percentage of those living in towns doubled between the Famine and the First World War (although the overall town and city population fell owing to emigration). Towns and cities also grew in importance as economic and administrative centres. There was, however, mixed economic prosperity in urban areas. Competition with more powerful British firms led to a decline in Irish industry in the 1870s. Dublin and Cork saw the percentage of workers involved in industry fall by almost half between the Famine and the First World War. But retailers gradually were able to offer customers more mass-produced (and usually cheaper) goods, and their profits were healthier than those in industry. Belfast was somewhat exceptional in this period in that, although its traditional primary industry, linen production, was decreasing, it was being replaced by shipbuilding and engineering. Living conditions were generally better than in Dublin, but they still lagged behind those in Britain and most of Europe. But in Belfast the bulk of industry was in Protestant and unionist control. Northeastern Ireland was being divided along economic, religious and political lines that the rest of the country generally did not witness. For the most part, the ownership and management of industry and retailing was Protestant (and increasingly unionist), while the bulk of Catholics were employed in low-wage jobs. Trade unions were more able to organize in Belfast than in Dublin, although sectarianism prevented a broad-based labour movement. In Dublin, the importance of Home Rule overshadowed attempts at unionization.

GAELIC REVIVAL

One of the effects of the death of Parnell and the continuing failure of the Home Rule movement was that many Irish people looked for other avenues to express what they thought of as Irish identity. This took many forms, but three distinct ones stand out: a new

Irish literary movement, the revival and promotion of the Irish language and the organization of traditional Irish games and sports.

The famous Anglo-Irish literary revival was led by a group of intellectuals who thought that a national literature and cultural life was vital to Irish nationality. They also thought that this literature should not just be old folktales (although they were considered important), but that it should be a vibrant and cultivated literature of the highest quality, one that would be regarded as highly as other national literatures. It was led by William Butler Yeats (1865–1939), a young poet who eventually came to symbolize the movement and much of what is now considered Irish literary culture. Yeats came from an artistic family (his father and brothers were successful and famous painters) with strong connections to County Sligo, where the young Yeats spent many holidays. His interest in the wild west of Ireland was to surface later in his poetry. He was born in Dublin and spent much of his youth in London, but he returned to Dublin to attend art school. After art school, he worked for a while as a literary correspondent for American newspapers, and began his serious work as a poet. His early poetry did not indicate a strong interest in native Irish literature, but Yeats soon came under the influence of John O'Leary, the Young Irelander, who had recently returned from exile in Paris. To Yeats and his friends, O'Leary symbolized early nationalist ideals of creating a nation in its entirety (culturally as well as politically). Yeats consulted O'Leary regularly while compiling some of his early works, such as *Folk Tales of the Irish Peasantry* (1888). He was also heavily influenced by Standish James O'Grady (1846–1928), who was writing heroic histories of Ireland. Between 1886 and the 1920s, Yeats revived Irish legends and folklore, with the help of other Irish literary figures such as the playwrights J.M. Synge (1871–1909) and Lady Augusta Gregory (1852–1932), and the Irish language scholar Douglas Hyde (1863–1947), who would also become the first president of Ireland (see chapter 7). They used folk imagery and ancient Irish heroes to symbolize the cultural history of Ireland. Rather than use historical figures such as the Gaelic chieftains of recent centuries, Yeats and his colleagues wrote about mythological or partly mythological figures, such as Cuchulainn [coo-cullen], the legendary Ulster warrior who came to symbolize the fighting spirit of the Irish. Yeats founded the Irish Literary Society of London in 1891 and joined the National Literary Society in Dublin in 1892. The Abbey Theatre in Dublin was founded in 1904 to provide a venue for the production of what was called 'Irish national drama'.

Many great poems, legends, stories, plays and other types of literature were produced during this fervent period of creative activity, but the significance for Irish identity was more complex. The literary revivalists were highly successful in creating a new national literature based on ancient ideas, and their work continues to be studied to this day. But their literature generally appealed to like-minded people, and really only captured the interest of educated and intellectual people. Most Irish people, Dubliners especially, were interested in more popular and light-hearted forms of entertainment, such as music halls and dance clubs. The revivalist Abbey Theatre, for instance, struggled financially until it was subsidized by the Irish Free State in 1924. Further, although the literary revivalists took many of their themes from the west of Ireland, they mainly worked in Dublin for a Dublin (and international) audience, rather than the country as a whole. Still, their literature had an impact on some nationalists, who drew inspiration from the vision of Ireland as an ancient nation and culture, and the revivalists succeeded in one of their most cherished goals, that of gaining international recognition for Irish literature and drama.

Another important Irish movement of this period was the Gaelic League, and it succeeded where the literary revival failed – in capturing the imagination of the whole nation. It was founded in 1893 by Douglas Hyde (1860–1949) and Eoin MacNeill (1867–1945). The League had two goals: to retain and support the Irish language where it was already spoken (which was mainly in the far west, in isolated pockets in Munster and Leinster and in Donegal); and to restore Irish as the spoken language of the country. The League organized Irish language classes and Irish-speaking social activities. Rather than looking solely towards the past (like many literary revivalists), Gaelic Leaguers tried to create the conditions for the Irish language to become the major language in the country for the future. Starting in 1897, it ran a national festival, published its own newspaper and paid for the publication of Irish language texts and literature. It was a subscription organization, and raised a lot of money. There were many Gaelic League successes. The Irish language became a central part of Irish education. In 1903 alone, 1,300 National Schools had Irish introduced into their curriculum, and in 1909 it became a compulsory subject. To the extent that it is part of contemporary Irish culture at all, the Irish language owes its survival, beyond the boundaries of antiquarianism, to the Gaelic League and groups like it. Douglas Hyde was one of those involved in the Gaelic revival who argued strongly that a separate Irish cultural nation had to be re-created. His idea was that this must come about through a process of de-Anglicization, which meant casting off English customs, dress, games, language and ideas. This brought back memories of the boycotts of English goods in the late 1700s and during the Famine. Hyde wanted to help build a self-sufficient Irish economy.

In these ways, the League grew from being simply an organization to promote the Irish language, to a movement to invigorate the country with what was, essentially, new-found Irishness. The League was successful in gaining broad support from many different classes, although the working class made up its smallest element. It was also popular among some unionists, partly because the League was initially apolitical and partly because many unionists did not see any contradiction between being culturally Irish and still part of the United Kingdom. In 1915–16, however, the League became politicized, as Patrick Pearse (1879–1916) became more involved in its activities. Outside politics, however, the League was very successful. They even persuaded pubs to close on St Patrick's Day and eventually had that day turned into a national holiday. Although they failed in their ultimate goal of making Ireland an Irish-speaking nation, the League, generally known under its Irish name Connradh na Gaeilge [conn-rah nah gale-geh] has continued to promote the language to the present day.

The other major surviving organization from this period is the Gaelic Athletic Association (GAA) which was founded by Michael Cusack in 1884. Cusack (1847–1906) had been a teacher and lecturer at a training college for aspiring civil servants. In his youth, he had enjoyed cricket and rugby, those quintessentially English games. But he became disillusioned with the way these games were run by exclusive social clubs and organizations. He also began to think that the gambling that was so prevalent at the time was an unwelcome English import, and that English games were damaging Irish identity. He founded the GAA with Maurice Davin (1864–1927), in an attempt to promote traditional Irish sports such as hurling, Gaelic football and camogie. Other athletic sports (such as foot races) which were not explictly English were promoted in the early stages, but they soon declined in popularity compared with team sports. The Archbishop of Cashel, Thomas William Croke (1824–1902), became the GAA's first patron. Other prominent figures included Michael Davitt and Charles Stewart Parnell. One of the first things that the GAA did was to ban its members from playing foreign sports (tellingly called 'imported games'; the ban was lifted in 1971) and from serving in the British military or police. It was organized on county lines, and county teams competed for their provincial titles, and then on to an 'All-Ireland' grand final. The Fenians quickly became involved in the GAA, and by 1886 they were in a dominant position. This soon brought disapproval from the Catholic Church, but after the fall of Parnell, the Fenian leaders reorganized the GAA so that it was clearly a nationalist organization, but also non-violent and non-revolutionary. The GAA also benefited from the general rise in interest in spectator sports that was taking place in Europe and America at the time. Crowds flocked to games and special trains were run to handle the flow of people. Participation in GAA events declined during the Anglo-Irish War and the civil war (see next section), but the organization soon recovered and has played an important part in Irish life ever since. Hurling and Gaelic football are perhaps unique in the western world in that they are mass spectator sports, but remain amateur.

NATIONALISM AND UNIONISM, 1891–1914

When Gladstone's second Home Rule bill was defeated by the House of Lords in 1893, he resigned. The new Liberal Prime Minister, Lord Rosebery (1847–1929), did not see Ireland as a priority and would not propose a Home Rule bill. But the Liberals were soon out of office, with the Conservatives coming to power under Lord Salisbury (1830–1903) in 1895. In opposition,

Rosebery and the Liberals concentrated mainly on British domestic problems and did not raise Irish issues seriously. At the same time, the Irish nationalist MPs in the House of Commons were struggling with their own problems. They were still divided over Parnell, even after his death. The small group of Parnellites were led by John Redmond (1856–1918), and the anti-Parnellites by John Dillon (1851–1927). Although fewer in number than the anti-Parnellites, the Parnellites had more support in the constituencies and were backed by the Irish Republican Brotherhood. Further, the anti-Parnellites argued over tactics. Dillon thought that too much emphasis was being placed on land reform, and wanted a strong, centralized organization such as O'Connell and Parnell had built. Other anti-Parnellites, such as William O'Brien (1852–1928), thought that the land issue was vital, and that the Irish party would lose popular support if they neglected it. Tim Healy (1855–1931) thought that the party should be decentralized, become more locally based, so that it could rebuild its strength. All this division amongst the Irish MPs, and lack of interest in Irish affairs among British Liberal politicians, left the question of Irish government open to action from the Conservatives and Unionists. Salisbury (1830–1903) and Arthur Balfour (1848–1930), Irish secretary from 1887 to 1891 and Prime Minister from 1902 to 1905, developed an Irish policy which focused on further land and social reforms, and largely left the national question alone. In addition to seeing genuine need for such reforms, they wanted to placate the Irish population, as well as assure Unionists in Ulster and Great Britain that the United Kingdom would stay intact. Their land reforms from 1887 to 1903 made it very easy for tenants to buy the land that they worked, offering them interest at three and a quarter per cent over sixty-eight and a half years. It was foolish to keep renting when the payments on their land loans were often cheaper, and so, by 1909, half of the country's farmland was in the hands of former tenant farmers. Balfour also pushed through poor relief and agricultural organization in Ireland that pre-dated most welfare state reforms in Britain and much of Europe. Cottage industries such as weaving and fishing were subsidized by the government, and agricultural institutes were set up to train farmers in new methods. Railways, roads and bridges were built in an effort to help rural trade flow better. Local government was reformed and taken out of the hands of the landlords in 1898. While all these reforms provided much needed relief from specific and long-standing problems, their emphasis on rural and agricultural matters may have meant that industrial and commercial development in Ireland was delayed by a few generations.

By 1900, however, the Irish Party in the House of Commons had reunited under John Redmond, with his anti-Parnellite opponent John Dillon agreeing to act as his deputy. But William O'Brien still argued that the main issue was land reform and Tim Healy wanted to decentralize the party. Redmond and Dillon finally had to force Healy out of the party, and O'Brien resigned. Still, the revitalized party had potential. While criticized from different quarters for being controlled by the Catholic Church or by the British Liberals, the party tried to assert its independence by renewing the call for Home Rule. One of the main problems, however, was that, by 1900, many of the MPs in the Irish party had actually found themselves distanced from their constituents back home. They had become used to parliamentary life in London, and had actually begun to admire the parliamentary system. As a result, Redmond and his party were often not as careful to listen to Irish opinion as they probably should have been, which meant that they did not pay enough attention to Irish social issues while they were concentrating on the national question.

In Ireland, other nationalist movements were beginning to take shape. Arthur Griffith (1871–1922), a journalist, had recently returned from South Africa in 1899. Like many other Irishmen, he supported the Boers against the British in the Boer War (1899–1902). He began to edit a weekly newspaper called the *United Irishmen* (reviving the title of the Young Ireland paper of the 1840s). Through this newspaper and his other writings (particularly his *Resurrection of Hungary: a Parallel for Ireland*, 1904), he began to outline a policy of non-Home Rule independence which he called Sinn Féin [shin fain]. Griffith argued for a completely independent Ireland, but one which would share a monarch with Great Britain. Griffith had seen Hungary gain its independence from Austria this way, and thought that it was the best route for Irish independence. He also argued that Ireland needed economic protectionism in order to build its own economy.

As a political vehicle for these ideas, Griffith and others founded Cumann na nGaedheal [cummann nah gale] in 1900, as an umbrella organization for co-ordinating the activities of smaller Irish nationalist groups. Among other things, they demanded in 1902 that the Irish Parliamentary Party withdraw from the British House of Commons. In 1905 Griffith and Bulmer Hobson (1883–1969) translated the idea of Sinn Féin into an official organization. Between 1905 and World War I, it attracted various nationalists who were finding it difficult to organize, and absorbed them into its organization (along with previously organized groups such as Cumann na nGaedheal). Other nationalist organizations were also starting to crawl out from under the long shadow of Parnell, including the Irish Republican Brotherhood, which was revived when Thomas Clarke (1857–1916) returned from jail in England via a stint in America in 1907. The IRB gradually attracted more members, and became very active in the Gaelic League and GAA, as well as Sinn Féin.

At roughly the same time, an infant Irish labour movement was beginning under James Larkin (1876–1947) and James Connolly (1868–1916). Although agricultural and rural labourers had been a major concern of Irish nationalists and reformers since the days of Young Ireland, urban workers had not received the same attention. Irish cities were amongst the most socially and economically backward in the United Kingdom. Undernourishment and disease were common. Inspired by labour and socialist movements in Britain and Europe, Larkin and Connolly organized the Irish Transport Workers Union (ITWU) in 1908. They were initially very successful in gaining concessions from employers, but a massive strike against the United Tramways Company in 1913 was a disaster. It lasted four months, and eventually, the ITWU had to surrender, which left its members with very little (and lacking four months' wages). Frustrated by the lack of help from nationalist organizations, Larkin went to America to raise money for the union. Connolly then took over Irish trade unionism, and created his 'citizen army' to protect labourers from the police and hostile employers. Connolly also began to make connections with militant nationalists because he began to think that revolution was the only way that an Irish workers' state could come about.

Meanwhile in Britain, the Liberals returned to power in 1906 with a large majority. They pushed through many reforms in Britain and Ireland, including setting up the National University of Ireland and extensions of land reform, and offering Redmond and the Irish Party an 'Irish Council' instead of an Irish parliament as a concession to Home Rule in 1907. Redmond refused. But the Liberals ran into trouble when the House of Lords vetoed their 1909 budget, and they had to call an election. Although they won the election, the Liberal majority was greatly reduced, and the Irish Party and the rising British Labour Party held the balance of power between the Liberals and the Conservatives. Redmond's Irish Party pledged support for the Liberals if they would reciprocate with Home Rule. After they reduced the Lords' veto powers in 1911, the Liberal Prime Minister, Herbert Asquith (1852–1928), introduced a third Home Rule bill on 11 April 1912. It was a moderate bill, which reserved British control of foreign affairs, currency and tariffs. Even so, it received the support of Redmond's party and Sinn Féin. Unionists, however, were outraged because they realized that this Home Rule bill had a good chance of passing. Their leaders, Sir Edward Carson (1854–1935) and Sir James Craig (1871–1940), rejected the bill and held many demonstrations against it throughout 1912. They also put together the Ulster Volunteers (a private army), and gun-running provided it with arms. The Conservatives in Britain backed the unionists. With all this controversy, the bill took until January 1913 to pass the House of Commons. It was defeated by the House of Lords, but since their veto powers had been reduced in 1911, the bill could only be delayed for two years. The agitation against it did not cease, however. Unionists refused to accept that Home Rule would become law within two years, and pledged to fight against it. The support they received from British Conservatives made the problem a serious crisis. The government would have to enforce Home Rule by using the military, but many important officers in Ulster and in Britain said they would refuse to enforce Home Rule and that they would support the unionists. This made many Liberal cabinet members worry that Home Rule could never become law in Ireland without a civil war in the United Kingdom. Some MPs tried to convince the government to partition Ulster and keep it in the United Kingdom, but these efforts failed.

Seeing that the unionists were arming against Home Rule, many nationalists decided to do the same. The IRB formed the Irish Volunteers in November 1913. Eventually, Redmond realized that he needed the Volunteers, and many of the Irish Party joined them, especially in command offices. Membership in the Volunteers grew very rapidly. Redmond tried to pacify the overall situation by offering the unionists temporary exclusion from a Home Rule Ireland, but it was rejected. King George V tried to solve the crisis over the Home Rule bill by inviting all the major participants to a conference at Buckingham Palace from 21 to 24 July 1914. The conference was a failure because none of the participants could agree on anything. In the meantime, the government had considered amending the Home Rule bill, giving Ulster a temporary exclusion. By this time, however, World War I had started and Britain entered it on 4 August 1914. The Home Rule bill, which had been lingering since January 1913, was then given the royal assent by King George on 18 September 1914. The government had insisted on this in order to quell Irish disturbances during the war. In a concession to unionists, however, it passed another bill which delayed the implementation of Home Rule until the war was over. The question of whether Ulster would take part in a future Home Rule Ireland was not resolved.

WAR IN EUROPE AND WAR IN IRELAND, 1914–22

The First World War split Irish nationalists. Some, like Redmond, thought that the war was for the freedom of small nations, and that Ireland should support the allies since it was a small nation struggling for freedom. He argued that if the Irish volunteered for the British army and fought in the war, then Irish claims for independence would be taken more seriously by both Britain and the international community after the war. But many other nationalists, including Sinn Féin and the IRB, were opposed to the war and could not conceive of an alliance with Britain. The effect of this was that the Irish Volunteers split into those who supported participation in the war (and who changed their name to the National Volunteers), and those who opposed entry into the war (who retained the name Irish Volunteers). The National

Volunteers were in the majority, and many of them joined the British army. Although they were a minority, the new Irish Volunteers were more militant in their thinking, and began planning for an insurrection. The IRB also became more heavily involved in militant nationalism when their organizational director, Patrick Pearse (1879–1916), began to strengthen links between the IRB and the Irish Volunteers. Pearse, along with Joseph Mary Plunkett (1887–1916) and Thomas MacDonagh (1878–1916), thought that a revolution was necessary not only to gain independence, but to cleanse Ireland of its confused efforts at Home Rule and to provide a blood sacrifice as a symbol to the Irish people. (This was not unique thinking at the time. Some British and French intellectuals thought that the First World War would prove to be a cleansing experience.) Pearse was a powerful orator and on 1 August 1915, he gave the funeral oration for Jeremiah O'Donovan Rossa, the old Fenian who had died in New York and whose body had been returned to Ireland. At Glasnevin Cemetery in Dublin, Pearse used O'Donovan Rossa's body to symbolize the dead heroes of Ireland's struggle against Britain, and said that, no matter how many weak Home Rule bills were passed, the Irish would not rest until they had achieved full independence. His oft-repeated words became slogans for militant nationalism.

> Life springs from death; and from the graves of patriot men and women spring living nations. The Defenders of this Realm ... think they have pacified Ireland ... but the fools, the fools, the fools! They have left us our Fenian dead, and while Ireland holds these graves, Ireland unfree shall never be at peace.

While these were to become inspirational words in April 1916, it should be remembered that this idea of the necessity of a blood sacrifice was a minority view even among nationalists.

From late 1914 until April 1916, the Irish Volunteers and James Connolly's Citizen Army organized and drilled in Dublin and Wicklow. Contacts were made with Germany to provide arms for an Irish rising. Sir Roger Casement (1864–1916), an Ulster Protestant and former British civil servant, went to the United States to raise money and to Germany to try to recruit Irish prisoners of war for the planned rebellion. Preoccupied with the European war, the British government only put up mild resistance to Irish nationalist propaganda. In January 1916, Pearse and the military council of the IRB planned a rebellion for Easter Sunday, 23 April 1916. Dublin was to be the centre, but there were rebellions planned for other cities as well. Some important members of the IRB and the Volunteers objected to what they thought would be a suicidal revolt, but they were quickly overwhelmed by Pearse and the others, who argued that, since German arms were already on the way, it was too late to call off the rebellion. But this organizational confusion meant that the German ship *Aud* was not able to land on the Kerry coast on Thursday or early Friday 20–21 April. It was intercepted by a British ship and scuttled by its captain, sending its cargo of 20,000 rifles to the bottom of the sea. Casement landed near Tralee in Kerry on the same day, but was soon arrested by the British. He was taken to London, put on trial for treason and executed on 3 August. When he heard about the *Aud* and Casement, Eoin MacNeill (1867–1945), the chief of staff of the Irish Volunteers, cancelled the planned Sunday rebellion. Some of the other rebels then met on Sunday 23 April and decided to go ahead with the rebellion the next day, Easter Monday. Because of the confusion and conflicting orders, the rising mainly took place in Dublin, with only scattered action in other parts of the country.

On Monday morning, Pearse led 1,558 Volunteers and Connolly led 219 members of his Citizen Army in a Dublin rebellion which captured the General Post Office (GPO) and other important strategic points in the city, including the Four Courts, Liberty Hall and City Hall. The GPO became headquarters for the rebellion, and it was here that Pearse read the Proclamation of the Irish Republic. The British army counterattacked on 25 April, recovering several important buildings and cordoning off many of the rebels' avenues of communication. British reinforcements soon arrived from Belfast and other military posts in Ireland. On 27 April, the army started to shell the GPO and the Four Courts. Pearse and his rebels retreated from the burning GPO on 28 April, and were captured the next day.

It is difficult, if not impossible, to gauge the reaction of Dublin citizens because there was no contemporary reporting of the events of the Rising until May. People were urged to stay at home, and it is very unlikely that any solid information about the Rising reached them. There were, however, a number of rumours which seemed to spread rapidly. The first and most prevalent was that the Rising was part of a German invasion, or that it was laying the grounds for one. This rumour caused many people to be disgusted with the rebels. These were most probably Dublin unionists, who may have had family members serving in the trenches in France. They were, of course, greatly opposed to the Rising, and thought it was a betrayal of the Irish men serving in the British army. Redmond stated in the House of Commons on 27 April that Irish people were horrified at the Rising, but he was in no position to know because he was in London. It is clear from many eyewitness reports that there was some sympathy for the rebels, and that this came from ordinary Dubliners who expressed regret that the Rising had failed. Sir John Maxwell (1859–1929), the British Commander, said that many people who witnessed the Rising and were on the streets immediately after it sympathized with the rebels. Any hostility which the rebels endured while being marched away was mainly from some Dublin unionists, and from the wives of soldiers in the British army.

Between 3 and 12 May, the British military court in Dublin tried and executed fifteen of the rebels, including Pearse and Connolly and those who had signed the Proclamation of the Irish Republic. Other participants in the rebellion were arrested and jailed in England and Ireland. The execution of the Rising's leaders was received with shock and outrage by many people in Dublin. As stated above, there was a base of sympathetic support for the rebels, but even those nationalists like Redmond, who had opposed them, condemned the executions. The poems and writings of Pearse and others became popular reading, and copies of their pictures were put up in many homes. Although it did not look likely when they surrendered, the rebels' idea of a blood sacrifice came true after the executions.

Because of this change in public opinion, the British government soon realized that it must make some concessions to avoid further trouble. Between August 1916 and July 1917, the imprisoned Easter rebels were released. They were welcomed back to Ireland as heroes. The new British Liberal Prime Minister, David Lloyd George (1863–1945), re-opened negotiations with Redmond on Home Rule, with the temporary exclusion of six Ulster counties

(Antrim, Armagh, Down, Fermanagh, Londonderry and Tyrone – the counties of Northern Ireland today). Redmond rejected this offer because he found out that Lloyd George had promised unionists that this arrangement would be permanent. Another meeting of all Irish parties was agreed to, and Home Rulers and unionists met in Dublin from July 1917 to April 1918. The Irish Volunteers and Sinn Féin, now militarized by Eamon de Valera (1882–1975), a commander during the Easter Rising, refused to attend the meeting because they thought it would end in partition of the island. But the meeting could not agree on a solution, and Redmond died suddenly during the conference in March 1918. De Valera was arrested on 17 May 1918 on a charge of plotting with the Germans, and imprisoned in Lincoln jail in England.

Redmond's death, along with the massive victory for Sinn Féin in the general election of December 1918, meant that Irish nationalism had been taken away from the Irish Parliamentary Party. Sinn Féin won seventy-three seats, the Irish Parliamentary Party six, and the unionists twenty-six. Sinn Féin, however, refused to accept the authority of the British parliament and to sit in the House of Commons. They set up Dáil Éireann [dawl air-un], an Irish parliament, at Mansion House in Dublin on 21 January 1919. The Dáil operated as a full government, setting up its own court system, land bank and other important offices. On 3 February 1919, Eamon de Valera escaped from Lincoln jail with the help of two important Dáil members, Michael Collins (1890–1922) and Harry Boland (1887–1922). De Valera returned to Dublin as President of the Dáil, and almost immediately went to the United States on a fund-raising trip. Although he succeeded in raising much money, disputes between Irish-American politicians and other problems prevented de Valera from gaining what he most wanted – official recognition of the Irish Republic as a sovereign state from the United States government. While he was gone, Michael Collins began to strengthen the Dáil's connections with the IRB and the Volunteers. Although some important Dáil members thought this was unconstitutional, Collins proceeded, building up an impressive, but unofficial, Irish guerrilla army.

The Easter Rising had left militant nationalism in disarray until Collins started to revive its organization. The Irish Volunteers became known as the Irish Republican Army (IRA) after January 1919, and they began a guerrilla war against British government in Ireland, which became known as the Anglo-Irish War (1919–21). The IRA focused primarily on the Royal Irish Constabulary (the paramilitary police force in Ireland). They attacked RIC outposts and barracks, killed RIC officers and constables and raided RIC weapons depots. The IRA were very successful initially, with the RIC defeated in many areas of the country. The British government responded by sending army troops to Ireland, and two new forces were created from British soldiers who had served in the First World War. These forces were intended to supplement the RIC (which was largely made up of local Catholic men). Owing to a shortage of RIC uniforms, many of these transferred soldiers wore khaki military trousers and dark green (almost black) police tunics, earning them the nickname Black and Tans. Along with the other new force, the Auxiliaries, the Black and Tans fought a counter-guerrilla war with the IRA, and earned a reputation for ferocity and brutality in their reprisals. British public opinion was often shocked at their actions, and a Peace with Ireland Council was formed. On the world stage, this war was a propaganda victory for the IRA. Many other nations saw an inconsistency in Britain being part of the dismantling of other European empires during the settlement of the First World War, yet retaining their empire and control of Ireland.

Although the Home Rule bill which was due to come into effect at the end of the war had been bypassed by militant Irish nationalism and stubborn Irish unionism, the British Prime Minister, David Lloyd George, put forward a new Home Rule solution for Ireland in 1920, during the height of the Anglo-Irish War. He proposed two parliaments in Ireland, one for the six Ulster counties, and another for the rest of the country. For the first time, unionists accepted a form of Home Rule (for themselves), but the nationalists in the south refused the offer. They argued that the Irish people wanted an Irish republic for the whole island. Their republican ideals were firmly held at this point, and so the Anglo-Irish War continued on its bloody and destructive path. Finally, Lloyd George realized that he must negotiate with the republicans. A general truce was called on 9 July 1921. Lloyd George offered Eamon de Valera and the Dáil dominion status within the British Empire, much like Canada. De Valera and the Dáil rejected this offer, but agreed to treaty negotiations in October 1921. De Valera sent Michael Collins, Arthur Griffith and four other members of the Dáil to London to meet with Lloyd George and the British cabinet. De Valera stayed in Dublin, possibly to keep an eye on extreme militants, or perhaps because he knew that he and Lloyd George were at a stalemate, and that different personalities might be better negotiators. He instructed the Irish delegation not to accept any partition of Ireland.

The negotiations which led to the Anglo-Irish Treaty of 6 December 1921 were difficult and trying. Lloyd George was under pressure from unionists to provide a measure of self-rule for some Ulster counties, and also from British public opinion, which desperately wanted peace with Ireland. The Dáil delegation was told by de Valera to retain the unity of the island of Ireland. The talks came down to two important issues, the question of partition and of allegiance to the British crown. After many fraught verbal battles, Lloyd George offered the republicans a partitioned Ireland, but with a boundary commission which would discuss the placing of the border according to public opinion in the affected counties (although the eventual treaty added that economic and other geographical considerations had to be taken into account as well). The southern part of the divided Ireland would take dominion status within the British Commonwealth. The Dáil in Dublin rejected this offer, and sent the Irish delegation back to London for further negotiations. The main figures in the delegation were starting to believe that Lloyd George's offer was the best that could be obtained under the circumstances. Griffith had always thought that a dual monarchy was the best avenue for Irish independence (indeed he had based some of his original Sinn Féin ideas on it). Dominion status was close enough for him. Perhaps more than anyone, Collins knew that the guerrilla Anglo-Irish War could not have gone on much longer before the IRA began to run out of resources and men. If there was a resumption of hostilities, the full might of the British army would be too much for them.

The full might of the British army was exactly what Lloyd George offered the Irish delegation on 5 December 1921 when they returned to tell him of the Dáil's rejection of his proposal. He said that if the Irish delegation did not sign the treaty, '... it is war, and war within three days'. Collins, Griffith and the rest of the Irish delegation signed the Anglo-Irish Treaty on 6 December 1921. It established the Irish Free State and the Province of Northern Ireland as separate political entities. Knowing that the treaty would spark off much hostility in Ireland, Michael Collins said, 'I may have signed my actual death-warrant.' The Irish delegation returned to Dublin, and the Dáil debated the treaty in early January. De Valera and other Sinn Féiners rejected the treaty outright. They also objected to remaining within the British Commonwealth; the issue of partition was surprisingly little discussed. After a bitter debate, the Dáil ratified the treaty by a slim margin of sixty-four to fifty-seven on 7 January 1922. De Valera resigned as president, and withdrew from the Dáil, along with many of his supporters. Although the Free State was to remain in the British Commonwealth until 1948, most of its domestic governance devolved to the Dáil. The province of Northern Ireland was to remain an integral part of the United Kingdom.

INTERPRETATIONS

In a confrontational, bloody and permanent way, the events described in this chapter symbolized ideas of nationalism, unionism and Irish identity. At the same time, they set the stage for what was to become the modern Irish Republic, the province of Northern Ireland and the political troubles that plague the province today. If we look at the interpretations of the Easter Rising, the collapse of Home Rule and the partition of Ireland, and ideas of nationalism and unionism, we can see just how ideas and attitudes were as central to this period as the events described above. Questions about nationalism, unionism and Irish identity were hopelessly bound up in the politics of this troubled time.

INTERPRETATIONS – THE EASTER RISING

For such a well-known event in modern Irish history, and one that has captured the public imagination in literature and film, the 1916 Easter Rising has had a curious history of interpretation. For much of the half-century after the Rising, very little scholarly work was done on it, even though it formed an important part of the political consciousness of the Free State and many prominent politicians (such as Eamonn de Valera) had either participated in the Rising or were of that generation. The first works that appeared about the Rising were mainly popular biographies of its leaders, such as Patrick Pearse, who were generally treated as heroes.

The first major scholarly contribution to interpretation of the Rising came from Professor F.X. Martin in an article in 1948 ('Eoin MacNeill on the 1916 Rising', *Irish Historical Studies*, vol. 11). He analysed some previously unused memoranda written by Eoin MacNeill, who had tried to call the rebellion off when arms shipments did not arrive and organizational problems made any rising seem hopeless. These documents showed that MacNeill was even more opposed to a hopeless rising than had been thought. MacNeill had argued that to continue with the rebellion when it had no chance of success was not only tactically foolish, but morally wrong. Anyone who would be killed in such an action, he said, would have been murdered, rather than having died in a legitimate military battle. Military legitimacy was important to men like O'Neill because they wanted the republic they sought to be founded on international principles of government, rather than being grabbed by terrorist action. MacNeill's ideas encapsulated a central point of debate about the planned Rising. Some thought that it should be the start of a general, and relatively orthodox, rebellion against the British. Others believed that Ireland needed to be shocked into action by a blood sacrifice and the creation of martyrs. Professor Martin's article received a great deal of attention (especially given that it appeared in an academic journal), but it was not until eighteen years later (the fiftieth anniversary of the Rising in 1966) that another important interpretative work appeared. This also came from Martin, in his edited book, *Leaders and Men of the Easter Rising*. In this book, the various contributors attempted to show that the Rising was more significant than just a mainly Dublin-based event of relatively short duration. It was part of a larger picture of the tense period since the Home Rule crisis starting in 1912. Whereas Martin's earlier article (and some popular studies of the Rising) had focused on the behind-the-scenes workings of the conspirators and the participants in the events of Easter week, this book concentrated very much on the public side of things. Looked at in this way, the Rising became part of a more general narrative of the politics of the period, and the events preceeding it had a great deal of effect on the planners and rebels. Many of the contributors to this volume, while broadening the focus of interpretation of the Rising, did not reject many of the more traditional ideas about its participants. In some cases, they were hailed as martyrs and as patriots who had the future happiness of all Irish people (Catholic and Protestant) in mind.

In the same year, T. Desmond Williams published *The Irish Struggle, 1916–1926*. Among other things, he emphasized what he saw as the ineffectual efforts of Connolly and his Irish socialist movement. W.I. Thompson argued in his 1967 *Imagination of the Insurrection: Dublin 1916* that the Easter rebels had concentrated too much on their visions of the kind of Ireland they wanted the Rising to bring about. Noble ideas about blood sacrifices, and poetry glorifying the struggle they were about to embark on, blinded them to what he saw as realism (i.e. the hopelessness of their plans). Other important questions about the Rising were raised around the time of its fiftieth anniversary. Perhaps the most important was: why did it fail to spark a more general uprising against British rule in Ireland? J.C. Beckett argued in 1967 that there were really two revolutions in nineteenth- and early twentieth-century Ireland. The first was a slow process of reform and change in religious rights (e.g. Catholic Emancipation), land ownership and education ultimately brought about by British legislation. The second revolution was not only the Easter Rising but the establishment of the Free State. Beckett did not argue that the first revolution necessarily laid the groundwork for the second, but that there seemed to be some connection. This led other historians to consider whether the conditions that the first revolution brought about by the time of the last major land reform in 1909 prevented the growth of mass discontent in the country as a whole. Patrick Lynch argued that land reforms may have been particularly instrumental in the absence of a general social uprising following the political and military one during Easter Week (Lynch, 'The Social Revolution that Never Was', in Desmond Williams (ed.), *The Irish Struggle*, 1966). Even though there may have been no general social rising to follow the militant one, it was clear that the Rising provided a political alternative to the constitutionalism of the Irish Parliamentary Party. This greatly affected the domestic politics of the Free State.

Another article which discussed the political (and, indeed, moral) after-effects of the Rising was written by a Jesuit priest and sent to *Irish Historical Studies* in 1966. It was not published until 1972, partly because it was highly critical of Pearse and of the effects of the Rising on subsequent Irish history. Father Francis Shaw's article was more of an essay about an historical event rather than a researched article, but it gained a lot of attention and encapsulated a strain of thought about the Rising that argued that it was damaging. For the most part, Shaw was highly critical of Pearse, especially his use of Christ as an allegory for Irish patriotism. Further, he said, Ireland was not in need of a blood sacrifice to cleanse itself, and the Irish nation was not generally suffering. Reforms under the Union had brought about general improvements in the lives of people. But most of all, Shaw argued, the Rising was politically damaging and led directly to partition, the civil war (see chapter 7), and the lack of recognition for the Irishmen who had died in the First World War. The Rising ended any hope that some sort of Home Rule might be put in place, because the unionists saw that nationalists would never be satisfied unless they could completely overthrow British rule. Partition was the result. Further, the civil war came about because the rebels and their ideological descendants could never accept the compromise solution of a twenty-six-county Free State. Their stringent republicanism ultimately caused more suffering, he argued. Finally, the lack of respect for the Irish dead of the First World War (because they had fought for what the rebels saw as a foreign and oppressing power) 'kept the fire of hatred burning', which hurt Irish families of the war dead. This could hardly ease the nation's wounds, he thought.

The next generation of historians, interestingly, turned back to biography in an attempt to analyse the meaning of the Rising. For Ruth Dudley Edwards and Austen Morgan, studying the psychological attributes of leaders of the Rising, and trying to understand the philosophical and literary influences on them, could bring to the surface the true motivations for the Rising.

Dudley Edwards concentrated on Patrick Pearse. Her 1977 biography of him explained his vision of a post-rebellion Ireland, which would be distinctly different from the kind proposed by John Redmond and the Home Rulers. Pearse saw Ireland after 1916 as Gaelic, self-sufficient economically, and, of course, politically independent. In this, he showed how important this vision of Irishness would be in creating a new nation based on ancient traditions and an unbroken link with past Irish heroes. Not only would this new Ireland be historically sound, it would bring about great changes in the Irish people. Ireland would become communal, removed from the excesses of the modern world, and the people would be happier and more considerate of their fellow countrymen. For Pearse, then, the Rising would not end in 1916. The ideas behind it would fashion the country, its people and its politics for generations. Austen Morgan's 1988 biography of James Connolly examined his writings fully and analytically. Morgan argued that, in the years before the Rising, Connolly gradually modified his ideas about socialism and internationalism. In short, he moved towards a more closed, national focus. He changed his ideas about the future of an Irish workers' state with broad support from the populace, to concentrating on the military overthrow of British government in Ireland. Morgan went so far as to argue that, at the time of his death in 1916, Connolly no longer held strong socialist convictions. Further, his internationalist ideas had also been abandoned, and he considered Irish politics only.

In the early 1990s, there was a reaction against these somewhat critical revisionist interpretations of the Easter Rising. The most important of these, interestingly, came from the Field Day Theatre Company. Their edited volume, *Revising the Rising* (1991), contained a mixture of essays from historians, literary critics and other non-academic commentators. Some of the more important ideas to come out of this collection were those of Declan Kiberd, Tom Garvin and Arthur Aughey. Kiberd argued that the connection between the Easter rebels and the modern IRA has been overstated. The ideals of the Easter rebels were far removed from those of the modern IRA. The rebels, therefore, cannot provide an enduring ideological inspiration for militant republicans in the second half of the twentieth century. Tom Garvin stressed that there was at least one important characteristic shared by the rebels and the constitutional nationalists led by the Irish Parliamentary Party. This was a kind of inclusiveness (or at the very least anti-sectarianism) common to both types of nationalism. Previous scholars, in their emphasis on the differences between the militant and the constitutional nationalists, have under-valued this important link, Garvin argued. Aughey, a unionist, argued that the 1916 Rising sits very uneasily with contemporary politics in the Irish Republic. In Northern Ireland, militant nationalist rhetoric relies heavily on the idea of a strong link between the rebels then and the rebels now. In the Republic, however, there is a recognition that nationalist politics have moved beyond the ideals of the Easter rebels. This has manifested itself, among other things, in the country's willingness to remove its constitutional claims on Northern Ireland (see chapter eight). Yet the Rising is considered part of the political history of the Republic, and generations of politicians (particularly those from Sinn Féin and Fianna Fáil) have used it as part of their rhetoric. This has caused an ideological tension within modern republicanism.

INTERPRETATIONS – PARTITION

The collapse of Home Rule and the partition of Ireland have also received a good deal of historical attention. The debate over the dividing of Ireland has taken a different course from that over the Rising. Its central concerns are to explain why the late attempts at Home Rule failed, and why the island was partitioned in 1921. As in interpretations of subsequent periods of Irish history, the debate has focused on nationalists, unionists and the role of the British government.

The traditional nationalist interpretation was most fully set out in Frank Gallagher's *The Indivisible Island: the History of the Partition of Ireland* (1957). He argued that partition was mainly a solution that helped British politicians solve British party-political problems. Gallagher thought that unionist attachment towards Britain was not as strong as it had appeared, and that their fervour had been whipped up by British Conservatives. This interference from Britain was what kept the division between nationalists and unionists alive. It was, therefore, the British who partitioned

Ireland. Although she does not argue as polemically, Catherine Shannon reached some of the same main conclusions in her *Arthur J. Balfour and Ireland* (1988). But she was more interested in perceptions of the Irish among British politicians than Gallagher was. Racial ideas about the difference between the British and Irish, and the attitude that the Irish might well be able to govern a backward and agricultural area like southern Ireland but would be lost trying to run the more sophisticated north-east Ulster economy, meant that British politicians could never have seriously considered a united Ireland run from Dublin.

The competing interpretation, however, stresses the depth of unionist feeling, and their severe opposition to a united Ireland. When most other explanations had been tested and found wanting (see the Interpretations section in chapter 8), it became clear to many historians that unionist feeling was deep and genuine, whether or not those feelings were based on a balanced reading of Irish history. Peter Gibbon's *Origins of Ulster Unionism* (1975) makes this case strongly. Patricia Jalland's *The Liberals and Ireland: the Ulster Question in British Politics to 1914* (1980) is perhaps the most sophisticated and in-depth analysis of the third Home Rule bill. She also found Ulster unionism to be a profoundly held ideology, but rather than blame Irish nationalists for not recognizing this, or British Conservatives for whipping it up, Jalland concentrated on the failure of British Liberals (from Gladstone onwards) to understand the depth of feeling. This meant that Home Rule started from a basically untenable position, and that partition was the inevitable result. Alvin Jackson has also shown how strong Ulster unionism was, but his *The Ulster Party: Irish Unionists in the House of Commons, 1884–1911* (1989) makes the case that, far from being strong allies of the Conservatives, unionists distanced themselves from both British parties because they trusted neither. Their die-hard political stance may be more accurately understood as a lonely one, based on self-interest and the survival of what they saw as their heritage. This ultimately tied the hands of both the British government and the Irish nationalists, and partition, although the 'least bad' option, was the only one left.

INTERPRETATIONS - NATIONALISM AND UNIONISM

Although nationalism and unionism certainly existed before (and after) the period covered by this chapter, the years under consideration were particularly important for the development of these two main political ideologies over the rest of the twentieth century.

As with the Easter Rising, much of the early work done on nationalism was based on biographies of those considered to be nationalist heroes. Much popular material argued that there was a continuity of nationalist ideology from Theobald Wolfe Tone in the late eighteenth century to Patrick Pearse in the early twentieth century. Like many other aspects of Irish history, this began to be revised between the two world wars. A main interpretative struggle took place over which individuals and groups could be said to have sustained Irish nationalism after the Famine. F.S.L. Lyons argued that the Irish Parliamentary Party had been the main vehicle for nationalist expression, rather than republican militants (see his *Irish Parliamentary Party 1890–1910*, 1951). He also tried to return Charles Stewart Parnell to the consititutional side of nationalism in his 1977 biography. Republicans, he argued, had ahistorically claimed him for their side. Also, later work, especially that by D. George Boyce and Tom Garvin, stressed the diversity of nationalist thinking and action. In his *Nationalism in Ireland* (1982), Boyce argued that there was no real continuity of nationalism from the late eighteenth century to the early twentieth century, and that diversity in nationalist thinking was set in place by the time of O'Connell (who had very different ideas of Irish nationalism from Tone, who, in turn, also had very different ideas from Henry Grattan). The differences in nationalism, he argued, grew from there. Tom Garvin argued that the differences between militant and constitutional nationalists in the nineteenth century were more complicated than previously thought. At times, their ideas and purposes merged, but often they were in complete opposition, and any reading of Irish history which shows them merging within the Home Rule movement is too simplistic.

Another aspect of the early interpretation of Irish nationalism was that its ideas and actions sprang from Irish brains alone. This can also be seen as part of the idea of separateness and self-sufficiency that would define much of political and economic policy in the Irish Free State and Republic in later years (see chapters 7 and 8). Alan O'Day's reinterpretation of this idea, however, argued that members of the Irish Parliamentary Party were heavily influenced by reform traditions within British politics. O'Day's 1977 *English Face of Irish Nationalism* shows how dependent radical Irish nationalism and republicanism were on British radical thinkers and political organizers. Further British influence was shown by Charles Townshend, who argued in an article in 1981 that much of the government's policies in the nineteenth century (such as the provision of elementary education since 1831) helped create an atmosphere wherein nationalism could grow.

Another important aspect of the continuing reinterpretation of Irish nationalism concerns geography. Traditional nationalist interpretations implied that nationalism was a countrywide ideology and was expressed in various parts of the country in similar ways. More recent interpretations, however, have stressed regional diversity, and, in fact, have argued that the national nature of the campaigns of O'Connell and Parnell were unusual, rather than commonplace. K. Theodore Hoppen argued that the immediate post-O'Connell period saw a revival of local political identities and loyalties (*Elections, Politics, and Society in Ireland 1832–55*, 1984). This built on earlier work which showed that not only were there different levels of nationalist activity in different areas, but that the activity itself was often of a different nature. Munster, for instance, saw a great deal of militant nationalism in the early twentieth century, whereas Connacht was less violent, but more expressive of nationalism at the ballot box. (See David Fitzpatrick, *Politics and Irish Life 1913–1921: Provincial Experience of War and Revolution*, 1977; and A.C. Hepburn and E. Rumpf, *Nationalism and Socialism in Ireland*, 1977.)

Revisionist ideas about Irish nationalism, as about other topics, have undergone re-appraisals. But nationalism as an issue has perhaps attracted the most attention, because it seems to go right to the heart of Irish identity and current Irish politics. The major critic of revisionism has been Brendan Bradshaw, who wrote a seminal piece in *Irish Historical Studies* ('Nationalism and Historical Scholarship in Modern Ireland', vol. 26, 1988–9). Although focusing mainly on the pre-modern period, Bradshaw had general criticisms to make about the revision of nationalism and Irish history in general. In short, he argued, revisionists have removed the professional study of history from the public sphere, and have ignored the importance of history in the popular mind as a way to understand the past and to give ideas about the future. Revisionism, with its emphasis on 'value-free history' (an early goal of the revisionists of the 1930s and 1940s), has, Bradshaw argued, produced work only of interest to scholars, which the public could not understand, or would find boring. The revisionist emphasis on the complexities of Irish history has also understated the level of suffering the native Irish endured during various conquests and other events such as the Famine, Bradshaw maintained. Nationalist heroes, movements and events have been been dissected too stringently by the revisionists, he argued, and this has resulted in the loss of a scholarly basis for an Irish national identity. Bradshaw's ideas, however, were heavily criticized, both in the pages of *Irish Historical Studies* and in the popular press, on a number of points. Much of this commentary has been on Bradshaw's specific examples from pre-modern history, but some of it has been on the broader implications of his ideas about nationalism and history. These include the argument (denied strongly by Bradshaw in subsequent writings) that his ideas present an uncritical approach to nationalism and seek to revive traditional interpretations. This, it has been said, only heightens the divisions in Irish society and between the Republic and Northern Ireland.

Unionism is as complex as nationalism, and its history has also been interpreted in a number of ways. Alvin Jackson has argued, however, that, like nationalism, the more complex that unionist history is shown to be, the more simplified the political unionist rhetoric becomes in contemporary Northern Ireland. What this means is that contemporary militant and extreme notions of nationalism and unionism must rely on simple explanations of history, and so the potential for greater understanding between the two communities through the reading of professional history is lost. Like nationalism, interpretations of unionism first appeared mainly in the form of biographies of great unionist leaders, and books written by participants in the Home Rule crisis of the early twentieth century.

A good example of an ideologically unionist, but nevertheless well-researched, history of the late nineteenth- and early twentieth-century battles over the political state of Ireland was Ronald McNeill's *Ulster's Stand for the Union* (1922). McNeill was a unionist, but claimed to have written a professional history of the period. This is true in the sense that he used recognizable historical sources, but his political stance skewed the interpretations towards the unionist cause. McNeill, however, was very successful in inspiring a number of important unionist-influenced histories throughout the middle decades of the twentieth century. Like the Easter Rising for nationalists, gun-running for the defence of unionism in 1914 has been seen as a seminal event for unionists. F.H. Crawford, one of the leading gun-runners, wrote *Guns for Ulster* in 1947 as not only a defence of the practice, but as a celebration of unionist backbone. Crawford was sponsored by the Northern Ireland government to publish his memories of these events, as was the case with several unionist historians who enjoyed official or semi-official patronage.

The most professional successor of McNeill, however, was A.T.Q. Stewart, whose *Ulster Crisis* (1967) was well received by the public. Although a professional historian who employed professional techniques, Stewart was openly sympathetic to unionism as both an historical movement and an enduring political ideology in the years just before the Northern Ireland Troubles broke out (see chapter 8). The main thrust of his *Ulster Crisis* was that the political separation of Northern Ireland from the south was an inevitability, based on major differences between the two parts of the island. Further, he argued that unionists such as Carson and Craig were heroes in standing up for this difference and demanding to remain within the Union.

After the start of the Troubles, however, more professional and academic historians became interested in unionism. Generally speaking, these scholars were not unionists themselves (or at least they did not discuss their political leanings). Much of this work concerned the state of Northern Ireland in the latter decades of the twentieth century, and so will be discussed in the Interpretations section of chapter eight. But several historians have tackled the issue of unionism during the period discussed in this chapter. Peter Gibbon's *Origins of Ulster Unionism* (1975) focuses on the different types of unionism found in town and country in Ulster. During this period, he argues, rural unionism (that is, the unionism of the landed elite which was generally preoccupied with issues of land) was gradually taken over by urban unionism (which was dominated by industrialists and merchants and not only catered for the economic demands of those interests, but also tried to enhance the image of Ulster as an industrial centre more like Britain than the rest of Ireland).

Perhaps the most important historian of unionism, however, has been Alvin Jackson, whose work has shown the extent and diversity of unionist ideology and action. Jackson has reminded historians that unionism sprang from many different sources (including the south of Ireland). For instance, its intellectual heart, he argues, was Trinity College Dublin, where many notable unionists (including Isaac Butt) were educated, and where a culture of 'advanced' (i.e. non-sectarian) unionism prevailed. He has also shown that many unionist myths and celebrated historical events (such as the siege of Derry in 1641, the Battle of the Boyne in 1690, and Ulstermen's participation in the First World War) have parallels among nationalists, and are held in the same esteem and veneration. Most importantly, like Gibbon and others, he has drawn out the complexities of unionism and the differences of opinion among unionists, to show that they were not a monolithic group of 'No Surrender' men, that even Carson had moments when he would have considered a compromise with nationalists over Home Rule, and that unionism never represented the unified threat to Britain that it was feared it did during that crisis. (See his *The Ulster Party: Irish Unionists in the House of Commons, 1884–1911*, 1989; *Sir Edward Carson*, 1993; and *Colonel Edward Saunderson: Land and Loyalty in Victorian Ireland*, 1995; as well as his *Ireland 1798–1998*, 1999.)

SEVEN

The Making of Two Irelands, 1922–66

The formal partition of Ireland happened in 1921, but the northern and southern parts of the island became more and more politically independent of each other in the first half of the twentieth century. Mutual mistrust and hostility, as well as very different economic and social circumstances, ensured that two very different societies would emerge. The Irish Free State went through two further constitutional transformations between 1922 and 1949, emerging as the modern and fully independent Republic of Ireland. Northern Ireland remained part of the United Kingdom, although it had its own parliament and governing executive. The Free State and the Republic had much economic difficulty in these years, as it struggled between defining itself as a largely agricultural nation or as a modern industrial country. Northern Ireland already had a relatively modern industrial economy. But Northern Irish society was based on inequalities between Protestants and Catholics, which would cause lasting resentment, and ultimately violence, from the late 1960s to the end of the century. The economic histories of both Irelands during this period varied widely between boom and bust, and protectionism and free trade. But even in the economic sphere, the national question was prominent. In Northern Ireland, there was a good deal of pride in its industrialization and higher living standards than in the Free State, as well as constant emphasis on the connection with Great Britain (it enjoyed free trade with Britain, of course, while Free State goods were charged a duty). Ideas of nation were reflected in the Free State's economic policies as well.

Especially during the 1930s, economic policies were designed to create a self-sufficient, largely agricultural country, which to many politicians embodied the ideal of Ireland. Eamonn de Valera, the Prime Minister from 1932 to 1948, publicly discussed the 'Ireland which we dreamed of'. This was 'a land whose countryside would be bright with cosy homesteads, whose fields and villages would be joyous with the sound of industry, with the romping of sturdy children ... and the laughter of comely maidens, whose firesides would be the forums of wisdom and serene old age.' This romantic vision was as completely out of step with European modernization as it was reflective of the hopes of Irish nationalists. In reality, neither the south's self-sufficiency agenda, nor Northern Ireland's mirroring many of the British economic policies, effected the desired outcomes. In the south, protectionism (although initially successful and probably necessary) and self-sufficiency created many more problems than they solved. And Northern Ireland was hampered by Britain's general economic woes in the post-war period. In the immediate years after the Treaty which partitioned the island, Northern Ireland was granted subsidies for farming and social security. The Free State no longer had to pay taxes to the British government and did not have to worry about funding Belfast's industrial unemployment. So at first it appeared as though both Irelands would benefit economically from partition.

THE IRISH FREE STATE, 1922–32

The Dáil's debate over the Anglo-Irish Treaty set the tone for the confrontational Irish politics that were to plague the early years of the Irish Free State. Those who supported the treaty called themselves Cumann na nGaedheal and the anti-treaty members under de Valera retained the name Sinn Féin. De Valera and Sinn Féin thought that the treaty was a betrayal of the Republic that had been proclaimed by Patrick Pearse during the Easter Rising. Since the Dáil had ratified the treaty, de Valera and his followers refused to recognize its authority and withdrew from it. Arthur Griffith, as the head of Cumann na nGaedheal, was elected president of the Dáil on 10 January 1922. In addition to this constitutional struggle, there was a serious problem with the IRA. Once the British forces and police started removing themselves from various posts across the country, they were usually taken over by the IRA. Michael Collins still had control of much of the Irish Republican Brotherhood, many of whom were in high positions in the IRA. He was able, therefore, to convince about half of the IRA to join the new Free State Army. The other half were more militantly republican and stayed loyal to the anti-treaty forces. This polarization of the main militant forces in the Free State led gradually to a destructive civil war between the pro- and anti-treaty groups. Anti-treaty IRA members created their own military formations (and were dubbed 'The Irregulars' by the pro-treaty side). In April 1922, the Irregulars occupied the Four Courts building in Dublin and set it up as their headquarters. After failed negotiations, Michael Collins, as head of the Free State Army, shelled the Four Courts on 28 June 1922. Although successful after two days of shelling, this attack further polarized opinion, and many non-militant Sinn Féiners, including de Valera, joined the Irregulars.

The Irish civil war had started, and, although the Free State Army easily won battles around Dublin, the Irregulars quickly began a guerrilla war in other areas of the country. The Church urged people to accept the Anglo-Irish Treaty of 1921 and said that the killing of Free State soldiers during the civil war was 'murder', and that those who did so could not receive absolution through confession or take communion. The church's stance on nationalism and the national ideal, however, was not as clear-cut as this would seem to indicate. Some priests were sympathetic to the anti-treaty forces, and there was a major disagreement between bishops in Ireland and the Vatican about the Church and the government hindering the nationalist movement. The heaviest fighting took place during the summer, and Michael Collins was killed in an ambush on 20 August in County Cork. But the Free State Army was eventually too much for the Irregulars. They called a cease-fire on 30 April 1923, and de Valera told his followers to lay down their arms on 24 May. In the meantime, Arthur Griffith had died of a brain haemorrhage on 12 August 1922. The deaths of Collins and Griffith left the Free State without its main leaders. The new leader of the Free State, William Cosgrave (1880–1965), and his minister for defence took a hard line with captured Irregulars, interning many and executing nearly eighty, including some who had fought in the Easter Rising. During the next decade, the Irish Free State under Cosgrave and the Cumann na nGaedheal party tried to repair the damage that the Anglo-Irish War and the civil war had caused, as well as form a police service (Gárda Siochána [garda she-ah-caw-nah], founded 8 August 1923), and other state infrastructure. Also, the Boundary Commission set up in the Anglo-Irish Treaty met in October 1924 to establish the future of the border between the Irish Free State and the province of Northern Ireland. Tense and controversial negotiations took place throughout 1924 and most of 1925. These culminated in a meeting in London in late November and early December 1925, in which the Free State accepted that Northern Ireland would never willingly join a United Ireland, and with the provision of financial concessions from the British government, agreed that the border would remain in place. In reaction to the Boundary Commission's report, Cosgrave tried to prevent nationalist opinion from deserting him by implementing a nationalist cultural policy. The first attempt was to use the Irish language to 're-gaelicize' the country through the educational system. The Irish language became a required part of elementary and secondary education, and an acceptable degree of fluency was required for the civil service and some of the professions and university positions. Irish history was to be taught in schools in a nationalistic way, arguing that independence had been the primary goal of all nationalists since Theobald Wolfe Tone and his United Irishmen in the 1780s and 1790s. Much of this effort coincided with public opinion in the Free State, which increasingly saw Irishness as synonymous with rural life, an agricultural economy, and the Catholic religion.

After their defeat in the civil war, de Valera and Sinn Féin stayed out of the Dáil for most of the 1920s. In March 1926, however, de Valera and Sinn Féin met to discuss whether they should return to mainstream politics and re-enter future Dáil elections. The IRA had withdrawn its support for de Valera because it thought he had not been militant enough against the Free State during the civil war. De Valera had maintained a fairly moderate stance (even though he had enlisted in the Irregulars), and he often tried to reach an agreement with the Free State by negotiation during the war. Freed from the extreme militancy of the IRA, de Valera thought that Sinn Féin would also be free to return to normal politics. But his proposals were largely rejected by Sinn Féin, and he decided to form a new party, Fianna Fáil [feena foil], on 16 May 1926. Many moderate Sinn Féiners and others joined de Valera, and they won forty-four seats in the election of June 1927. But the Fianna Fáil members refused to take the oath to the British crown, which was still required under the dominion status that the Free State held in the British Common-wealth. This meant they could not take their seats in the Dáil. Cosgrave held on to his administration. The government then decided that Fianna Fáil's refusal to take the oath (which left some Dáil seats empty) was unfair to other parties, and passed a bill which made the practice illegal. This forced de Valera to chose between taking an oath he despised or being left out of official politics permanently. On 10 August 1927, de Valera and his party took the oath and entered the Dáil. Fianna Fáil held enough seats, in coalition with some smaller parties, to force a no-confidence motion in Cosgrave's Cumann na nGaedheal government. This was passed, and another election was held in September 1927. At this election, Fianna Fáil won fifty-seven seats and Cumann na nGaedheal sixty-seven (staying in government). The major effect of this election, however, was that the other, smaller parties that had held seats before Fianna Fáil came back into the Dáil lost much of their representation. From this election, then, the Free State was to have a (mainly) two-party system. At the next election in 1932, de Valera's Fianna Fáil party won seventy-two seats and formed a government made up of many of the men who had taken up arms against the pro-treaty Free State ten years previously.

The strength of the political tension between the pro- and anti-treaty sides during this period meant that the ideological division in Irish politics was largely based on ideas of the nation, rather than on economic or social theories as in other European countries. Throughout the rest of the twentieth century, it became nearly impossible to talk about Irish politics in left/right or conservative/socialist terms. The long struggle for some sort of independence, combined with limited social and economic reforms brought in by the British, meant that it was the sovereignty question that preoccupied Irish political minds for nearly fifty years. Another influential element in the process, however, was the fact that, in its early years, Fianna Fáil cast itself as a populist party and (within the limits of a heavily Catholic and largely conservative country like the Free State) adopted many of the more moderate policies of the Irish Labour Party. Fianna Fáil, therefore, marginalized the labour movement by stealing some of its clothes. The electorate then saw no real reason to support the Labour Party in significant numbers. Now that Fianna Fáil had come in from the cold, and the major dispute over the Anglo-Irish Treaty was over, the difficult questions of building a nation could begin to be addressed. Throughout the 1920s, the Free State government pursued generally conservative economic policies. The Department of Finance kept a fairly tight grip on government spending, only loosening the purse strings when a project showed overwhelming need and popular support. One such project was the massive hydro-electric power plant built on the River Shannon. Further, the Free State more or less adopted British economic models during the 1920s. The Irish pound was tied to the British pound. The Free State passed the Land Purchase Act in 1923, the effect of which was that nearly all farms became owned by the people who worked them. A similar act was passed in Northern Ireland. Generally speaking, the conservative nature of economic policies benefited farmers with large holdings, as well as cattle ranchers. This angered smaller farmers. But agriculture in the south suffered during this period. Spending on the poor in the 1920s was not extensive. Proposals for unemployment insurance were rejected, hospitals and health care systems were antiquated and stayed that way without an increase in government spending, and old-age pensions were reduced. Overall, though, the 1920s were good years economically (even though agricultural prices remained low). Wages rose, and the Wall Street Crash and subsequent financial panic did not affect the Free State immediately. But these facts hid the uneven distribution of economic success across the country, and de Valera and Fianna Fáil were able to exploit them during the election of 1932.

NORTHERN IRELAND, 1922–32

King George opened the first Northern Ireland parliament on 22 June 1921. It contained an overwhelming number of unionist members, who had been elected on 21 May. Sir James Craig (1871–1940) was the first Prime Minister of the province. Nationalists were represented by the Nationalist Party of Northern Ireland and Sinn Féin, but they only held twelve seats between them. Sinn Féin refused to take their seats, but the Nationalist Party entered parliament in 1924. The ultimate difficulty for political nationalists was that they generally refused to recognize the legitimacy of the Northern Ireland parliament. Even the Nationalist Party, who sat in the parliament, did not act as an official opposition since that would mean that they supported the idea of a separate Northern Ireland government. This only reinforced the idea held by some unionists that nationalists were not able to handle governmental affairs, and that the largely nationalist Catholic population of Northern Ireland were not loyal to the government, nor were they good citizens. This is not to say, however, that unionists and Protestants were always united in their aims for Northern Ireland. There was much diversity of opinion among them, and the Northern Irish governments of the 1920s often had to contend with discontented Protestant churches and the revived Orange Order (who, for instance, agitated against non-denominational schools set up in 1923), as well as temperance reformers fighting for local power over licensing laws. Political measures were taken throughout the 1920s to lessen the effectiveness of these groups, and to forestall any political power that Northern Ireland Catholics might build up. Although elections were originally designed using proportional representation (which usually provides minorities with more potential for electing people to parliament), the Northern Ireland parliament abolished this system for local and central government by 1929. Business owners (mainly unionist) were given an extra vote for owning business property, and constituency boundaries were often redrawn to guarantee unionist majorities. But the abolition of proportional representation also ensured that only the main unionist parties would be successful. Smaller, fringe unionist parties (as well as socialist parties) were marginalized into oblivion. This system generally produced what Prime Minister James Craig called 'a Protestant parliament for a Protestant people'.

An early Catholic civil rights group, the National League, was founded in 1928 to press for reforms for Catholics, to agitate for a united Ireland, and to reduce tensions between Catholics and Protestants. But it was largely ineffective because there were so many institutional structures that kept Northern Ireland divided. From the foundation of Northern Ireland, the IRA refused to accept its legitimacy, and fought a terrorist campaign to disrupt its operation. Over two hundred people were killed and nearly one thousand wounded in 1922 alone. The British government responded by bringing in troops and establishing an armed police force.

Not only were there political difficulties. The Northern Irish economy had an uneasy start. Unemployment throughout the 1920s and 1930s ran at nearly twenty-five per cent, and social services were hard hit. There were not enough hospitals, the old Victorian workhouses still served as relief for the destitute and the provision of public housing was generally inadequate. In Northern Ireland, one of the major problems during the 1920s and 1930s was the decline of the linen industry and shipbuilding. The linen market had more or less disappeared, and the shipbuilding industry did not adequately adjust to the fall in demand after the end of the First World War. Since over half of Northern Ireland's workers were employed in industry (and less than a third in agriculture), these losses hit the economy hard.

But the permanence of the Northern Irish state was symbolically secured by the building of Stormont, the massive neo-classical home for the Northern Irish parliament. Its foundation stone was laid in 1928, and it was opened by the Prince of Wales (1894–1972, who later became Edward VIII) on 17 November 1932. Nationalist members of parliament refused to take part in the ceremony, and the erection of a statue to the arch-unionist Sir Edward Carson outside the building provided another strong symbol of the political imbalance that was to plague Northern Ireland many decades later.

THE FREE STATE AND ÉIRE, 1932–49

The 1930s and 1940s saw the assertion of final independence of the Irish Free State from any British connection. This happened in three main ways – by an economic war with Britain in the early 1930s, the evolution of the Free State to Éire [air-uh] in 1937, and Éire's neutrality during the Second World War.

Eamon de Valera and Fianna Fáil won the 1932 Dáil election and came to power in March, a position they would maintain until 1948. Their main goal was to remove the Free State's links with Britain, especially the oath of allegiance to the British monarch. First, though, de Valera withheld unpopular land annuities from the British Treasury. These annuities were payments made by farmers who had purchased their land under the various land reforms from 1870 to 1909. After the founding of the Free State, these were paid to the Dáil, which would then forward them to London. The Fianna Fáil government withheld these payments almost immediately. The British government retaliated by imposing duties on Irish imports, mainly livestock and dairy products. De Valera responded by placing prohibitive duties on British coal and heavy industrial goods. This 'economic war' hurt both sides considerably, and made the effects of the 1930s depression even worse in Ireland. A series of agreements were reached between 1935 and 1938, which at first alleviated some of the harsher aspects of the economic war. These agreements culminated in a meeting of the two governments in 1938. De Valera tried to revive the question of the partition of Ireland, but was unsuccessful. The meetings then focused on economics. The two governments agreed that the question of annuities would be settled by a one-time payment of £10 million to London. In return, the British government gave the Free State control of the ports that it had retained under the Anglo-Irish Treaty of 1921 (this was to become very important during the Second World War).

Meanwhile, the Free State government faced immense difficulty with militant republicans and proto-fascists in Ireland. The IRA had been largely excluded when de Valera formed his political party Fianna Fáil in 1926, and they re-activated shortly thereafter. They were committed to a united Irish republic. A more extreme movement also arose in the early 1930s when a militant group of soldiers nicknamed the 'Blueshirts' adopted some of Mussolini's political ideas. They formed military groups and armed themselves. In the beginning, de Valera needed the IRA to counterbalance the Blueshirts. The Blueshirts even made an alliance with the new political party, Fine Gael [finna gale], which had grown out of a merger of Cumann na nGaedheal and smaller parties. Although there were negotiations in the early 1930s to stave off violence, there were sporadic outbreaks in various parts of the country. The Blueshirt movement gradually faded, however, when the Fine Gael party realized that they did not want to be allied with them. By 1936, they were a spent force. The IRA, however, were not. Since he no longer needed them as a counterbalance to the Blueshirts, and in reaction to their increase in violence in 1935, de Valera banned the IRA in 1936 and imprisoned many of its members. But other IRA members continued their campaign of violence against both the British and Irish governments. In January 1939, they demanded that all British forces leave Ireland. When this was ignored, the IRA brought its campaign to Britain. During early 1939, they bombed various targets in Britain, killing seven people and injuring 137. Special acts were passed in the north and south of Ireland to quell IRA violence during 1939, and many hundreds of IRA men were imprisoned. This continued throughout the Second World War in an attempt to prevent any IRA contact with Germany.

During the mid-1930s, de Valera had also been working on a new constitution to replace the 1922 Free State one. His goal was to remove all references to the British government, eliminate the oath of allegiance to the crown and make the Free State a republic in all but name. De Valera stopped short of renaming the Free State a republic because he wanted to reserve that term for a future united Ireland. During the abdication crisis in 1936 (involving King Edward VIII in Britain), de Valera had passed the External Relations Act. He used the opportunity of the monarchy's problems (and the fact that there would be a new king crowned in Britain soon) to push this act through the Dáil. It said that the Free State would remain part of the Commonwealth of Nations, but would reserve foreign policy to itself rather than to the British government (except in the case of some diplomatic and consular appointments). This was a major step towards a new constitution. De Valera consulted with Irish academics, legal scholars and leading churchmen while drafting the new constitution. It was published on 1 May 1937, and retained many elements of the Free State government, but changed others. Perhaps most importantly, it changed the name of the country to Éire (in English, 'Ireland') and laid claim to 'the whole island of Ireland, its islands, and territorial seas'. This, of course, included Northern Ireland, and was a complete expression of de Valera's idea of nationhood (although article three of the constitution allowed that 'pending integration of the national territory', the new constitution would apply to the Free State area only). The Irish language was made the official language of the country, with English being named the second official language. The president of the executive council was replaced with the office of taoiseach [tee-shook], which was somewhat more powerful and more like a prime minister. There was also to be an appointed President of Ireland, who would perform the ceremonial functions of head of state. The constitution also expressly recognized the Catholic Church as the church of the majority of the population, but also established freedom of religion. (Special recognition for the Catholic Church was rescinded in 1972.) It also attempted to support the family through the abolition of divorce. The church was heavily involved in the censorship of films and books. Bishops were consulted about legislation banning divorce and regulating alcohol. De Valera's government also responded to church pressure and banned contraceptives in 1935, and attempted to regulate dance halls in the same year. Jazz and some other popular music was frowned upon. These ideas and restrictions, however, were not solely the product of the church. Public opinion in this period generally desired a strong sense of public moral rectitude. Further, economic and social customs (especially late marriage and celibacy) were common enough not to need much help from the church to gain broader acceptance. The church also had a great influence in education, but here again, its ideas coincided with the thrust of public opinion. One of the strongest aspects was in the way Irish history and culture were taught, and the degree to which they were emphasized over the study of the rest of the world. This is not to say that world history and geography were ignored, but that the balance was tipped very far towards studying Ireland. This was not only a function of the young state's nationalism, but also of the idea that Ireland and its history could be presented in such a way as to improve the nation's morality. Irish history, language, music and traditions were seen as presenting moral values in the best possible light, and therefore educational emphasis was distinctly Irish. This was the general trend in state schools and Catholic schools, in which Irish history was presented as the noble struggle against the British oppressor. Protestant schools in the Republic resisted this tradition. The *Catholic Bulletin* wrote that

> the Irish nation is the Gaelic nation; its language and literature is the Gaelic language; its history is the history of the Gael. All other elements have no place in Irish national life, literature and tradition, save as far as they are assimilated into the very substance of Gaelic speech, life and thought.

Catholic bishops forbade Catholic attendance at the Protestant Trinity College Dublin. (This ban was lifted in 1970.)

Both the External Relations Act and the new constitution faced a difficult passage through the Dáil. Opposition members argued that they violated the Anglo-Irish Treaty of 1921, and that too much power was to be invested in the new office of taoiseach. De Valera's constitution passed the Dáil on 14 June 1937, however, and was approved in a national referendum by roughly fifty-seven per cent to forty-three per cent. Rather than expel Éire from the Commonwealth (and risk other Commonwealth nations developing similar independence plans), the British Prime Minister Neville Chamberlain (1869–1940) decided to let the matter pass and do nothing. Officially, in the British government's eyes, Éire was still part of the Commonwealth, but unofficially they knew it had become a republic in all but name. One of the reasons that the British government did not become overly concerned with Irish affairs was that war loomed in Europe. De Valera had stated at the League of Nations (where he had been president of the Council and of the Assembly in the 1930s) that Ireland would remain neutral in any forthcoming European war. He repeated this emphatically to the Dáil in April 1939, when it was clear that Germany was preparing for war. He had general support from Dáil members of most parties, and when war broke out in September 1939, the government set up a special council to deal with what became known in Ireland as 'the Emergency'. As in Britain, rationing of essential goods was enforced almost immediately. A plan of compulsory tillage put many extra acres of land into agricultural production, and food supplies increased by nearly seventeen per cent. But being on the western edge of Europe, and on the vital shipping routes from the New World, Ireland could not avoid some of the ravages of the war. Wayward German bombs fell on Counties Wexford, Wicklow, Kildare, Louth and Monaghan in 1940–1. Dublin was bombed in May 1941, with the loss of thirty-four lives. The German government paid compensation for these bombings in 1943 and 1958.

Except for refusing the use of Irish ports (which would have caused Germany to attack Irish targets), Éire's neutrality was certainly friendly to the Allies. German pilots who crashed in Ireland were interned, while Allied pilots were rescued and returned to Britain. German spies were arrested, while British intelligence pilots were allowed to use a base in County Limerick to land their sea planes. Diplomatic relations were maintained with Germany, and amongst the most controversial of de Valera's acts during the war was to go to the German embassy in Dublin and sign a book of condolence upon the death of Hitler in May 1945. He had done the same at the American embassy for Roosevelt a few months earlier, but since news reports of the Nazi death camps had appeared by this time, many people (including many in Éire) thought that this showed callous disregard for the victims of the Holocaust. In a radio address on 13 May 1945 at the end of the war, the British Prime Minister, Winston Churchill, severely criticized de Valera's government for not allowing Allied use of Irish ports. Further, Churchill said, Britain had showed great restraint in not taking the ports by force of arms. De Valera replied in a radio address on 17 May, saying that Churchill had placed British interests on some sort of moral plane that overlooked the rights of other nations. Further, he said, Churchill should have found sympathy with Ireland, a country which had withstood tyranny for hundreds of years, while Britain had withstood Germany for two years before the United States entered the war. De Valera's reply was hailed in Éire, and certainly overcame the damage that his condolences to the German embassy had done to his political standing. But the war had done much to damage the Irish economy. The compulsory tillage programme had depleted much farming soil, and rationing had more or less halted industrial development.

An election was held in 1948, and de Valera's Fianna Fáil party could not form a government. A coalition of Fine Gael and other parties took over. This Inter-Party Government tried to deal with post-war problems, including industrial development, a housing shortage and uneven healthcare across the country. They also tried to deal finally with the question of 'the republic', which had vexed Irish politics since 1916. De Valera's constitution had made Éire a republic in all but name, and the new taoiseach, John Costello (1891–1976), thought that finalizing the process would stamp out the ardour of militant republicans and, as he said, 'take the gun out of Irish politics'. Costello's inter-party government repealed the 1936 External Relations Act and passed the Republic of Ireland Act on 21 December 1948. This removed the final few diplomatic powers that the British monarch had over Éire, and changed the English name of the country to the Republic of Ireland. This became official on Easter Monday, 18 April 1949. The British government, under Prime Minister Clement Attlee (1883–1967), then passed the Ireland Act on 2 June 1949. This recognized that the Republic of Ireland was no longer a part of the British dominions, but also said that Northern Ireland would stay a part of the United Kingdom as long as the Northern Ireland parliament desired.

The economic policies of the Free State and Éire governments of this period were based on increased protectionism and tariffs, more welfare provision and benefits for small farmers and agricultural labourers. In government, de Valera broadened the base of unemployment payments to include more people, boosted pensions of all kinds (including widows' and orphans' as well as old-age pensions), and embarked on a dramatic public housing project. These, however, did not completely protect the south from the worldwide depression of the 1930s. Some social services, particularly health and education, remained under-funded. Protectionism and attempts at national self-sufficiency were the hallmarks of de Valera's industrial and trade plans. During the 1930s, this seemed to provide a boost to native industries in the south, but they were, in many ways, too protected. Exports plummeted and the attending lack of revenue was sorely missed. These protected industries also struggled in the post-war period. While protectionism was the general European reaction to the depression and southern Ireland followed suit, self-sufficiency proved impossible to attain. In the 1930s, the south exported roughly the same percentage of its domestic cattle market to Britain as Northern Ireland did. So trade with Britain was still vital, despite ideas of self-sufficiency. What was certain was that the state grew in order to handle the adminstration of these new economic policies.

NORTHERN IRELAND, 1932–66

The 1930s were a difficult time for Northern Ireland economically. Unemployment ran at roughly twenty-five per cent throughout the decade, as the two biggest industries, shipbuilding in Belfast and the linen industry across the province, went into decline. But this did not mean that things were much easier for farmers in the north. In fact, they may have been less well off. Farm labourers were being paid less than the amount given as unemployment support in Belfast. One of the major problems was that the British government, trapped itself in serious economic problems, did not give Northern Ireland's economy the attention that it required. Even with all these problems, living conditions in Northern Ireland were generally better than in the south. Wages increased gradually during this period, and social services were generally better than in the Free State. Like the Free State, Northern Ireland had stunted development in the early decades of the century because of the long-term decline in heavy industry there. Access to clean water was poor in rural areas, tuberculosis was a serious problem amongst young people, and housing and hospitals were in short supply. These deprivations (particularly unemployment) hit both Protestant and Catholic communities, and led to increased sectarian strife. Attacks on Orange parades and unionist reprisals plagued the early 1930s, and serious rioting in Belfast in the summer of 1935 ended in several deaths. The Northern Ireland parliament passed several coercive measures to combat violence (similar to those passed by de Valera in the south). The reaction in the North to the dramatic events in the Free State and Éire during the 1930s was also important. Nationalists were generally pleased to witness what they thought was an emerging Irish republic. Unionist fears of nationalist insistence on a united Ireland were confirmed, however. Throughout the 1930s, the Northern Irish Prime Minister, Sir James Craig (now Viscount Craigavon), sought to strengthen the ties with Britain. He wanted to ensure that Northern Ireland would remain within the United Kingdom.

The coming of the Second World War was a very significant moment for Northern Ireland. Not only were there the usual deprivations and difficulties faced in wartime: Northern Ireland's participation in the war further cemented its emotional and national ties with Britain (particularly when contrasted with Éire's neutrality). Since the ports of Éire were closed to Allied use, the ports of Northern Ireland became all the more important to the British war effort. Northern Ireland also proved an important industrial centre during the war. Shipbuilding was revived in Belfast. A hundred and fifty ships were built there during the war, as were nearly six hundred tanks, and a thousand planes and bombers. Unemployment plummeted as the shipyards filled again, and nearly sixty thousand people emigrated to Britain to work. Incomes and employment shot up to an even higher level than in Britain. Employment prospects had improved so dramatically that some people from Éire emigrated north to work, although they were forbidden from remaining permanently (perhaps because of fears that they might boost Catholic voting numbers). Agricultural output was also increased, and wages nearly doubled. Belfast, Derry and Larne became vital naval bases, and were the first point of landing for American ships in late 1941 and 1942 (against which de Valera protested). Allied personnel were trained in Northern Ireland, and several important D-Day training operations were held there. Belfast suffered air raids in April and May of 1941. More than seven hundred people were killed and four hundred wounded.

Like the Republic, the Northern Ireland government tried to concentrate on social and economic questions after the war, particularly in housing, industrial development and the establishment of a welfare state. After the war, the Northern Ireland government was able to participate in the British Labour government's welfare programmes, though these were introduced incrementally. Some new industries were attracted to Belfast and new jobs created between 1945 and 1966. This was offset, however, by the continued loss of jobs in the traditional industries. Government subsidies and tax incentives brought much new industry to the province. These even went so far as to include buying or leasing land for businesses, as well as building and leasing factories. Agriculture was similarly supported. These developments generally raised wages and the standard of living in the north, which was often contrasted with the slower-developing south. Mainland Britain was witnessing a rapid acceleration in the development of the welfare state under Prime Minister Clement Attlee. The Northern Ireland government followed a 'step-by-step' policy in an attempt to keep pace with improvements in Britain. Massive housing projects were begun in an attempt to modernize living standards. Education and health reforms were brought in, as well as unemployment benefits.

Education in Northern Ireland was very different from that in the south. Whereas in the Free State and the Republic, the manifestation of a good nation was held to be 'Ireland', in Northern Ireland, it was Britain. (Significantly, Northern Ireland itself was not used as the guide, so schoolchildren were brought up to think goodness came from the connection with Britain.) Many Protestants, especially those who were strong unionists, looked upon the religious life of the Republic with horror. The influence that the Catholic Church seemed to have in government and society confirmed all their fears of 'Rome Rule' in a united Ireland. The Northern Ireland government instituted a series of discriminatory measures against Catholics. Many Catholics responded by retreating into their own communities. This meant that both communities increasingly lived completely within their own communities, which allowed sectarianism, tribalism and misunderstanding to grow without check. Throughout Northern Ireland, there were two distinct, and *complete*, communities. 'Complete' is as important as 'distinct' here, because there were separate neighbourhoods, schools, shops, clubs and associations, professions and almost all aspects of daily life. Education particularly was segregated and there was a great deal of argument over how the funding of Catholic and Protestant schools should be handled by the government. What this meant was that Catholic schools generally became independent of government funding (which also meant they had less money). The Catholic minority (including the clergy) looked to the Republic (and the activities of the Catholic Church there) as the model of what Irish Catholicism should be.

Although there appeared to be a great deal of difference in the speed with which the two Irelands were modernizing, there were also several examples of co-operation between the two governments on shared projects near or around the border. These included land drainage, the development of hydro-electric power, modernizing railways, and sharing responsibilities for the fisheries in the north of the island in the early 1950s. But old questions about nationality continued after the war. The IRA started a militant campaign again in 1956, and police and military posts in Northern Ireland were attacked. The campaign ultimately failed, however, because they could get no real support from Catholics in the North, and because both the Republic and Northern Ireland governments interned suspected IRA members without trial. With the depletion of its numbers through internment, and the hostility of many nationalists and Catholics in the north, the IRA were forced to end their campaign in 1962. Other, less violent, divisions continued, however. Nationalists started small-scale demonstrations against discrimination in social benefits (especially in employment and housing). Many of these demonstrations were broken up by strong police action. Unionists countered by organizing massive public displays of loyalty to the British crown whenever they could, especially during Queen Elizabeth's visit in July 1953. There were many Protestant demonstrations against the lowering of the flag over Belfast City Hall to half-mast on the death of Pope John XXIII in June 1963, as there had been when Pope Pius XII died in October 1958.

There were, however, other signs of potential understanding between the two governments when the new Northern Ireland Prime Minister, Terence O'Neill (1914–92), met with the taoiseach of the Republic, Sean Lemass (1900–71), at Stormont in February 1965. O'Neill visited Dublin in 1966. Although there were no real agreements reached at these meetings (they were intended mainly as friendly gatherings), they did seem to signal a thaw in north–south relations. Many hard-line unionists in Northern Ireland called O'Neill a traitor, including the Reverend Ian Paisley (1926–), a Free Presbyterian minister who was rising in northern politics. This was not improved when O'Neill allowed fiftieth anniversary celebrations of the 1916 Easter Rising to take place in Northern Ireland.

The mid-1960s, therefore, were crucial years in the history of Northern Ireland. On the one hand, there seemed to be an easing of restrictions on nationalists, yet the reaction of some unionists (including the revival of the paramilitary Ulster Volunteer Force) brought up the possibility of a continuing misunderstanding and prompted a reaction from nationalist extremists.

THE REPUBLIC OF IRELAND, 1949–66

The Republic tried to concentrate on social and economic matters after the end of the Emergency. In 1949, a large-scale land rehabilitation programme was implemented, in an attempt to revive land that had been depleted during the wartime compulsory tillage scheme or was underdeveloped for other reasons. In the same year, industrial investment and expansion was promoted through the Industrial Development Authority, which gave tax and other incentives for companies to build industries in Ireland, or to expand existing industries.

Costello's inter-party government ran into trouble in 1950–1 when the health minister, Dr Noel Browne (1915–1997), put forward a plan for non-compulsory free heath care for mothers and for children under sixteen. By European standards at this time, there was a high level of infant mortality in Ireland. Browne had been instrumental in eradicating tuberculosis in Ireland in the late 1940s, and he wanted to attack infant mortality next. His 'Mother and Child Scheme' proposed pre- and post-natal care, as well as education 'in respect of motherhood' for women and girls. But the Irish Medical Association and the Catholic hierarchy opposed the plan vigorously. The IMA argued that this would lead to socialized medicine (which they said the state could not afford) and would interfere with the patient–doctor relationship. The Catholic Church thought that the Mother and Child Scheme violated the sanctity of the family, that it was the family's right and responsibility to provide for health care, and that the proposed sex education would lead to an increase in immorality. The pressure from the IMA and the church proved too much. Browne was forced to resign, the government was wounded and fell in April 1951. Although the hostility of doctors was at least as responsible for the scheme's failure, the church received most of the blame. Public and press opinion was generally upset with the bishops' actions, and the whole affair served to deepen the impression held by many in Britain and Northern Ireland that the government of the Republic was in the grip of the Roman Catholic hierarchy. De Valera and Fianna Fáil took over as a minority government in 1951. In 1953, they passed public health legislation not that different from the Mother and Child Scheme, except that it included a means test, which meant that only those who could not afford to pay for medical care would qualify (twenty-nine per cent of the population were covered by this programme). Other social reforms were also passed, dealing with adoption, state benefits for widows and orphans and employment insurance. By 1954, therefore, the Republic had a fully functioning, if limited, welfare state.

Rationing had continued since the war, and other economic problems were quite serious in the early 1950s. Fianna Fáil lost the 1954 election on these issues, and a coalition government headed by Fine Gael came into power. This election was important because it set the trend for Republic politics up to the present. By 1954, Fianna Fáil and Fine Gael were clearly the dominant parties, with the Labour Party the third largest (although much smaller than the other two) and only a few seats being gained by other parties. John Costello became taoiseach again and tried to implement economic reforms, based largely on massive capital investment. Perhaps the most significant, and paradoxical, change in the Irish economy between 1932 and 1966 was the increase in the number of large farms. This seemed to go against the spirit of the Land Acts of the late nineteenth and early twentieth centuries, which tried to create a rural economy based on a large number of (relatively) small owner-occupiers. But as the twentieth century wore on, social changes made this unlikely. More people moved into towns, and the number of people involved in agriculture almost halved between 1926 and 1961. This was reflected in a drop in the number of small farms and an increase in the number of large ones. Twenty-four per cent of farms were larger than fifty acres in 1931, but this had grown to nearly thirty per cent in 1960 (and would continue to increase). The post-war period was difficult for the Republic. Agriculture was stagnant (except for cattle, which by 1960 made up seventy per cent of agricultural exports), and industry lagged behind Britain and Europe in technology and scale (although it did enjoy a brief period of prosperity immediately after the war). The main economic issue during the 1950s was the balance of payments, when imports increased and exports fell. This meant that wages hardly rose at all during the 1950s, and that economic growth was amongst the lowest in Europe (even amongst the war-ravaged countries). Unemployment grew, and with it, emigration (especially to Britain). Between 1946 and 1956, emigration more than doubled.

Another election in 1957 brought de Valera and Fianna Fáil back into power. In 1959, de Valera resigned as taoiseach when he was elected President. His deputy, Sean Lemass (1899–1971) took over as taoiseach. In 1958, this government put forward its First Programme for Economic Expansion, which was generally made up of the ideas of finance minister T.K. Whittaker (1916–). He proposed more state planning, fewer and lower taxes on imports and greater investment in those industries likely to be the most productive. The First Programme was a success in many ways. There were some increases in employment and some rise in the standard of living, although modest. A Second Programme was implemented in 1963 to extend this work. Ultimately, however, these Programmes did not provide the sort of economic prosperity that was hoped for. The Republic still lagged behind most of the rest of Europe. The Programmes were successful, however, in laying the groundwork for greater Irish participation in the world economy. In the late 1950s, the Republic made its economy more a part of the world economy by starting to reduce some import tariffs (a reform which lasted throughout the 1960s). While protectionism remained in many industries, it was gradually being brought down, and general economic growth in the Western world during the 1960s brought benefits to the more open Irish economy. By the end of the 1960s, over 350 foreign companies had set up shop in the Republic.

The problem with the Economic Expansion Programmes was that many elements of the economy failed to perform in the way the planners thought they would, including agriculture. The original idea of reducing government spending and taxation did not work because social welfare spending outstripped expectations. The economic buoyancy of the 1960s was, therefore, not so much the result of the Republic's economic planning as it was of the Republic's economy being more open than it had been. During the 1960s, government spending was able to increase because of this growth. This created a sense of prosperity and of having finally set the Irish economy on a successful path. Unemployment and emigration were reduced dramatically. Emigration had been as high as 42,400 per year between 1956 and 1961, but dropped to 16,100 between 1961 and 1966 (and further to 10,800 between 1966 and 1971). Economic growth was four per cent per year between 1958 and 1965, which was good, steady growth. There was another balance of payments crisis in 1965, however, and some government action was required to slow down the economy. This had an impact on growth, of course, but the Republic had learned the lessons of the early 1950s and the difficulties faced were not great.

In the meantime, the Republic was admitted to the United Nations in 1955 (without giving up its firm commitment to neutrality), and Irish soldiers served in UN actions in Lebanon in 1958, the Congo in 1960 and Cyprus in 1974. Along with Britain, the Republic applied for membership in the European Economic Community in 1961, but stayed out after Britain's application was rejected in 1963. Since most of the Republic's trade was with Britain, it seemed prudent to wait until both nations could join (which happened in 1973). An Anglo-Irish free-trade agreement was signed with the British government in December 1965, which gradually eliminated trade barriers by 1975. Initially, however, this hurt Irish exports because they could not compete with cheaper British and European goods, but the situation was remedied, however, when the Republic entered the EEC and began trading more freely with Europe.

Educational reform at the elementary, secondary, vocational and university level was also brought forward in the early 1960s. This was mainly in the form of increased financial support from the government. In other areas of social policy, slums were cleared and much of Dublin rebuilt and restored. The Republic, therefore, went through a similar modernization period to that witnessed in Northern Ireland during this period. Economic stability was not secured, however, and reliance on foreign investment could not be permanent. The Republic entered the late 1960s with great potential for economic growth and social change.

INTERPRETATIONS

Despite the drama of partition and the civil war, the succeeding decades in the histories of the two Irelands are no less interesting and important. Since these years are fairly recent in historical terms, they may not have seen the depth of historical interpretation that previous periods have. They have become.the subject of some very important historical work, however, and many myths about Irish history in this period have been dispelled. There is a popular perception that, after the struggles over Home Rule and partition, Ireland (albeit divided) settled down to a relatively calm period until the coming of the Troubles in the late 1960s. While there may not have been as much violence as appeared at the beginning of the century, historians have shown that there were tremendous differences between groups in the Free State and the Republic, as well as in Northern Ireland. Furthermore, many historians have been highly critical of the way the Free State and the Republic handled its economic and cultural affairs, and of the exclusive nature of Northern Irish society during this period.

Much recent historical work has shown that there were strong differences between the two main political groups in the Free State/Republic, which were greater than generally thought, and that these differences come from long-standing divisions in ideas about the nature of the country and its political future. Jeffrey Prager argued that one of the fundamentally important political aspects of the Free State was the difference between those who supported the Treaty (and eventually became Cumann na nGaedheal) and those who opposed the Treaty (and who became Fianna Fáil). This was a difference in political ideological background, which has not received adequate attention from scholars (who have concentrated on divisions surrounding the Treaty and the civil war). Free Staters, he argues, belonged to an 'Irish Enlightenment' background, which can be traced all the way back to the 1790s. Republicans belonged to a 'Gaelic-Romantic' ideology, which had its roots in the cultural and militant nationalism of the late eighteenth century. Since the supporters of the Treaty were the first governing party in the Free State, they set the early political agenda, and later Fianna Fáil governments had to respond to it. This agenda was preoccupied with building an Irish democracy, and the 'national question' (over partition and the border) was sidelined (Jeffrey Prager, *Building Democracy in Ireland 1986*).

In *The Making of Fianna Fáil Power in Ireland, 1923–1948* (1995), Richard Dunphy further advances the argument that the national question did not completely define party politics in the Free State and the Republic during this period. Internal party-political issues and questions also had a broad impact on events. One of the problems that Cumann na nGaedheal had was that they not only let Fianna Fáil capture the 'more nationalist' label, but also they did not concentrate sufficiently on party politics, to the detriment of their electoral successes. Cumann na nGaedheal, he argues, spent a great deal of time ensuring that the Free State population became generally loyal to the new institutions of Irish government, and not enough time defining themselves as a political party and building up a core base of support. One way of looking at the early years of independent Ireland, therefore, was that Cumann na nGaedheal toiled to build institutions that Fianna Fáil were then able to use to gain further support after their first term in government. In other words, Fianna Fáil were able to capitalize on the popular good will that Cumann na nGaedheal had built up with governmental institutions. This helped to cause the general wandering of Cumann na nGaedheal/Fine Gael in the political desert.

In his big book, *Ireland 1912–1985: Politics and Society* (1989), Joseph Lee argues that the national question was not pursued forthrightly by either nationalists or unionists. He emphasizes that there was a great deal of self-deception amongst nationalists (and unionists, although he does not treat them as extensively since the book is mainly about the Free State and the Republic). This deception meant that meaningful dialogue between the south and north was delayed much further than it should have been, which gave the extremists on both sides time to solidify their opinions.

Lee also carefully examines economics. His main argument is that the Irish Free State and the Republic in the twentieth century failed the Irish people through mis-management of the economy. He claims that Ireland was behind all western European countries, even Britain, in economic performance. His comparative analysis with other European countries did much to break the historiographical tradition of looking at modern Irish political and economic history as a relationship between Britain and Ireland alone. On government economic policy before 1960, Mary Daly has argued that the much-lauded semi-state (or state-sponsored) industries were not as successful as generally perceived. In the first place, the Irish industries of this type were not as extensive as they had been in other European countries, and this prevented them from making sufficient economic impact. In the second place, because they could rely on a certain level of state support, they did not really compete with private businesses. This led them to become sluggish and non-innovative. Joseph Lee termed them 'rats who could not run'. (See Mary Daly, *Industrial Development and Irish National Identity, 1922–1939*, 1992, and Joseph Lee (ed.), *Ireland 1945–1970*, 1979.) In other ways that influenced economics, Lee argues, the Free State and the Republic remained behind Europe. Academic life and the flourishing of universities in Ireland only began in the second half of the twentieth century. In many other European countries, even those ravaged by the two world wars, universities had begun to expand earlier and were more professionally run in the first half of the century. This not only caused problems in Irish education, but in economic and industrial life.

Religious life in the Free State and Republic has also gained much attention, partly because it was so important to the defining of southern society, and also because it became a significant aspect of how the south was viewed in Northern Ireland. Most historians agree that the influence of the Catholic Church on society and politics in the Free State and the Republic increased from 1922 until after the Second World War, and that it has decreased since the early 1950s. John Whyte's *Church and State in Modern Ireland, 1923–1979* (1980) shows that there was close dialogue between the Church and government ministers in the Free State period. Importantly, public opinion generally supported this connection. During the 1950s and 1960s, however, church influence suffered a few important blows. One was the public's reaction to what was seen as church interference over the Mother and Child Scheme in 1951. Book bans and other censorship were also reduced during these years, which Whyte analyses carefully. Dermot Keogh's *The Vatican, the Bishops, and Irish Politics,*

1919–46: International Relations, Diplomacy, and Politics (1986) also shows the strong influence that the Church hierarchy had over government policy. His research in government archives has shown that, during the 1920s and 1930s, church attempts at influencing government policy were even greater than was publicly admitted. Tom Inglis, while agreeing with Whyte and Keogh about the depth of church influence and involvement in Free State politics and society, goes further to condemn the church for 'limiting' Irish society during this period. His *Moral Monopoly: the Rise and Fall of the Catholic Church in Modern Ireland* (1988) argues this strongly, saying that the church was a 'coercive organization' during this period, and that it hemmed in the development of Irish society.

Northern Ireland has also received extensive critical scrutiny. Some of the strongest criticism of the Northern Ireland government in the period between the Treaty and the Troubles relates to the question of discrimination against the Catholic minority. *The State in Northern Ireland, 1921–72: Political Forces and Social Classes* (1979), written by Paul Bew, Peter Gibbon and Henry Patterson, argues that discrimination against Catholics in Northern Ireland was serious, deliberate and part of the policy of the Northern Ireland government. Patrick Buckland, in his *The Factory of Grievances: Devolved Government in Northern Ireland 1921–39* (1979) details this more extensively. This discrimination, however, was more complicated than might appear on the surface, and all of the above writers (Bew, Gibbon, Patterson and Buckland) are careful to make distinctions between government officials who were extreme in their ideas of defending Northern Irish Protestantism by restricting Catholics, and those who were much less discriminatory and who tried to implement even-handedness. Some politicians and commentators on both sides in Northern Ireland have tried to exaggerate the levels of discrimination. Some nationalists compared it to South Africa under apartheid, and some unionists claimed that there was very little discrimination, and that, where it did exist, it was justifiable to discriminate against a disloyal minority. The majority of scholarly opinion, however, agrees with Patrick Buckland, who wrote in his *History of Northern Ireland* (1981) that,

> The fact remains that, owing to local conditions, the power of the government was used in the interests of Unionists and Protestants, with scant regard for the interests of the region as a whole or for the claims and susceptibilities of the substantial minority. (p. 72)

Interpretations of this period of Irish history, therefore, have shown that the great diversity which defined Irish politics, culture and society was reflected in the events of the time. This diversity continued to the end of the twentieth century, and was the base upon which the troubles and triumphs of the following chapter were built.

EIGHT

Troubles and Triumphs, 1966–2000

The second half of the twentieth century saw great troubles in Ireland, as well as economic and cultural triumphs. Sectarian violence in Northern Ireland reached a peak in the late 1960s and early 1970s, the Northern Ireland parliament was suspended and direct rule from London reimposed. The Republic entered the European Monetary System in 1979, and enjoyed a crescendo of prosperity in the 1990s. These decades also saw the export of Irish culture and music throughout the west, and Irish artists became some of the best known in the world.

THE REPUBLIC OF IRELAND, 1966–82

Economic change continued to be the preoccupation of the Republic during this period. Sean Lemass had resigned as taoiseach in November 1966, and was succeeded by Jack Lynch (1917–99). The economic plans that had been put in place in the earlier 1960s had to be abandoned or reformed. Several times during these two decades, the Republic's economy went through serious difficulty, such as in 1974–5, when the oil crisis and other worldwide economic problems hit small countries like Ireland very hard. The recession of the late 1970s and early 1980s had similar effects, one of which was increased emigration. But there seemed to be a fundamental stability in the Republic's economy though it might not have been very noticeable during each crisis. Average growth during this period remained steady. The work of the Industrial Development Authority in attracting new industries seemed to have diversified the Republic's economy. Lynch and Fianna Fáil won the 1969 general election, and began working for Ireland's introduction into the European Community. Fianna Fáil ran into difficulty, however, when two of its important ministers, Charles Haughey (1925–) and Neal Blaney (1922–), were implicated in an IRA arms-smuggling operation in 1970. Lynch removed them from the government, and they were arrested on these charges, but they were acquitted in October. All this showed that difficulties in Northern Ireland continued to impinge on politics in the Republic.

A new focus emerged in the life of the Republic when it became a member of the European Community on 1 January 1973 (along with Britain and Denmark). This brought immediate benefits, especially for farmers (who received nearly half of their income from European and government subsidies). In the late 1970s, Ireland was receiving over £400 million from the EEC, while contributing just over £40 million. The net gain from the EEC climbed even higher by the mid-1980s, to over £500 million. This meant that farming would remain a large part of the economy, and that farming incomes rose dramatically. But the economic benefits of EEC membership that were to become so apparent in later decades could not help the Republic during the economic slump of the early 1970s. The oil crises of the 1970s hit the Republic's economy hard, but the responses of the various governments probably did not help. Having seen the benefits that expansion and government borrowing had brought during the 1960s, they pursued more or less the same policies. Budget deficits were allowed to rise out of control, and governments seemed to think they could spend their way out of the problems of the 1970s. Inflation and unemployment were two important reasons for the rejection of Fianna Fáil at the 1973 election. A Fine Gael–Labour coalition came into power under Liam Cosgrave (1920–). One of the most important things that the new government did was to declare a state of emergency during the revival of IRA terrorism in Britain and Northern Ireland. Police and the military were given increased powers to arrest and detain suspected terrorists, and many militant republican organizations were banned.

The election of 1977 proved to be a Fianna Fáil victory. Fine Gael had spent a lot of time between 1973 and 1977 improving their electoral and political organizations, and were widely expected to win the 1977 election, but the election result showed that there was little perception of ideological difference between the two parties, and often very minor issues (such as certain types of property and vehicle taxes in 1977) could sway the electorate. Jack Lynch became taoiseach again, but many of his own supporters disagreed with his moderate stance towards unionists in Northern Ireland. Further, there were sharp economic difficulties in the immediate aftermath of the Republic joining the European Monetary System in late 1978 and early 1979. This broke the market connection between the Irish pound and the British pound, and tied the value of the Irish pound to other European currencies. As with the Republic's entry into the European Community, the idea behind the move to the European Monetary System was to free the Irish economy from the overwhelming influence of the British economy. This would reduce the Republic's dependency on British markets, and open up more markets in Europe. Initially, however, the move to the European Monetary System caused the value of the Irish pound to fall dramatically. Trade union problems also plagued the country (the postal service was on strike for nearly six months in 1979), and fuel shortages were severe in the wake of another international oil crisis. Also, by the end of the 1970s, the degree of European support for agriculture reduced significantly, and prices fell sharply. The late 1970s and early 1980s were characterized by massive public debts, and failed attempts to solve the problems that they created.

Jack Lynch resigned unexpectedly as taoiseach in December 1979, and was replaced by Charles Haughey. Haughey's priorities were to improve the economy and to tackle Northern Irish and British relations. Agreements were reached with trade unions and others in October 1980, which ended many disputes and meant that services were renewed. Haughey met with the new British Prime Minister, Margaret Thatcher (1925–), on 21 May 1980, and held discussions on Northern Ireland. Although no agreements were reached (none had been proposed at this stage), the meeting was said to be friendly. They met again in December, and took the step of agreeing to an examination of the 'totality of the relationship within these islands'. Some unionists in Northern Ireland expressed alarm at this statement, and Thatcher was forced to state publicly that the British government would never force Northern Ireland to unite with the Republic if a majority of the people did not wish it. The strength of this statement caused many nationalists in the south to withdraw their support for Haughey. This, combined with the stubborn recession, led to Haughey losing the 1981 election, and a Fine Gael–Labour coalition coming in under Garrett FitzGerald (1926–). FitzGerald had productive meetings with Thatcher (they set up the Anglo-Irish Intergovernmental Council to discuss common concerns), and he brought up the subject of amending the Irish constitution to make it less objectionable to Northern Ireland unionists (which faced serious opposition in the Dáil). But FitzGerald's remedy for the economy was strict, and his austere budget of January 1982 was rejected by one vote in the Dáil. He called an election in February 1982. This time, Haughey and Fianna Fáil were more successful in building a coalition.

Haughey's previous good relations with Thatcher were highly strained when he rejected the idea of a devolved assembly for Northern Ireland (which he thought would not provide security for Catholics) and he asked the UN Security Council to intervene in the Falklands war between Britain and Argentina. But Haughey's government was plagued by administrative scandals, and the continued recession did much to bite into his government's acceptability in the country. He lost a no-confidence vote on 4 November 1982, and had to call another general election (the third in an eighteen-month period). The Haughey–Fitzgerald see-saw swung back in favour of FitzGerald, who put together another Fine Gael–Labour coalition in early December. From 1982 onwards, the pace of dialogue between Dublin and London increased dramatically, and social issues in the Republic again became prominent.

In addition to these rapid-fire political changes, there were also important social and economic changes during this period. The population of the Republic grew dramatically. It increased by over half a million between 1961 and 1981 (from 2,818,000 to 3,440,000). Other social factors changed. Marriage age fell, but married couples were having fewer and fewer children. The population became younger, a fact that was exploited in the Republic's advertisements to attract industry and development from abroad during the 1980s – 'We're the Young Europeans'. Emigration to countries on the European continent increased, providing an alternative to the traditional patterns of leaving Ireland for the USA, Britain and Australia. Educational reforms were sweeping. Many smaller schools were closed or amalgamated with larger ones nearby. Provision for equipment was improved, and secondary schools became free for most students, which, among other things, improved retention. Universities were given funds to expand, and technical and vocational colleges spread. Censorship of what had been considered indecent or obscene books and magazines was relaxed in 1966. Contraception, long banned in the Republic, was permitted (with certain restrictions) in 1979. By the mid-1980s, however, this policy was seen to have many difficulties, and in 1985 condoms were made legal for all those over eighteen. And the bans on divorce and abortion were coming under criticism. Women's groups formed and pushed for greater equality, and equal pay and equal opportunity legislation was passed in this period.

The Catholic Church tried to make itself 'more relevant to modern times' during the 1960s and 1970s. Dictates from the Second Vatican Council, which contained many liberalizing measures, meant that Irish Catholicism could not continue to be as inward-looking as it had been. There was also a gradual relaxation of censorship. Religion still retained a strong hold on Irish life, however. More than ninety per cent of Catholics described themselves as 'practising' (that is, they attended mass at least once per week) in the early 1970s. There was some evidence, and fear, that young Catholics were not as devout as older generations, and that this might cause a decline in religious practice in later decades (which turned out to be true).

NORTHERN IRELAND AND THE TROUBLES, 1966–82

There were two major, and opposing, new forces in Northern Ireland in the mid-1960s. The first was the extremist, the Revd Ian Paisley, who had emerged as the spokesman for many hard-line unionists in the late 1950s and early 1960s. The second was the Northern Ireland Civil Rights Association, which was founded in Belfast in 1967 to press for reforms in local government, the removal of the extra vote for business property, equality of housing and equal civil rights for everyone in Northern Ireland. Although the Association was intended to appeal to all religions and traditions in the north, it soon had a Catholic majority, and, in fact, most of the things it opposed were essentially restrictions (formal and informal) on Catholics in the province. The crucial difference between the Northern Ireland Civil Rights Association and other organizations that proposed to support the Catholic minority was that the Association did not question the political existence of Northern Ireland. Their concern was to press for equality in housing, employment and elections. Following an investigation into severe housing discrimination in County Tyrone in 1968, the Association held protest marches throughout Northern Ireland in late 1968 and early 1969. A Derry protest on 5 October 1968 was a violently suppressed by the police. This was captured on news cameras, and much of the world became shocked at the brutality of the police action. The police force, the Royal Ulster Constabulary, soon lost credibility with Northern Irish Catholics.

Disorder in Northern Ireland became rife. A new organization, the People's Democracy, rose after the October confrontation between the Northern Ireland Civil Rights Association and the police. Led by Bernadette Devlin (1948–) and others, the People's Democracy was a more radical group than the Association, and it attracted severe criticism from some unionist groups and from Northern Ireland's Prime Minister, Terence O'Neill. They led various civil rights marches, including a famous one from Derry to Belfast in early January 1969. Although the People's Democracy gradually faded by the early 1970s, Bernadette Devlin was elected to the British House of Commons in April 1969. Continuing sectarian violence between Catholics and Protestants and between nationalists and unionists sparked widespread concern in Ireland and Britain. O'Neill came under heavy criticism from all sides for the government's handling of the situation. He called a general election on 24 February 1969, and lost unionist support in many important constituencies, although he remained in government. This election was important because it saw a rise in support for Ian Paisley. Also, on the nationalist side, the Nationalist Party's leader, Eddie McAteer (1914–86), lost his seat to John Hume (1937–), who would come to lead the non-militant nationalist campaign for the rest of the century. O'Neill ended the multiple vote system (whereby business owners, mainly unionists, got an extra vote for owning business property) and introduced 'one person, one vote'. The negative reaction from his own party was so great that he resigned on 28 April. His successor was Major James Chichester-Clark (1923–). But Chichester-Clark was unable to calm the situation, and in August 1969, his government asked the British government to send in troops to restore order. In many Catholic areas of Belfast and Derry, the British troops were welcomed as protectors from the police and unionist extremists. The British government, under Prime Minister Harold Wilson (1916–95), insisted on a number of reforms from the Northern Ireland government. Public housing was to be allocated by a non-partisan body, electoral gerrymandering was to end and discrimination in employment was made illegal. On 19 August 1969, the British government issued the 'Downing Street Declaration', which said that every person in Northern Ireland was 'entitled to the same equality of treatment and freedom from discrimination as obtains in the rest of the United Kingdom'. Although welcomed by the minority community, these reforms and the Declaration were seen as coming a little late. They were also bitterly resented by many unionists, and some militant groups saw an increase in membership and financing.

In the Catholic streets of Derry and Belfast, the initial goodwill that the British troops had enjoyed in late 1969 was lost quickly during arms searches of Catholic homes. Many Catholics found this insulting, and the harsh behaviour of the soldiers during these searches turned Catholic opinion against them. This was a highly significant moment, because much of nationalist and Catholic opinion had seen the British government as a protector of the minority against the unionist and Protestant majority in Northern Ireland. These months were also crucial for the IRA. Although it had largely been militarily inactive since 1962, it had retained its structural organization and membership. The movement became interested in issues broader than the national question and began to embrace Marxist socialism as a cure for Ireland's ills (north and south). But when hostilities began to mount in Northern Ireland, two opposing camps in the IRA began to emerge. Those in the north thought that the idea of a socialist Ireland would have to be put on hold until the Catholics and nationalists had been protected, and the national question had been settled in the north. The southern command of the IRA stuck to its plan to agitate for a socialist republic. The northern IRA finally split from the southern IRA on 11 January 1970. The militants became known as the Provisional IRA, and the socialists as the Official IRA. The IRA members who would make up the Provisionals had essentially reactivated their military campaign in 1969, in reaction to the attacks on civil rights marchers and the arms searches in Derry and Belfast. They declared war on the British army in late 1969. The Official IRA ceased to be a significant force in Irish politics, north and south, and the term IRA now generally refers to the Provisionals, as it will throughout the rest of this book.

Meanwhile, the nationalist Social Democratic Labour Party (SDLP) was founded in August 1970 to provide a party and forum for non-militant nationalists, civil rights campaigners and trade unionists. It quickly grew in popularity under its leaders, one of whom was John Hume. Northern Ireland governments (under Chichester-Clark until March 1971, and under Brian Faulkner until March 1972) put in place some of the reforms that had been announced in the Downing Street Declaration in 1969. But the government soon put reforms on hold, and concentrated on destroying the IRA. The IRA had begun its campaign in earnest in early 1971. The first British soldier was killed on 6 February. Bombing campaigns began throughout the province. Faulkner (1921–77) responded by introducing 'internment' for suspected IRA members in August 1971. Internment was imprisonment without trial or charge until the violence ceased, but it was not a new idea. It had been used both in the Free State and in Northern Ireland in 1922, 1939 and 1956. Initially, internment in 1971 only targeted republicans, over three hundred of whom were arrested (many of these had to be released because they were not connected with the IRA). Internment seemed like the action of a police state, and many people (nationalists and Catholics, as well as moderates) were strongly opposed to it. Internment, however, only helped the IRA. Many nationalists who had been unwilling to commit themselves to militancy joined the organization in 1971 and 1972 in reaction to what they saw as repression. Violence increased dramatically, with twice as many bombings between August and December 1971 as there had been between January and July. There were demonstrations against internment almost immediately after it was imposed; the most notorious of these was in Derry on 30 January 1972. On this 'Bloody Sunday', thirteen civilians were shot dead by British Army paratroopers during a banned civil rights demonstration. Massive protests against these killings were held across Ireland, and the British Embassy in Dublin was burned down on 2 February.

Faulkner was summoned to London to meet with Conservative British Prime Minister Edward Heath (1916–). Faulkner was warned that if the Northern Ireland government could not contain the political violence, direct rule would be implemented from London and the Northern Ireland parliament would be suspended. But the violence continued at alarmingly high levels (some of it at military bases in England) and on 24 March 1972, the London government took political control of Northern Ireland, and the Northern Ireland parliament at Stormont was suspended 'temporarily'. A new British cabinet office, the Secretary of State for Northern Ireland, was created and William Whitelaw (1918–99) was appointed. 1972 continued to see horrific violence in Northern Ireland. Although there was a very brief truce between the IRA and the British army from 26 June until 9 July, its breakdown prompted even more violence. In response to IRA action, unionist and Protestant militant groups, such as the Ulster Volunteer Force, were revived, and new groups, such as the Ulster Defence Association, were founded. Even though violence declined in late 1972, the death toll by the end of the year was 474.

The next few years saw many attempts at constitutional settlements to the divisiveness in Northern Ireland. The first was the creation of a Northern Ireland Assembly. William Whitelaw tried to bring the non-militant parties together in an effort to create a new governing body for Northern Ireland. Unionists were promised that Northern Ireland would remain part of the United Kingdom as long as a majority of its residents desired it. Nationalists, represented in this instance by the SDLP, were promised a share in the executive power in the new assembly. This was agreed to in December 1973, and the British government met with the government of the Irish Republic at a conference at

Sunningdale in Berkshire to discuss the founding of a Council of Ireland. This Council was to be made up of representatives from the Republic and from Northern Ireland, and was to discuss and manage issues of common concern to both governments. The new Northern Ireland Assembly met during the first week of 1974, but many hard-line unionists refused to accept the Council of Ireland agreement that Faulkner had signed at Sunningdale, and they withdrew from the Assembly. Faulkner then had to deal with a massive strike against the Sunningdale agreement by the Ulster Workers' Council, called on 14 May. Over the next two weeks, the strike gradually gained support, bringing most of Northern Ireland to a standstill. This was the last straw, and Faulkner and his party members resigned from the executive of the Assembly on 28 May 1974. The executive then broke down, and any hope of an effective assembly was gone.

In 1975, another attempt was made at restoring government to Northern Ireland. A Convention was set up, and seventy-eight members elected in May, with the intention of putting forward proposals for governing the province. But no agreement could be reached on how to balance majority power with minority rights, and the Convention was eventually dissolved in March 1976. Internment was ended on 5 December 1975, but violence in Northern Ireland continued. Other groups tried to bring about a peaceful solution. The Peace Movement (also known as the Peace People) was founded in 1976 by Mairead Corrigan (1944–) and Betty Williams (1943–), after political violence had taken the lives of many children in Northern Ireland. They organized huge demonstrations and, in the short term, seemed to gain a lot of attention and to question some fundamental aspects of the divide in Northern Ireland. Although the Movement did not last much past the mid-1970s, Corrigan and Williams were awarded the 1977 Nobel Peace Prize for their work.

Further proposals to devolve power to Northern Ireland in 1977 and 1979 failed to satisfy nationalists or unionists, and the continued stalemate seemed to entrench the different parties in their positions. The decade of the 1970s was undoubtedly the worst that Northern Ireland had lived through in the twentieth century, but the 1980s saw only limited progress towards greater understanding. 1980 and 1981 were the years of hunger strikes. In late 1980, republican prisoners (including women) in various Northern Ireland prisons went on hunger strike for nearly two months. 1981 saw more severe hunger strikes, led by Bobby Sands, who initially protested against treatment in the Maze prison. Sands began his hunger strike on 1 March, and was soon joined by fellow republicans. This strike attracted worldwide attention, and Sands was even elected a Sinn Féin MP for the British parliament at a by-election on 20 April. The British government refused to give in to the strikers' demands to be treated as political prisoners, and Sands and nine other hunger strikers died in early May.

The next year, the British Conservative government under Margaret Thatcher made another attempt at setting up a Northern Ireland Assembly, and elections were held in October. This time, however, nationalists refused to take their seats in protest at what had gone on in the late 1970s and early 1980s. The plan for the Assembly then collapsed. Attempts at co-operation between the British and Irish governments were also troubled during this period. Thatcher had met with Charles Haughey, the Irish taoiseach, in December 1980, with the intention of examining the 'totality of relationships' between Ireland and Britain, and an Anglo-Irish Council was set up in November 1981. But this progress stopped completely and quickly in 1982, partly over the Irish government's refusal to support Britain's war in the Falkland islands, and partly because of Conservative pressure on Thatcher to support Northern Ireland unionists. Politically, Northern Ireland began this period with an awakening of minority consciousness of their rights and powers of protest and disturbance. But the period ended in entrenched stalemate.

Economically, important changes had taken place, even in the midst of violence and instability. While the Northern Irish economy had expanded until 1973, it began to contract and decline in 1974. This was partly due to general British economic woes, as well as political violence frightening off potential investors. All this led to the 'de-industrialization' of Northern Ireland, where the manufacturing sector dropped to less than a quarter of the whole economy. Unemployment became intractable, reaching twenty per cent in 1982. Overall, Northern Ireland became a 'kept province' in that the British government was sending much more money to Northern Ireland than it was receiving from the province in taxes. Even though there had been some growth in the Northern Ireland economy during the 1960s, the problems with the drastic decline of the shipbuilding industry and the slow pace of industrial and commercial modernization meant that living standards were not as high as they were in the rest of the United Kingdom (although they were still higher than in the Irish Republic). These economic problems, and slow growth, meant that Northern Ireland's economy was not strong enough to handle the shock that the Troubles brought. It struggled throughout the 1970s, 1980s and early 1990s, although it was always heavily subsidized by the British treasury which ensured its viability.

IRELAND, 1982–2000

The last two decades of the twentieth century saw the solidification of the idea of co-operation between Dublin and London in bringing about a solution to the problems in Northern Ireland. The 1990s saw the start of the 'peace process', but the 1980s started with what looked like a continuation of opposing attitudes in Northern Ireland, the Republic and Britain. The British Prime Minister, Margaret Thatcher, said in July 1982 that her government had no reason to consult with the Irish Republic over affairs in Northern Ireland. The idea of an assembly for Northern Ireland was revived in 1982, however, and the Assembly election showed an increase in political support for Sinn Féin in October. This caused some concern amongst nationalists because the moderate SDLP gained only slightly, and many nationalists wondered if Sinn Féin would eventually become the dominant nationalist party. This concern grew when the new leader of Sinn Féin, Gerry Adams (1948–), was elected to the British parliament as MP for West Belfast in June 1983. Adams refused to take his seat in protest at the British presence in Northern Ireland.

In 1983, the Irish government made an attempt to bring about greater dialogue between the constitutional and non-violent political parties in the Republic and the North. Established as the New Ireland Forum, it was made up of the SDLP from Northern Ireland, and Fianna Fáil, Fine Gael and Labour from the Republic. Meeting in May 1983, one of the recommendations that the Forum put forward was that Northern Ireland could be governed jointly by the British and Irish governments. This symbolized a new direction amongst nationalists, a direction which not only recognized the 'equal validity' of the unionist tradition in Northern Ireland, but indicated that co-operation between Dublin and London was potentially the most viable way towards a solution to problems in the North. Although the British government's reaction to the Forum's report was lukewarm, a meeting between Margaret Thatcher and the new taoiseach, Garrett FitzGerald, in November 1984, encouraged this sort of thinking when they announced that 'the identities of both the majority and the minority communities in Northern Ireland should be recognized and respected and reflected in the structures and processes of Northern Ireland in ways acceptable to both communities.' This was further advanced by the Anglo-Irish Agreement, signed by Thatcher and FitzGerald on 15 November 1985 and approved by both the London and Dublin parliaments. In this agreement, a new, co-operative approach seemed to have been taken. It recognized the right of the majority of the people in Northern Ireland to determine the province's governance, and stated that any change in its status would have to be approved by a majority vote. If a change were ever to be desired by a majority of the people in the north, the Agreement stated, it would be supported by the Dublin and London governments. A British–Irish Intergovernment Conference was set up so that civil servants from Dublin and London could meet to discuss issues of common concern. The reaction to the Agreement was cautious optimism from most moderate and constitutional parties, distrust from militant nationalists and fierce opposition from extreme unionists, who saw this as the first step to a united Ireland. But optimism for a non-violent solution grew when the SDLP gained strength at the 1987 British parliamentary elections, at the expense of Sinn Féin. This optimism was tempered, however, by the spectre of renewed violence in Northern Ireland. In May 1987, the IRA attacked an RUC station in County Armagh, and eight IRA men were killed. During a Remembrance Day ceremony in Enniskillen, County Fermanagh, an IRA bomb killed eleven people. And three unarmed IRA members were killed by British forces in Gibraltar.

THE PEACE PROCESS

The British government took two further steps towards resolving the Northern Ireland problem when it stated in late 1989 that it would respond positively to an end to IRA violence, and said in late 1990 that Britain had no 'strategic or economic interest' in Northern Ireland, which meant that it would only retain the province on the basis that the majority of the people there wished it to. The Secretary of State for Northern Ireland, Peter Brooke (1934–), also tried to build inter-party co-operation in what came to be known as the Brooke Initiative in early 1990 (which was more or less the start of the peace process). Brooke tried to base this on the idea that the constitutional parties in Northern Ireland had no real barriers to talking to one another, and, hence, moving the 1985 Anglo-Irish Agreement forward. Various proposals for a change in how Northern Ireland was to be governed (by a commission made up of members from Northern Ireland, London, Dublin and the European Community) were put forward by the SDLP, but were rejected by unionists. Although these talks and the issues they raised lasted through 1991 and most of 1992, the problems and disagreements (which included such matters as the venue of the meetings and who would chair them, as well as more long-standing issues) between the various parties caused them to collapse by November 1992.

Throughout the early years of the 1990s, John Hume, the leader of the SDLP, had been holding talks with Gerry Adams from Sinn Féin, attempting to bring Adams's party into the constitutional process of seeking reform in Northern Ireland. The British government, under the new Secretary of State, Patrick Mayhew (1929–), had publicly stated its willingness to allow Sinn Féin to participate in political talks if they would renounce violence and try to convince other hard-line republicans to do the same. A further sense of Sinn Féin taking a more moderate stand came on 24 April 1993, when Hume and Adams issued a joint statement that the Irish people had a right to self-determination, and, more importantly, that the way this right was to be exercised was 'a matter of agreement between the people of Ireland'. This seemed to indicate that Sinn Féin were willing to take the concerns of unionists into account. Mayhew had also publicly stated that, although the identity and aspirations of unionists were safe-guarded in national and international law, there was 'also the aspiration to a united Ireland, an aspiration that is no less legitimate'. This recognition of nationalist feelings was a major step forward in understanding the different groups in Northern Ireland.

In December 1993, the British Prime Minister, John Major (1943–), and the Irish taoiseach, Albert Reynolds (1932–), issued their Joint Declaration that 'it is for the people of Ireland alone, by agreement between the two parts respectively, to exercise their right of self-determination on the basis of consent, freely and concurrently given, North and South, to bring about a united Ireland, if that is their wish.' The 1993 Declaration also emphasized the need for all interested parties (including those in Britain and the United States) to have 'full respect for the rights and identities of both traditions in Ireland'. This was welcomed by constitutional nationalists, who saw the British withdrawal from specific interest in Northern Ireland as a positive step forward. Militant nationalists, however, resented the renewed emphasis on the separateness of Northern Ireland. Unionists remained worried that the British government was gradually accepting moderate nationalist arguments about the future of Northern Ireland. One of the most important things about the Declaration, however, happened privately. Reynolds made it known to militant repub-licans that, if the Declaration was not enough to stop the violence, he would continue to work with the British government to bring about peace in the north, even if it meant leaving republican parties such as Sinn Féin out of the negotiations. This seems to have helped bring about the IRA ceasefire of 31 August 1994.

SOCIAL AND POLITICAL LIFE IN THE REPUBLIC

The Northern Ireland troubles were not the only important issue in Ireland. During the 1980s and early 1990s, the Republic addressed important social concerns. Two main social issues, abortion and divorce, rose in the Republic in the 1980s. These would attract worldwide attention and have some influence on how Protestants in Northern Ireland perceived the Republic. From 1981 to 1983 there was a campaign to add a ban on abortion as an amendment to the Irish constitution. Previously, there had been strong laws against abortion, but many anti-abortion activists thought that only a constitutional ban would prevent the legalization of abortion in the future. A Pro-Life Amendment Campaign and Anti-Amendment Campaign fought a heated battle during the public debate. In the September 1983 referendum on the issue, the amendment was passed by a majority of sixty-seven per cent to thirty-three per cent, with a low turnout. Also, the taoiseach during these years, Garrett FitzGerald, attempted to make some aspects of the Republic's social life and constitution more palatable to northern unionists and Protestants. In 1986, he proposed to remove the Republic's constitutional ban on divorce. Not only was this a needed reform for the Republic, he argued, it would improve relations with the north, and make any future co-operation between the Dublin and London governments seem less worrisome to northern Protestants. As in the referendum on abortion, those who opposed divorce liberalization were more organized and more powerful. In the June 1986 divorce referendum, the constitutional ban was upheld by 63.5% to 36.5%. But the votes against the liberalization of abortion and divorce law cannot be solely explained in terms of the influence of the Catholic Church. Public opinion amongst Protestants in Northern Ireland was also strongly opposed to abortion, and the anti-divorce campaign made much of the complicated changes that would have to be made to property inheritance law if divorce had been approved. FitzGerald, however, saw the defeat of the legalization of divorce as a blow to his plans to improve north–south relations (in November 1995, however, another divorce referendum passed with a slim majority). In 1992, other referendums removed the restriction from travelling abroad to obtain an abortion, and made contraception more available.

Other important changes in the religious life of the Republic were taking place. In the 1980s, there was a renewal of devotional practices such as pilgrimages (which had always been popular, but which had a boost during this time). Also, there were several cases of reported visitations by the Virgin Mary in the form of statues that moved, smiled and even spoke in 1985. There was also, however, a reduction in the number of men entering the priesthood. Further, there seems to have been an 'Americanization' of Catholic practice, meaning that increasing numbers of Catholics came to believe in the broad message of the church, without feeling compelled to follow the specific social and personal demands of their bishops and the Pope. Perhaps the most damage was caused to the church by the scandals that rocked it in the early 1990s. The Bishop of Kerry was revealed in 1992 to have fathered a child and used church money to support it. Priests were caught in shady Dublin men's clubs. And the most damaging were the revelations that some priests had abused children, and that their church hierarchy had attempted a cover-up. But even with all these problems, the Catholic Church was still a powerful part of life in the Irish Republic at the end of the twentieth century. Attendance at religious services is higher than almost anywhere else in the world.

Party politics also changed during this period, and the diversification of support for parties changed politics in the Republic significantly. A new political party, the Progressive Democrats, was founded in 1985 and quickly garnered much support for their idea of reducing the size of government and its role in running the economy. The Labour party continued to play its role as coalition-maker, although Fine Gael–Labour relations weakened when Fine Gael tried to rein in government spending. And, in 1989, Fianna Fáil went into coalition with the Progressive Democrats, the first time that Fianna Fáil had to rely on another party to form a government. Further, a major change in the appearance of Irish politics took place on 9 November 1990, when Mary Robinson (1944–) was elected president. Robinson, a noted international lawyer and human rights campaigner, was the first woman president of the Republic. Her election has been seen as a triumph of the diversification of party politics (she was nominated by the Labour party, while most previous presidents had been Fianna Fáil members), and of an emergence of a more progressive attitude towards women. But her election owed more to a scandal that ruined the Fianna Fáil candidate than to these other interpretations. All this, however, was not nearly as important as the changes that Robinson seemed to symbolize in Irish life. Her high international profile, and her campaigning for human rights, drew international attention immediately, something which previous presidents simply had not done. The presidency is a largely ceremonial office, and although Robinson pushed the limits of ceremonial restriction by increasing her own public exposure, there was ultimately little that she could directly change in Irish politics. But the symbol of a female head of state and the serious consideration that she attracted outside Ireland did a great deal to modernize the international view of Ireland. Ireland's international profile was further enhanced in the 1980s and 1990s by the popularity of Irish music groups. Both traditional Irish music (as played by groups such as the Chieftains) and modern pop music (represented by U2 and other groups) gained worldwide recognition.

Perhaps most important, however, was the further close development of the Irish Republic and the European Community, and the dramatic economic improvements of the late 1980s and early 1990s. The economy recovered in the late 1980s and 1990s as a result of reforms in finance and government economics, as well as more sophisticated economic relationships with the international community. By the mid-1990s, economic growth in the Republic was much higher than anywhere else in the developed world, which prompted the nickname 'The Celtic Tiger', and the 'greening' of economic relations with Britain and the rest of the European Union. Irish exports to the EU rose dramatically in the final decade of the twentieth century (and at a time when overall EU growth was not as healthy). Problems remain, however. Unemployment is higher than expected in a buoyant economy, and the economic successes of the 1990s have not been followed by enough improvements in social conditions (although this is changing very rapidly). Many commentators see these important changes as resulting from three basic trends in economics in the Republic. The first is a more moderate and prudent level of government borrowing and more vigilant attention to the balance of payments and inflation. The second is a move away from economic shadowing of Britain, and of comparing economic successes with Britain. And the third is a much greater emphasis on the Republic's place in Europe and the international market. Not being blinkered by looking only at the British economy (which, in the second half of the twentieth century, has been a poor performer over the long term), and thinking of itself in European and world terms has made the economy much more flexible and potentially powerful. Joining 'Euroland' (the eleven countries that adopted the Euro as a currency) in 1999, while Britain stayed on the sidelines, is symbolic of this highly significant change in outlook and economic sophistication. In a May 1987 referendum, Irish voters approved the Single European Act, which was designed to bring about closer co-operation between members of the European Community. This pro-European attitude in the Republic was further enhanced by an approval of the 1992 Maastricht treaty (also by referendum), which further strengthened the ties between countries, and deepened commitments to a central European system.

THE GOOD FRIDAY AGREEMENT AND BEYOND

Northern Irish affairs again preoccupied Irish people in the mid- to late-1990s. In October 1994, loyalist terrorists called a ceasefire, which, along with the IRA ceasefire called in August, meant that large-scale violent campaigns in Northern Ireland were put on hold. In July 1995, Orangemen were prevented from marching in a mainly nationalist area of Portadown in County Armagh. There was a stand-off between the Orangemen and the police, and the marchers were ultimately allowed to go through the area without drums or music. The tensions caused by this problem were overwhelming, and the peace talks that had been going on were suspended. Also, the Ulster Unionist party elected a new leader, David Trimble (1944–), in September 1995, in what came to be seen as an important move towards real negotiations. Although generally perceived as a hard-line unionist, Trimble was also known in Northern Ireland as a pragmatist (he was, Alvin Jackson has said, a mixture of 'public defiance and private realism'). And United States' President Bill Clinton visited Northern Ireland in late November, in an attempt to kick-start the talks again. He was warmly welcomed, and his visit was seen as a boost to the peace process.

Early 1996 saw both strong hope and deep despair concerning terrorists. In January, an arms decommissioning body was created with the intention of convincing militants to 'put their weapons beyond use' during the peace negotiations. It asked all parties to subscribe fully to democratic methods and to reject violence as a political tool. But the optimism that this created was dashed in February, when the IRA (frustrated with what it saw as unionist obstruction to the peace process, with British collusion) ended its ceasefire with a bomb in London's Canary Wharf district, killing two people. Despite the best efforts of the Dublin and London governments to get the talks going, they were stalled until June. Again, sectarian activities led to another breakdown. In early July, Orangemen were prevented from marching in Drumcree in County Antrim. After a stand-off lasting several days, the police backed down and allowed the march to continue. The nationalist SDLP withdrew from the talks in reaction to what it saw as an unacceptable concession to extreme unionists.

1997 saw changes of administration in London and Dublin, with Tony Blair (1953–) and his Labour Party coming to power with a massive majority in May, and Bertie Ahern (1951–) and his Fianna Fáil–Progressive Democrat coalition gaining office in June. These were significant developments because Blair was not reliant on support from Ulster Unionists within the House of Commons (as his predecessor, John Major, had been), and Bertie Ahern was well-known to be an excellent diplomat and negotiator. Both of these changes may have had a significant effect on the continuing talks in Northern Ireland. In early June, the talks revived at Stormont, and in July the IRA resumed its ceasefire, which they called 'a complete cessation of military operations'. Although unionists were dissatisfied that the word 'permanent' was not used, this was seen as being enough for Sinn Féin to join the talks in September, and to meet with the Blair government in London in December. A mood of cautious optimism carried through the end of 1997 and beginning of 1998. In January, the British and Irish governments published their plan for the future of Northern Ireland, which provided for a devolved assembly in Northern Ireland, an intergovernmental 'Council of the Isles', a north–south ministerial council and other cross-border bodies. The plan implied that the Republic would give up its territorial claims to Northern Ireland, and that, because of demographics, the Northern Ireland assembly would have a unionist majority.

But punishment beatings amongst paramilitaries, especially republicans, continued. This was seen as a violation of the principles of non-violence, as set down by former United States' Senator, George Mitchell, the chairman of the talks. Sinn Féin were temporarily suspended from the peace table in late February 1998 because of the beatings, but they returned in early March after making further commitments to exclusively peaceful means. Further, Gerry Adams made a public statement to the effect that the prospect of a united Ireland was unlikely in the near future. This went a long way to convincing the British and Irish governments that militant republicans might take unionist identity seriously.

At the end of March 1998, George Mitchell set a deadline for the conclusion of the talks. 'The time for discussion' was over, he said, and it was 'now time for a decision'. The parties knew what needed to be done, he argued, and it was now time to do it. He set the deadline at 9 April. As it neared, Prime Minister Blair flew to Belfast to take a direct part in the negotiations. One of the main sticking points was the unwillingness of the Ulster Unionist party to accept the idea of a north–south body to discuss common concerns between the Republic and Northern Ireland. Earlier on, the Ulster Unionists had called the group of proposals put forward by George Mitchell a 'Sinn Féin wish list' and argued that the north–south arrangements were simply the first step towards a united Ireland. Ulster Unionists were also opposed to members of political groups with connections to terrorists being part of the proposed Northern Ireland Assembly, and wanted Tony Blair to make amendments to the proposals. Blair refused, but gave the unionists a promise that politicians linked to terrorists could not hold office in the new Northern Ireland government, and that the decommissioning of terrorist weapons would begin after the Northern Ireland Assembly was set up. These negotiations took place privately between the parties involved. The public face of these problems was shown in bitter words being exchanged between Sinn Féin and the Ulster Unionists in press conferences and interviews.

The final negotiations in early April lasted thirty-two hours. At nearly every moment, there were fears that the chance of an agreement might collapse. The representatives from each party worked throughout the night of 9 April, with a deadline of midnight. The deadline passed in an atmosphere of great tension, but also great expectation that an agreement would be signed. Finally, at 5.36 pm on 10 April, Senator George Mitchell announced that an agreement had been reached between eight Northern Ireland political parties and the British and Irish governments. The Good Friday Agreement was signed on 10

April, and immediately came to symbolize hope that the politics of Northern Ireland would change. In the thirty years since the Troubles started in 1969, nearly 3,500 people had been killed, and countless injured.

The Agreement addressed constitutional issues concerning Northern Ireland, the Republic of Ireland and the United Kingdom. The right of the people of Northern Ireland to determine their own future was affirmed. The possibility of bringing about a united Ireland by the consent of the population of Northern Ireland was also agreed to, while recognizing that the majority of the people of the north wished to remain within the United Kingdom, and that that desire was legitimate. The British government was to devolve some power to the Northern Ireland Assembly, and the Irish government was to give up its constitutional claim on Northern Ireland. The Northern Ireland Assembly would consist of 108 members elected by proportional representation, and there would be a North–South Ministerial Council to facilitate relations between the Republic and Northern Ireland. There would also be a British–Irish Council, also called the 'Council of the Isles', which would be a consultative body made up of representatives from all the governments in the United Kingdom and the Republic of Ireland. Human rights and equality of opportunity were also agreed to, as well as providing instruments whereby these would be safeguarded. An Independent Commission on Decommissioning was set up to deal with the elimination of terrorist weapons, which was to be completed within two years of the Agreement being ratified by votes in the Republic and in Northern Ireland. The Royal Ulster Constabulary, long a point of contention between nationalists and unionists, was also to be reformed. Although held by unionists as an important symbol of the connection with Britain, the RUC had been generally distrusted by nationalists. The vast majority of RUC officers came from the unionist community, and at the very least there was distrust of their impartiality, and at most, extreme nationalists thought of them as state terrorists. Many unionists, however, saw the RUC as a safeguard for remaining part of the United Kingdom. A Policing Commission was to be set up to review the RUC and propose reforms, and British politician Chris Patten (1944–) was appointed to head it. The criminal justice system was also to be reviewed, and prisoners connected with political groups which had signed the Good Friday Agreement would be released under appropriate circumstances. Although they had put their names to the Agreement, some of the major parties had serious reservations about its provisions. Unionists generally did not trust Sinn Féin's promise to begin the decommissioning of IRA weapons once the Northern Ireland Assembly had been set up. They were also unhappy with the powers given to the North–South Council and proposals to reform the RUC. Nationalists were wary of the British government's commitment to hold unionists to the agreement, and were concerned that it would collapse.

The Agreement was then put to a referendum in both Northern Ireland and the Republic. A massive four-week campaign across Ireland saw a revival of some of the major arguments and mistrust amongst the main parties. Although the Ulster Unionist Party under its leader David Trimble campaigned hard for a 'yes' vote in the Northern Ireland referendum, some members of the party were opposed to the Agreement and campaigned openly for a 'no' vote. Harder-line unionists, such as the Reverend Ian Paisley and his Democratic Unionist Party, argued fiercely that the Agreement was a cave-in to nationalists and opened the door to a united Ireland. The full membership of Sinn Féin voted in support of the Agreement by a ninety-four per cent majority. This included support for Sinn Féin sitting in a Northern Ireland Assembly, which was a departure from their previous position of boycotting Northern Ireland assemblies and parliaments because they implied support for the idea of partition. It soon became clear that the nationalist community supported the Agreement overwhelmingly, with the SDLP and Sinn Féin campaigning vigorously for it. The main concern for supporters of the Agreement was not that unionists would reject it (the support of moderate unionists looked to be enough to gain an overall 'yes' majority), but that the level of unionist support would not be high enough for the supporters of the Agreement to claim a convincing victory and a mandate for implementing the Agreement's provisions.

Tony Blair campaigned extensively in Northern Ireland for a 'yes' vote, and made several further promises to wavering unionists. He assured them that the North–South bodies would work on the principle of consent amongst differing parties, that they would be accountable to the Northern Ireland Assembly (which was bound to contain a unionist majority), as well as being accountable to the Dáil in the Republic, and that terrorists and their political spokesmen who did not renounce violence and follow strictly democratic methods would be excluded from the governance of Northern Ireland. Blair's immediate predecessor, John Major, joined the 'yes' campaign, and Bill Clinton campaigned for it as well, promising greatly increased international investment in Northern Ireland if the referendum was positive. In an unprecedented move, nationalist SDLP leader John Hume and Ulster Unionist leader David Trimble campaigned together for a 'yes' vote, appearing together at political rallies and cultural events. They made a special effort to increase the youth vote (thought to be overwhelmingly in favour of the Agreement) by appearing at rock concerts and with other cultural celebrities.

Although a 'yes' vote looked generally promising (especially in the Republic), the campaign on both sides was intense and, at times, acrimonious. The appearance of released terrorists at various nationalist and unionist political meetings was particularly galling to the relatives of their victims. But on 22 May, voters in both the Republic and Northern Ireland voted overwhelmingly in favour of the Good Friday Agreement. The 'yes' vote in the Republic was ninety-four per cent, and in Northern Ireland was seventy-one per cent. Although the turnout in the Republic was only fifty-six per cent, participation was eighty-one per cent in Northern Ireland. Supporters of the agreement celebrated greatly across the island, and the international press hailed it as the beginning of peace and understanding in Northern Ireland. But the difficulty in reaching the Agreement meant that several important points were still contentious, and the less formal (and unwritten) promises made to sceptical unionists by the British government meant that there was still a lot of work to do. David Trimble, who would become the First Minister in the Northern Ireland Assembly, used the euphoria of the post-referendum celebrations to push the decommissioning of IRA weapons along faster. He called on Gerry Adams to use the momentum of the referendum to convince the IRA to begin decommissioning early. Adams and Sinn Féin argued that early decommissioning was not part of the Agreement, and that unionists had to give ground on the controversial question of the marching season (see below) before arms decommissioning could begin.

One of the most important effects of the Agreement was somewhat overlooked by the media. During the campaign for the referendum, the British Chancellor of the Exchequer, Gordon Brown (1951–), pledged a £350 million economic development package for the province. Although some criticized this as a bribe to gain a 'yes' vote, Brown emphasized that the money was for long-term development so that Northern Ireland could gain a genuine 'peace dividend'.

In late June, voters in Northern Ireland elected members to the Northern Ireland Assembly. Like the referendum campaign, the Assembly election was dominated by concern over the unionists who were uneasy with the Good Friday Agreement. David Trimble urged the waverers in his Ulster Unionist Party to elect Agreement supporters to the Assembly. Abandoning the Agreement would, he said, be 'irresponsible and reckless'. Many unionists were unconvinced that terrorist organizations really would begin decommissioning their weapons under the terms of the Agreement, and wanted some sort of show of good faith before they would support the Assembly. Trimble also kept the rhetorical pressure on Sinn Féin high by insisting that decommissioning had to be a reality. While early decommissioning was not forthcoming from either nationalist or loyalist terrorist groups, pro-Agreement parties won a large majority in the Assembly elections.

The Assembly elections seemed like another important step to a solution to the problems of Northern Ireland, and the relatively successful way they were conducted gave many people cause for hope. David Trimble was elected First Minster on 1 July, and Seamus Mallon (1936–) of the SDLP was elected as his deputy. Yet further issues remained which could wreck the Assembly's future. The British government had set up a Parades Commission to decide whether certain traditional marches of the Orange Order and other Protestant groups should modify their routes so as not to pass through nationalist and Catholic communities. The Commission ruled that the Orange Order parade through Drumcree, near Portadown in County Armagh, could not follow its traditional route (which would lead it down the Garvaghy Road, a largely Catholic area). The local Orange Order pledged to defy the government ban. The Orangemen were determined to follow their preferred route, but were prevented by a large contingent of the RUC and British army soldiers on 5 July 1998. Nearly 1,500 Orangemen and their supporters camped near Drumcree Church in a massive protest, hoping to wear out the government's patience. There were violent clashes between Orangemen and security forces, and ten Catholic churches were struck by arsonists during this tense period. As the tension reached breaking-point, three young boys were killed by a petrol bomb thrown through the windows of their home in Ballymoney, County Antrim on 12 July. Although they were being brought up as Protestants, their mother was a Catholic, and the RUC declared that these were sectarian murders. Revulsion over these killings swept through Northern Ireland, including the vast majority of the Protestant and unionist communities. The Drumcree Orangemen were urged to halt their protest, even by some senior Orangemen and unionist politicians. The tragedy took the force out of the Orange protest. Most left Drumcree, and the police and army removed the last few hard-liners on 15 July.

Just when Northern Ireland seemed not to be able to stand another tragedy, and when it appeared that the reaction against the killings in Ballymoney might prove to be the end of senseless violence, a massive car bomb exploded in Omagh in County Tyrone. In the most deadly single incident since the troubles began in 1969, twenty-eight people were killed and two hundred and twenty injured. In the early afternoon of 15 August, a coded warning was sent, reportedly saying that there was a bomb planted at the Omagh courthouse. Police evacuated people to the other end of the town's main street. But this was exactly where the actual car bomb was, and the massive loss of life was directly related to this confusion. Another wave of revulsion swept through Northern Ireland, the Republic and Great Britain. The Real IRA, an extreme nationalist splinter group, claimed responsibility for the attack and was condemned by all sides, including Sinn Féin and the IRA. The British and Irish governments met to decide on new anti-terrorism measures. The Irish taoiseach, Bertie Ahern, introduced new laws in the Republic which even he described as 'extremely draconian'. Tony Blair responded by pushing similar legislation through the British parliament.

Throughout the rest of 1998, the arms decommissioning issue continued to delay the setting up of an executive for the Northern Ireland Assembly. Although Sinn Féin leaders met with David Trimble in early September (the first public meeting of republicans and unionists since 1922), no real progress was made. Amid the decommissioning impasse and in the wake of the Omagh bombing, a sense of hope was rekindled when John Hume and David Trimble were awarded the 1998 Nobel Peace Prize in October. Hailing Hume's long career as a civil rights campaigner, and Trimble's courage in convincing his party to moderate its views, the Nobel Committee praised the two men for 'laying the foundations of peace' in Northern Ireland.

As eight months had passed since the signing of the Good Friday Agreement, the decommissioning difficulties continued, and were added to by a rise in terrorist punishment beatings in late 1998 and early 1999. Tony Blair and the Irish taoiseach, Bertie Ahern, travelled to Northern Ireland at the end of March 1999 in an attempt to save the peace process, which was in grave danger of falling apart. Meeting with the major parties at Hillsborough Castle, Blair and Ahern boiled down the decommissioning disagreement to a question of 'timing and dates'. They reached an agreement, called the Hillsborough Declaration, which outlined the steps that would have to be made in order for the Northern Ireland Assembly to meet and for decommissioning to begin. The spring and summer of 1999 saw the peace process at its lowest point. Trimble and the Ulster Unionists would not agree to sit in an executive with Sinn Féin unless there was actual arms decommissioning, rather than plans for decommissioning. They were heavily criticized in Britain and in Ireland for taking a highly inflexible stand.

Following another round of talks with party leaders in July, the British government announced that Senator George Mitchell, who had chaired the negotiations leading up to the Good Friday Agreement, would hold a review of the peace process in order to help reach a settlement. Mitchell stressed that he was not in Northern Ireland to renegotiate the Good Friday Agreement, but to discuss how its provisions could be implemented. Failure to do so, he said, would be 'unforgivable'. He met with the main parties, but had to suspend his review when the report of the Patten

Commission on reform of the Royal Ulster Constabulary was published on 9th September. The Commission recommended that the name of the RUC, its oath and official symbols be changed, with the effect of removing the 'royal' elements. Further, there should be an increase in Catholic recruits to the police force in Northern Ireland, and an elected committee should be established to oversee policing, which would be made up of people from all groups in Northern Ireland. This was strongly opposed by unionists and another talks breakdown seemed likely. October and November were tense months but there was optimism on 17 November, when the IRA put out a statement saying that they agreed to begin decommissioning and that they would nominate a representative to the decommissioning body. The next day, Mitchell brought his review to a close, saying that there was nothing now to prevent the implementation of the Good Friday Agreement. He outlined the careful way in which this should occur: 'devolution should take effect [meaning that the British government should cede powers to the Northern Ireland Assembly], then the executive should meet, and then the paramilitary groups should appoint their authorised representatives, all on the same day, in that order.' Further, he said, the review process and the implementation of the Good Friday Agreement meant that 'neither side will get all it wanted and both will endure severe political pain. But there is no other way forward. Prolonging this stalemate will leave this society uncertain and vulnerable.' The Ulster Unionist Party met on 27 November to decide whether to accept the IRA's statement as a basis for allowing Sinn Féin to sit in the Northern Ireland executive. At that meeting, a majority of 57.9 per cent voted in favour of accepting this compromise – the promise of decommissioning and putting in place the elements of the process, rather than seeing arms decommissioning itself first. But there was a sting in the tail. In February 2000, there was to be a review of decommissioning, and if it were found that progress had not been made, Trimble would resign as leader of the UUP, which would probably mean that the party would withdraw from the executive and the Northern Ireland Assembly would collapse. In this way, Trimble and the UUP changed from demanding decommissioning as a pre-condition for the formation of an executive to allowing it as a post-condition. In a press conference following the vote, Trimble made two important statements which symbolized both the difficulties of the previous months' negotiations, and the faith that supporters of the Good Friday Agreement had in its ultimate success. The Ulster Unionist Party's vote, he said, 'clears the stalemate'. He addressed Gerry Adams and Sinn Féin directly when he said, 'We have done our bit. Mr. Adams, it is over to you. We have jumped, you follow.' This 'jumping' was a tremendous leap of conviction for Trimble and his slight majority of supporters. Not only would their personal political futures depend on it, but so would the whole peace process.

After this vote, the process of devolution of power to the Northern Ireland Assembly was swift. Within days, the political parties nominated their members for executive seats, the formal act of handing over certain powers to the Northern Ireland Assembly was introduced and passed in the British parliament, and the Irish Republic's Constitution was amended to remove claims on Northern Ireland. On 2 December 1999, the Northern Ireland Assembly Executive met for the first time, amid high-minded speeches and mundane administrative work. Although Ian Paisley's anti-Agreement Executive members boycotted the meeting, the other ministers, including Sinn Féin's two ministerial appointments attended.

Decommissioning matters continued to progress throughout December, with the major loyalist paramilitary groups appointing their representatives to the decommissioning body, and that body reporting that initial meetings with these representatives (and the one from the IRA) had taken place, and that these developments represented 'some progress'. Other aspects of the Good Friday Agreement also fell into place, such as the North–South Ministerial Council, and the establishment of cross-border bodies, and the first meeting of the British–Irish Council. Most contentious, however, were the proposals of the Patten commission on reform of the Royal Ulster Constabulary. As the year ended, the British government had not yet decided on the extent to which it would accept the Commission's proposals. But in mid-January 2000, it announced that it would accept most of them, including the highly contentious changes to name and uniform. This was greeted by strong protest from many unionists, including David Trimble, who said that the British government had 'shamed itself' with these proposals. But it appeared that the government would press ahead with these plans, in an attempt to make the force more acceptable to the whole Northern Irish community, and to attract a better balance of recruits from the different groups in the North.

The Ulster Unionist deadline for decommissioning progress came and went in mid-February without any evidence of IRA action on the issue. In accordance with their party vote in November, the Unionists met to decide whether to pull out of the Northern Ireland Assembly. Rather than see this force a collapse of the Assembly (which would be incredibly difficult to revive), the British Northern Ireland Secretary, Peter Mandelson (1953–), suspended it on 11 February 2000 and reinstituted direct rule from London. Although heavily criticized by nationalists for caving in to the unionists, to Mandelson this seemed the least bad option (as it had to many during the partition question in 1920–21). The Northern Ireland Assembly was then put on hold and further private negotiations continued.

The suspension of the Northern Ireland Assembly was derided by nationalists and republicans because they thought it was a violation of the Good Friday Agreement. The IRA announced on 15 February that they would no longer co-operate with the decommissioning body, and it appeared that it would be very difficult to get militant republicans involved in the negotiations again. Hope for a solution was renewed, however, when David Trimble said that he was prepared to return to the Assembly without a prior commitment by the IRA on decommissioning, as long as it was clear that the issue was going to be addressed in the months ahead. The symbolism of his statement being made on 17 March (St. Patrick's Day) in New York (where so many militant republican groups had found support in the past) was not lost on commentators and participants in the peace process. Many members of his party, however, thought that he had gone too far. They put his leadership to a vote on 23 March, which Trimble won by fifty-seven per cent to forty-three per cent. Trimble's attempt to re-engage the republicans in negotiations seemed to have paid off when, on 6 June 2000, the IRA issued a statement that, among other things, promised to 'initiate a process that will completely and verifiably put the IRA arms beyond use.' They would also

resume contact with the Independent Commission on Decommissioning. The details of the statement outlined how all this
would be verified. 'The contents of a number of arms dumps will be
inspected by agreed third parties ... the dumps will be reinspected
regularly to ensure that the weapons have remained secure.' All
this, they claimed, meant that, 'there is no threat to the peace
process from the IRA'. Trimble's response was quick and cautiously
optimistic, and Peter Mandelson announced that he would soon
restore the Northern Ireland Assembly. The Ulster Unionist party,
however, still had to be persuaded to go back into the Assembly. At
a party meeting on 27 May, Trimble won a slight majority vote
(fifty-three per cent to forty-seven per cent) for accepting the IRA
statement as the basis for returning to the Assembly. He argued
that the only way to hold the IRA to decommissioning was to call
their bluff by going back into government, which would force the
IRA to take further decommissioning steps. Finally, the Northern
Ireland Assembly reconvened on 5 June, and the executive started
work again on the governance of the province.

Problems remain, however, and it is by no means certain that
the Assembly will not break down again. The reform of the Royal
Ulster Constabulary continues to be a major point of contention
between nationalists and unionists. The British government
published its bill for RUC reform on 16 May. Most of the
recommendations of the Patten Commission were included in the
bill, but, significantly, the change in the name and symbols of the
RUC will be negotiated by the British government's Secretary of
State for Northern Ireland and the new Police Board of Northern
Ireland. Less contentious is the procedure for recruitment of new
officers, which requires that fifty per cent come from Catholic
backgrounds. Also, Ian Paisley's Democratic Unionist Party have
decided that they will try to disrupt the working of the Northern
Ireland executive by rotating its party members in the ministerial
offices that they occupy. This will mean that, for those offices at
least, the lack of permanent members will make some aspects of
the executive's work more difficult. Finally, questions of identity
have arisen in a dispute over the flying of the Union flag (the flag of
the United Kingdom) over government buildings in Northern
Ireland. Nationalists and republicans (especially Sinn Féin) have
objected to it (with Sinn Féin arguing that, if the Union flag is

flown, then the tricolour of the Republic of Ireland should be flown alongside it). Unionists, particularly Paisley's Democratic Unionists, have reacted equally strongly in favour of flying the Union flag. Although the DUP's motion to have the Union flag flown over all government buildings in Northern Ireland was defeated on 6 June 2000, this sort of issue of identity is bound to arise many times in the future. It symbolizes the difficulties in reaching agreement and understanding between different groups in Northern Ireland, not just over practical issues such as discrimination and policing, but over the deeper issues of national identity that have been a central part of Irish history for centuries. Whether understanding will eventually be reached, and whether the peace process is a success, remains to be seen.

INTERPRETATIONS

The Troubles in Northern Ireland have been interpreted in a number of different ways, but perhaps more than any other aspect of Irish history, the difficulties in the north have had their own impact on how historians have considered Irish history of all periods, and in some cases have changed the ways those histories have been written. The Troubles have been so influential that they have caused some of the most prominent Irish historians to change their own interpretations in subsequent editions of their books.

The most important work on interpreting the situation in Northern Ireland is John Whyte's *Interpreting Northern Ireland* (1989). In it, he outlines four major schools of interpretation. But those four schools are actually based on how the conflict in Northern Ireland is perceived, and who the antagonists are. Most scholars do not, however, attribute the complexity of the Northern Ireland problem so simply to one of these conflicts. They almost all agree that it is a combination of two or more. Many of those who have been committed to one political ideology have generally relied on one explanation for the bulk of their interpretations. Whyte argued that those who think that the dominant conflict in Northern Ireland is between Britain and Ireland may be termed 'traditional nationalists'. Those who see the two main antagonists as Southern Ireland against Northern Ireland may be said to belong to the 'traditional unionist' interpretation. A perceived capitalist versus worker conflict feeds the Marxist interpretation. And Protestant/unionist against Catholic/nationalist within Northern Ireland itself is called the 'two-community' or 'internal conflict' school. Whyte used 'traditional' to refer to the historical nationalist and historical unionist interpretations of.the problems in Northern Ireland, but many nationalists and unionists today think that the major conflict is within the Northern Ireland community (and so belong to the fourth interpretative school). This does not mean, however, that modern-day nationalists do not wish for a united Ireland, or that modern-day unionists do not wish to retain the Union with Great Britain. What it does mean is that these two contemporary groups believe different explanations about the causes of the Troubles than their political forebears did, but that they still desire the political outcomes that previous generations of nationalists and unionists wanted. Identifying these four different interpretative groups, however, should not imply that each of them has retained fossilized ideas for generations. All four interpretative schools, especially the traditional nationalist and the traditional unionist, have undergone transformations and subtle reinterpretations within their general framework of ideas.

The traditional nationalist interpretation of the partition of Northern Ireland and the Troubles since 1968 is based on the idea that Ireland is (and has been for hundreds of years) one nation, and that the British are responsible for partition and keeping Ireland divided. This interpretation has its origins in the period 1916–23. Soon after the partition of Ireland, various commentators (including government commissions) in the Irish Free State published books and pamphlets explaining the division of the island as largely the fault of the British government. This idea lasted until the late 1950s. The basic argument was that the British government stoked up unionist opposition to the idea of a unified Ireland with a parliament in Dublin, and that unionists and Protestants in Northern Ireland have only been able to sustain their dominance with British support. The best example of this interpretation is Frank Gallagher's *The Indivisible Island: the History of the Partition of Ireland* (1957). He argued that partition was mainly a solution that helped British politicians solve British party political problems, that Prime Minister Balfour, for instance, insisted on it to maintain his position in the House of Commons and prevent a rebellion of those British Conservatives who allied with recalcitrant unionists (see chapter 6). Without this interference from Britain, he claimed, the nationalist and unionists groups in the early twentieth century would have been able to reach some sort of agreement for a unified Ireland. Further, he said it was only British economic support and subsidies that kept the border a viable political division. Without such propping up, Irish groups on both sides of the divide would have united because they shared a number of common interests.

This interpretation was quite influential in the Irish Free State and in the first two decades of the Republic. It was used as justification for article two of the constitution of Éire, which laid claim to the counties of Northern Ireland. By the late 1950s, however, many nationalists had begun to question the validity of this interpretation. Strong majorities in Northern Ireland continually voted to retain the union with Great Britain. This led to a recognition amongst some influential nationalist writers that there were two distinct groups in Ireland, nationalists and unionists, and that the unbridgeable gap that existed between their ideas of what should comprise the Irish nation was the main reason that the British were forced to use partition. These nationalists, such as Donal Barrington (who published a pamphlet entitled *Uniting Ireland* in 1959), argued that the problem in Northern Ireland lay with the unionists being unwilling to join a united Ireland. The solution, according to this revision of the nationalist interpretation, was to persuade these unionists to change their minds. The advent of the Troubles in the late 1960s caused nationalists to revise their interpretation even further. Garrett FitzGerald, an economist from University College Dublin who would later become taoiseach, argued in his *Towards a New Ireland* (1972) that, although Ireland was one nation, a significant group within that nation, the Ulster Protestants, mistrusted the rest of the country. They were afraid of what would happen to them under what they saw as 'an authoritarian Southern Catholic state'. What needed to be done, according to FitzGerald, was to change those things in the Republic that kept northern Protestants opposed to unification. These included reducing the formal and informal power of the Catholic Church in the governance of the Republic, amending laws (such as that on divorce) that Protestants found offensive, and to change the attitude of many in the Republic who saw northern Protestants as British imports and not native Irish. This gradual change in nationalist writing has come a little closer to the internal conflict interpretation, which will be discussed below. It is important, however, to remember that most nationalists, by definition, have not changed their fundamental political view that Ireland should be united. They have, however, shifted their emphasis of explanation away from the responsibility of Britain in ultimately causing the problems in Northern Ireland.

The traditional unionist interpretation says that Ireland is not one nation, that it is made up of two distinct groups (nationalists and unionists), and that the main reason behind the continued problems in Northern Ireland is the inability of nationalists (particularly militant nationalists) to accept the distinctiveness of unionists as a group with rights of self-determination. The traditional unionist attitude to Britain is also different from the traditional nationalist interpretation, but not the polar opposite. Although the traditional unionist school tends to see nationalists (in the north and south of Ireland) as the main cause of the Troubles, they do not see the British government as their tried and true allies. Traditional unionists are suspicious of the level of commitment that the British government has to retaining and supporting Northern Ireland. Like the traditional nationalist interpretation, the traditional unionist view started in the period around and after partition. A number of books came out from the late 1920s to the late 1950s, praising the unionist stand during the Home Rule and Anglo-Irish Treaty period (roughly 1880–1922). Their titles are symbolic of their biases: Ronald McNeill's *Ulster's Stand for the Union* (1922) and Hugh Sherman's *Not an Inch* (1942). A Dutch scholar, M.W. Heslinga, put forward the fullest and strongest scholarly statement of this interpretation. His book, *The Irish Border as a Cultural Divide* (1962), argues that, far from being two distinct countries, the British Isles operate more or less as one. But within that larger community, there were several distinct groups of people. In short, Heslinga argued, there are more cultural fault lines between Britain, the Republic and Northern Ireland than nationalists have been willing to see. The strongest of these divisions is the one between Northern Ireland and the Republic, and the political border between them is a relatively accurate reflection of those differences. The people in Ulster, Heslinga concluded, are a distinct nation, and there is no real reason why Ireland should be a unified country.

Like the traditional nationalist view, however, the unionist view can be seen to have supporting evidence from a certain reading of history. One of the central ideas of this school of thought is that Northern Ireland and Northern Irish identity were constantly under threat from the south. Not only did the partition arising from the Anglo-Irish Treaty result in a civil war in the south, it occasioned much anti-partition rhetoric and violence in the decades following it. The IRA attacked Northern Ireland from the south in two major campaigns (1921-2 and 1956-66). The Éire constitution of 1937 laid claim to Northern Ireland, and there was much anti-partition propaganda in the Republic up until the late 1950s. But the traditional unionist view also reassessed some of its main ideas in the last few decades of the twentieth century. In the late 1960s, some unionists began to think that the Troubles were not so much the fault of the southern nationalists as they were of northern nationalists. A.T.Q. Stewart, for instance, argued in his 1977 *Narrow Ground: Aspects of Ulster, 1609–1969* that the cause of the Troubles lay within Northern Ireland, and had been there since the beginnings of plantation and the initial clash of cultures (which, he argues, never really stopped).

Unlike the traditional nationalist interpretation (which has been successfully revised, with that revision being accepted by most nationalists), the traditional unionist interpretation remains strong in that community. This strength is mostly found amongst politicians and unionist activists, such as Ian Paisley, rather than amongst academics, within Northern Ireland. Many commentators argue that these unionists see themselves as a community under siege, and therefore, they hold on to this traditional interpretation (as well as other traditions, such as marches and parades) in order to retain their identity. Traditional unionists also argue that the unionist cause is supported by purely Northern Irish rather than British interests. In other words, unionists have their own reasons to wish to remain in the United Kingdom, whether or not those are shared by the people in Great Britain. These are based on three main grounds: economics, nationality and religion. Most traditional unionists think that the British economy is, in the long term, more stable and prosperous than the economy in the Republic (despite their prosperity in the 1990s and the prospect of a more unified European economy in the twenty-first century). Northern Ireland, therefore, would be better off in the British economy. Nationality, however, is more important to unionists than economics. Although they have been in perpetual fear of being sold out by a British government seeking a final solution to the problem of Northern Ireland, they have generally thought of themselves as British (in addition to being Northern Irish). Further, they find great psychological links with Britain which seem to transcend politics and economics. Finally, and most importantly, traditional unionists cling strongly to the belief that the only way that their Protestantism can be successfully defended in Ireland is for Northern Ireland to remain separate from the Republic. This goes beyond fearing discrimination on specific issues in a united Ireland with an overall Catholic majority. It is a perception that the Republic is a Catholic country with a Catholic atmosphere, and that Protestants would be perpetual second-class citizens there.

The Marxist interpretation of the problems in Northern Ireland is based on economics, and argues, essentially, that there would be no real national or religious conflict between the two main groups in Northern Ireland if there had not been an even more basic conflict between capitalist employers and workers. The intellectual founders of modern communism and socialism, Karl Marx (1818–83) and Frederick Engels (1820–95), wrote directly about Ireland in the nineteenth century. But it was when their ideas were taken up by James Connolly in late nineteenth- and early twentieth-century Ireland that they were applied more specifically to the question of the two communities in the north. Connolly argued in his *Labour in Irish History* (1910) that the only way that class considerations would not overcome the national question in north-east Ulster was if Ireland were to be partitioned. Partition, he argued, would artificially keep the question of nation alive, and would prevent working-class Catholics and working-class Protestants from realizing that their true struggle was against their industrial overlords. Connolly, of course, was executed in the wake of the 1916 Easter Rising, and did not see his fear become reality. Subsequent Marxist historians in the twentieth century argued that partition had accomplished exactly what Connolly had warned against. Northern Ireland was preoccupied with the national question, while biting economic problems were being left to fester. As the Troubles consumed Northern Ireland in the late 1960s and early 1970s, Marxist interpretations enjoyed a good deal of attention (partly owing to the fact that they were being heavily used in other fields of history as well). Connolly's interpretations and predictions about Northern Ireland were refreshed and extended with greater historical research. Of particular note is Michael Farrell's *Northern Ireland: the Orange State* (1980), which argued that Northern Irish capitalists kept the population divided and conquered. This was accomplished in two ways. First, sectarianism was kept alive by raising Protestant fears about Catholics whenever it appeared that workers from each group might be uniting in industrial action. Second, this sectarianism was further sustained by making sure that Protestant workers were less discriminated against than Catholic workers. Although both groups were exploited, a hierarchical system was employed so that Protestant workers would feel at least marginally superior to Catholic workers, and would unite with Protestant employers to keep Catholics down.

But like the other interpretations, the Marxist one has undergone revision. One of the reasons for this was that the ferocity of reaction against the civil rights movement in Northern Ireland amongst many Protestants and unionists seemed to go far beyond economic and class-based explanations. Michael Farrell modified his earlier interpretations in his 1983 *Arming the Protestants*, in which he recognized that non-economic factors such as national feeling and religion played an important role in the beliefs and actions of working-class Protestants and unionists. A group of revisionist Marxists also began to analyse the situation somewhat differently. Much of this newer work has focused on class differences within the Protestant community in Northern Ireland. And, according to this interpretation, nationalist attempts to overthrow or dismantle Northern Ireland (with or without violence) have forced working-class Protestants to be more vigorous in their defence of what they see as their nationality than they otherwise would be. The best example of this argument may be found in Paul Bew, Peter Gibbon and Henry Patterson, *The State in Northern Ireland* (1979). Marxist analyses of Northern

Ireland continued to be somewhat fragmented through the 1980s, and lost much favour in the 1990s. This, however, may not have been owing to insufficiencies in the Marxist interpretation (although there are many), but mainly to do with the rise in popularity of the final interpretative school that John Whyte defined – the internal conflict interpretation.

The three preceding interpretations of the Northern Ireland conflict share one important argument – that the problems in the north are largely the fault of external factors. For the traditional nationalists, the British are to blame; for the traditional unionists, it is nationalists in the north and the south; for Marxists, it is the capitalists and the capitalist system. The internal conflict interpretation departs from the basic idea of external blame. As its name suggests, it argues that, although external factors have certainly played a part, the major causes of the Troubles may be found within Northern Ireland. This is now by far the most accepted explanation, but it has a much shorter pedigree than the other three schools of thought. It arose after the publication of Denis Barritt and Charles Carter's *The Northern Ireland Problem* in 1962. In this book, Barritt and Carter examined the sociological workings of Northern Ireland society, and particularly concentrated on areas of friction such as social relations, education and employment. They found deeper-held divisions in Northern Ireland than could possibly be explained by external factors alone. Attitudes and perceptions in both major communities seemed to be of longer standing than Marxist analyses would allow, and seemed to be more directly related to local problems than either the nationalist or unionist interpretations could explain.

By the time violence erupted in Northern Ireland in the late 1960s and early 1970s, this interpretation was gaining much attention and popularity, partly, it has been argued, because it seemed as if an internal conflict might be more easily solved than one involving other governments or economic structures. The Northern Ireland government's 1969 Cameron Commission, appointed to look into the cause of the violence, came to a similar conclusion. It argued that the Troubles largely arose because of Catholic grievances over discrimination and Protestant fears about a rise in Catholic population and potential political power. Conor Cruise O'Brien's highly influential *States of Ireland* (1972) was largely an internal-conflict interpretation, and one which argued that outsiders not only could not understand Northern Ireland, but their proposed solutions were bound to be flawed.

As stated in the introduction to this 'Interpretations' section, not only have the Northern Ireland troubles been interpreted in various ways, but they have also influenced how historians have viewed other aspects and periods of Irish history. Perhaps the clearest example of how such disturbing contemporary events can influence writing about previous centuries is shown in T.W. Moody's *The Ulster Question 1603–1973*, published in 1974, but written during the height of the violence in Northern Ireland (1968–72). In it, Moody argued that the current problems and divisions in the north could be traced all the way back to the original Stuart plantations in the seventeenth century (see chapter 1). The plantations, he argued, were intended to build a British supremacy in Ulster, which could then be the base for dominance of the rest of the island. Further, the success of the Ulster plantations, and the consequent economic and political suppression of the native population, ensured that long-lasting bitterness would characterize attitudes that grew up between the two major groups in the north. Moody was criticized for tracing the origins of the problem too far back, however. The Ulster plantations were clearly planned and relatively successful and prosperous, but critics contended that this did not mean that entrenched bitterness between Protestants and Catholics would inevitably result. There were too many different influences and problems in Ulster between 1603 and 1968 for the Troubles of the late twentieth century to be blamed on plantation. One of the strongest critiques of Moody's argument has been that the major problem in Ulster in the 1700s was between rival Protestant groups, particularly radical Presbyterians.

A less risky analysis was offered by Brian Walker, in his *Ulster Politics: the Formative Years, 1868–86* (1989). He argued that the Northern Ireland troubles were indeed of historic origin, but were one hundred years old, rather than three hundred and fifty. The Home Rule period (especially Gladstone's first Home Rule bill efforts in 1885–6), he argues, was the start of the sectarian split in Ulster (see chapter 5). It was Home Rule which added a political dimension to a religious difference that had existed for centuries.

Without this added element (without, in other words, the attempted application of a political solution), attitudes may not have hardened in Ulster. Another example is Conor Cruise O'Brien, who had also written on the Home Rule period as central to the evolution of the difficulties in Ulster. When his *Parnell and His Party* was first published in 1957, O'Brien argued that Parnell and his Home Rule proposals provided perhaps the best possible chance of accommodating a Protestant Ulster within an Ireland ruled from Dublin. In the book's second edition, published in 1978 (after a decade of violence in Northern Ireland), he changed his argument to the effect that Parnell could not see that his Home Rule proposals were perceived by Ulster Protestants as solely addressed to Catholics. Parnell, in short, had failed to understand the need to recognize a diversity of Irish identities, and Home Rule could never have proved acceptable to the majority in the north.

Similar ideas about identity preoccupied F.S.L. Lyons, who was also strongly influenced by the violence of the late 1960s and early 1970s. Lyons, one of Ireland's most prestigious historians, is also generally thought to have changed his interpretation of Irish history based on what has happened in the north during the Troubles. In his 1968 biography of John Dillon, he blamed the failure of Home Rule on the inability of some important unionists to see how reasonable and moderate the proposals of Parnell, Dillon and Redmond had been. Their steely rejection of Home Rule was, to Lyons, a strange mystery. A decade later, in his 1977 biography of Parnell, Lyons had changed his mind a great deal. The failure of Home Rule was not so much the result of obstinate unionists, as the inability of Parnell to understand the complexities of Irish identity. Unionist identity had been ignored by most major Home Rulers, and if they had paid more attention to it, a more acceptable proposal may have been found. These ideas were further elaborated in Lyons' *Culture and Anarchy in Ireland, 1890–1939* (1979), in which he found that identity in the north was split into three groups – Gaelic, Anglican and Presbyterian. This meant that the divisions and conflicts in Northern Ireland went beyond politics into culture, and that those cultural differences were too great to be bridged by political solutions, either during the Home Rule period or during the late twentieth century. It was, he said, the recognition of these differences that would ultimately lead to 'peaceful co-existence'.

The troubles in Northern Ireland have also had the effect of creating greater historical interest in that region. While Irish historians in the Republic had largely concentrated on the southern part of the island for much of the twentieth century, and historians in Northern Ireland focused on larger questions in British history, historical questions about Northern Ireland, Ulster nationalism and Ulster unionism were more rare. Since the late 1960s, however, there has been a real growth in historical attention paid to the north, amongst historians on both sides of the border and around the world (particularly in Australia and the United States).

NINE

Conclusion: Themes
in Irish History

Several important themes have appeared throughout this book, as indeed they run through Irish history from very early times. Some of the most significant are: politics, religion, the land, Irish identity and history itself. While it would be impossible to show unbroken thematic links across the centuries, some interesting things stand out.

Irish politics has been nothing if not complex. Political groups have sometimes shared common ideologies and strategies, but this has been the exception rather than the rule. In medieval and early modern Ireland, different groups allied themselves politically in very different ways, and not always with the groups closest to them in religion, class or economic status. Some looked to outside allies, such as the Vikings and the Normans, to help change politics and power in Ireland. Other groups tried to form 'native' power blocks in an effort to keep out foreigners and invaders. In the modern period, political behaviour was equally diverse. Theobald Wolfe Tone looked to the French to help gain Irish independence from Britain, whereas Daniel O'Connell used the British political system to gain rights for Catholics and to attempt to repeal the Act of Union. Young Irelanders and Fenians were more radical than O'Connell, and broadened Irish politics by using propaganda and social activities to gain support. Yet they too looked to supporters in the United States and Australia in attempts to bring about political change. Home Rulers disagreed not only over tactics, but also over the legacy of Parnell after his fall. Those who wished to retain the Union were also not monolithic in their political ideas and activities. Some, such as the Orange Order and the Brunswick Clubs, mirrored O'Connell's political tactics, and insisted that the defence of the Union was also the defence of Protestantism. In the early twentieth century, politics was equally complicated. Nationalists were split between supporters of John Redmond and parliamentary tactics, and Sinn Féin and militant separatism. The Irish Civil War symbolized the continuing divisions over strategy, as well as the nature of Ireland as a country. Unionists clung desperately to their connection to Britain, yet stockpiled arms to fight against the threat of Home Rule imposed by the British government. And throughout the twentieth century, in both the Free State/Republic and in Northern Ireland, politics did not settle down to the mundane aspects of running each country, as chapter 7 has shown. Most dramatic, perhaps, were the changes that occurred at the end of the twentieth century. This was particularly the case in Northern Ireland, where unionists and republicans have made massive shifts towards the centre. David Trimble and a slight majority of his Ulster Unionist party have been willing to sit in government with Sinn Féin, which would have been unthinkable twenty years ago. Similarly, republicans such as Gerry Adams now recognize the political existence of Northern Ireland by agreeing to sit in a Northern Ireland Assembly. The fact that Gerry Adams' salary as a member of the Assembly ultimately comes from the British Treasury is something that would have shocked republicans of earlier decades. Politics in Éire has also undergone significant change. Two women presidents, Mary Robinson and Mary McAleese (1951–), were elected in the 1990s, and an increasing presence of women in Irish politics has been a feature of recent decades. New parties have arrived on the scene, and many young people now participate in political pressure groups outside mainstream politics. In fact, young people on both sides of the border are increasingly unwilling to ally themselves with political parties, as evidenced by the significant numbers of non-aligned, twenty-something voters who campaigned hard for a 'yes' vote in the referendum on the Good Friday Agreement.

Religion in Irish history is an equally diverse theme. Reading the Irish past as a struggle between Catholics and Protestants is not only too simplistic, it ignores the work of a great many Irish historians of recent decades. Chapter 1 has shown that alignments between different groups often did not follow religious identity. The Catholic Old English and Native Irish were opposed to the settlement of the Protestant New English and Scots in the period of the Stuart plantations (1603–60). Yet at the end of that century, the battle between the Protestant William of Orange and the Catholic James II found members of both religions on either side. The interpretations section of chapter 1 has further shown that the age of the Penal Laws (1691–1778) was much more complex than previously thought. Rather than being a universal system of 'apartheid' against Catholics, the Penal Laws were unevenly applied (and, indeed, ignored in some cases). At the end of the eighteenth century, nationalists such as Tone appealed to Protestants and Catholics to consider their rights as Irish people paramount, and that the only way to secure those rights was to break the connection with Britain. His United Irishmen were drawn from both religions. Even though O'Connell's Catholic Association used the clergy of the Catholic Church in extremely effective ways, he was ultimately fighting for a political right – to sit in parliament. The fact that his agitation helped link Irish nationalism with Catholicism may not have been what he wished. The growth in power of the Catholic Church in the pre-Famine and post-Famine years also shows the diversity of religious life in the early nineteenth century. The increase in devotional practices and in hierarchical control over local clergy during this period shows that previous years had seen less devotion and less power radiating from bishops. In north-eastern Ulster, the influence of evangelical preachers coming over from England greatly added to the religious diversity of that area. Although Methodism and other denominations never gained the strength that Presbyterianism and Anglicanism had reached, their presence from the late eighteenth century to the present day indicates that northern Ireland was not impervious to new religious influence. Evangelical influence was minimal in relation to the number of Catholics and Church of Ireland members in the south. Nevertheless, it made a contribution to the religious diversity of the country. The twentieth century saw an equally complex religious picture. Although the influence of the Catholic Church in the Free State and Republic is undoubted, it was not without its critics. W.B. Yeats protested against those parts of the constitution of Éire that he thought were objectionable to Protestants. The reaction against the Church's role in the defeat of the Mother and Child Scheme showed that Irish people were not uncritical of church involvement in state affairs. The divorce and contraception referendums of the 1980s and 1990s also showed that it is impossible to characterize the Republic as a Catholic state. In the same way, it is inaccurate to argue that Northern Ireland was in the grip of extreme Protestantism in the second half of the twentieth century. Chapters 7 and 8 show that there was a great deal of sectarianism and discrimination, but there were also significant instances of religious understanding, such as when the flag over Belfast City Hall was lowered to half-mast on the death of Pope Pius XII in 1958 and Pope John XIII in 1963.

'The land' has been a consistently strong theme in Irish history. Not only did it become a specific political and social issue in the nineteenth century; land questions from previous periods have been mythologized and romanticized almost from the beginning of Irish history. In one important sense, the land has been tied to Irish identity. Centuries of invasion, settlement and plantation have given rise to the popular idea that land has consistently been taken away, or stolen from, the native Irish, and that this was an injustice that has never been rectified. Much of nationalist ideology, for instance, blames the troubles in Northern Ireland on the importation of foreign settlers and the granting of Irish land to them. While there are undoubtedly true elements to this (as in the case of the Stuart and Cromwellian plantations), the historical picture is much more complicated. Chapter 1 has shown how many different groups (including native Irish) held land during these centuries, but also that plantation was a mixed success. Chapters 4–6 have also shown the complexities in trying to solve the 'land issue' in the nineteenth century. The various land reforms of the late nineteenth and early twentieth centuries accomplished something that perhaps no other country in Europe was able to do, however; that is, the large-scale transfer of land from landlords to farmers through government incentive and pressure. But even here it is inaccurate to say that Irish land was 'given back to the people' through these reforms. As successful as the land reforms were in making Ireland a country of 'owner-occupiers', they were less successful in creating a nation of 'peasant proprietors', as one historian has written. Agricultural labourers found it difficult to gain land, and prosperous farmers were able to expand their holdings and become significant landlords in their own right as the early twentieth century progressed. Land and agricultural issues continue to claim a great deal of attention in the contemporary Republic, as well. The ministry of agriculture is one of the most important government departments, and agricultural matters often dominate the news.

One of the strongest themes of this book has been the nature and diversity of Irish identity, and its centrality in Irish history cannot be doubted. Conceptions of Irishness have changed a great deal over the centuries. Regional differences were paramount in ancient and medieval Ireland, and although there was a great deal of cultural and linguistic unity, there were very few instances where this transferred to political unity. Early modern Ireland was also manifold in identity, with all the different groups discussed in chapter 1 competing for economic and political dominance. The modern period saw no less of a difference in ideas of Irishness. Some nationalists such as Tone argued for political separation from Britain as the greatest expression of Irish identity, while O'Connell and Isaac Butt would have been satisfied with remaining loyal to the British crown, and did not see any major inconsistency with being Irish under an English monarch, as long as there was an acceptable degree of home rule in Ireland. This mirrored the thinking of many Protestant nationalists such as Grattan in the late eighteenth century. The idea of a 'loyalist nationalist' was not unusual then, no matter how incompatible it would have sounded to twentieth century Irish people on both sides of the border. Young Ireland and the Fenians had stronger ideas of Irish identity, but even they disagreed amongst themselves at times. The late nineteenth and early twentieth centuries saw fervent assertions of types of Irishness through the literary revival, the Gaelic League, the Gaelic Athletic Association and Sinn Féin. These groups, however, chose different avenues for their expression of national identity. As chapters 7 and 8 have shown, questions of identity not only became highly prominent in the Free State/Republic and in Northern Ireland, but they often erupted into violent confrontation. Most historians agree that the twentieth century (particularly from the 1960s through to the

1980s) has witnessed the least willingness to accept different ideas of Irishness, particularly in Northern Ireland. Whether the hope of more understanding in Northern Ireland at the start of the twenty-first century is fulfilled remains to be seen.

Finally, the theme of history itself has been highly visible in this book, as well as in Irish history. As stated in the introduction, perhaps in no other country has history and the work of professional historians been so important to cultural and political life. Different (sometimes wildly divergent) ideas of Irish history have been used as justification for political organization and action, for violence, and in attempts to create specific types of cultures on both sides of the border. As chapters 7 and 8 have shown, this is particularly true of the teaching of history in schools in the Free State/Republic and Northern Ireland from the 1920s until the 1980s. Deliberate renderings of history have been used to craft cultural belief on both sides of the border. As shown throughout this book, there are traditional nationalist readings of Irish history, traditional unionist readings, and more recent revisionist and counter-revisionist readings. Further, historians of other countries are almost always amazed at the level and sophistication of popular historical discussion. When the 'revisionist controversy' broke out during the 1980s, it was not only debated in academic circles, but in the popular media of radio, television, and newspapers. Readers of this book will now know, however, that this sort of sensitivity to history is not a new thing in Ireland. As each of the interpretations sections of this book has tried to show, various ideas about Irish history have long (and sometimes distinguished) pedigrees. All the major schools of thought discussed here, although perhaps partly based on myths and misunderstandings, were not arrived at casually. They were wrought with a purpose (whether political, cultural, or professional), and argued strongly. History is a serious business in Ireland and, except for the extreme uses to which it has been put, Irish society is to be admired for that attention and sophistication.

Bibliography and Further Reading

As mentioned in the Preface, Irish history has become a very well-researched field since the middle of the twentieth century. In addition to general studies, there is a wealth of specialized work on the various topics introduced in this book. One of the purposes of this book was to give readers a basic grasp of the narrative and interpretations of Irish history. After reading it, they should find the more sophisticated general works listed below (especially those by Foster, Hoppen and Jackson) more accessible. This Bibliography and Further Reading section, therefore, is divided into General Works, Thematic Works, Specialist Works (organized by chapter headings from this book), and Periodicals and Journals. Most of the general works should still be in print, but the more specialized works may be available only in libraries.

GENERAL WORKS

Beckett, J.C., *The Making of Modern Ireland, 1603–1921*. London, 1966, reprinted 1987
—— *A Short History of Ireland*. London, reprinted 1981
Boyce, D. George, *The Irish Question and English Politics, 1868–1986*. Dublin, 1991
—— *Nineteenth Century Ireland: the Search for Stability*. Dublin, 1991
Boyce, D. George and O'Day, Alan (eds.), *The Making of Modern Irish History: Revisionism and the Revisionist Controversy*. London, 1996
Brady, Ciaran (ed.), *Interpreting Irish History: the Debate on Historical Revisionism*. Dublin, 1994
Buckland, P., *A History of Northern Ireland*. Dublin, 1981

Connolly, S.J. (ed.), *The Oxford Companion to Irish History*. Oxford, 1998

Cullen, L.M., *The Emergence of Modern Ireland 1600–1980*. London, 1983

De Paor, L., *The Peoples of Ireland from Prehistory to Modern Times*. London, 1986

Foster, R.F., *Modern Ireland 1600–1972*. London, 1989

Hoppen, K., Theodore *Elections, Politics, and Society in Ireland, 1832–1885*. Oxford, 1984

—— *Ireland Since 1800: Conflict and Conformity*. London, second edition 1999

Jackson, Alvin, *Ireland 1798–1998: Politics and War*. Oxford, 1999

Lyndon, James, *The Making of Modern Ireland: from Ancient Times to the Present*. London, 1999

Lyons, F.S.L., *Ireland Since the Famine*. London 1971, reprinted 1985

Moody, T.W., *The Ulster Question, 1603–1973*. Dublin, 1974

Moody, T.W. and Martin, F.X. (eds.), *The Course of Irish History*. Cork, 1994

Ranelagh, John O'Beirne, *A Short History of Ireland*. Cambridge, second edition 1999

Whyte, John, *Interpreting Northern Ireland*. Oxford, 1989

THEMATIC WORKS

Economic and Demographic History

Barry, Frank, *Understanding Ireland's Economic Growth*. London, 1999

Connell, Kenneth, *Population of Ireland 1750–1845*. Oxford, 1951

Cullen, L.M., *An Economic History of Ireland Since 1660*. London, 1972

Daly, M.E., *Social and Economic History of Ireland since 1800*. Dublin, 1981

Guinnane, Timothy W., *The Vanishing Irish: Household, Migration, and the Rural Economy*. Princeton, 1997

Ó Gráda, Cormac, *Ireland Before and After the Famine: Explorations in Economic History, 1800–1925*. Manchester, 1993

—— *Ireland: a New Economic History 1780–1939*. Oxford, 1994

—— *A Rocky Road: the Irish Economy Since the 1920s*. Manchester, 1997

Turner, Michael (ed.), *After the Famine: Irish Agriculture, 1850–1914*. Cambridge, 1996

Social and Cultural History

Bartlett, Thomas and Jeffrey, Keith, *A Military History of Ireland*. Cambridge, 1996

Brown, Terence, *Ireland: a Social and Cultural History 1922–1985*. London, 1985

Cullen, L. M., *Life in Ireland*. London, 1968

Donnelly, J.S. and Miller, Kerby (eds.), *Irish Popular Culture*. Dublin, 1998
Fitzpatrick, David, *Irish Emigration, 1801–1921*. Dundalk, 1984
Graham, Brian (ed.), *In Search of Ireland: a Cultural Geography*. London, 1997
Harkness, D. and O'Dowd, M. (eds.), *The Town in Ireland*. Belfast, 1981

Religion

Akenson, D.H., *The Church of Ireland: Ecclesiastical Reform and Revolution, 1800–1885*. New Haven, CT, 1971
Bartlett, Thomas, *The Fall and Rise of the Irish Nation: the Catholic Question, 1690–1830*. Dublin, 1992
Bowen, Desmond, *Paul Cullen and the Shaping of Modern Irish Catholicism*. Dublin, 1983
—— *The Protestant Crusade in Ireland, 1800–70: a Study of Protestant–Catholic Relations between the Act of Union and Disestablishment*. Dublin, 1978
Brooke, Peter, *Ulster Presbyterianism: the Historical Perspective, 1610–1970*. Dublin, 1987
Connolly, S.J., *Priests and People in Pre-Famine Ireland, 1780–1845*. Dublin, 1982
—— *Religion and Society in Nineteenth Century Ireland*. Dundalk, 1985
Corish, Patrick, *The Irish Catholic Experience: a Historical Survey*. Dublin, 1985
Keenan, D.J., *The Catholic Church in Nineteenth Century Ireland*. Dublin, 1983
Larkin, Emmet, *The Roman Catholic Church and the Creation of the Modern Irish State, 1878–86*. Dublin, 1975
McDowell, R.B., *The Church of Ireland: a History*. Dublin, 1978

IRELAND BEFORE 1800

Bartlett, Thomas, *Theobald Wolfe Tone*. Dublin, 1997
Beckett, J.C., 'Anglo-Irish Constitutional Relations in the Later Eighteenth Century'. *Irish Historical Studies*, vol. 14, 1964
Canny, Nicholas, *From Reformation to Restoration: Ireland, 1534–1660*. Dublin, 1987
Corkery, Daniel, *Hidden Ireland: a Study of Gaelic Munster in the Eighteenth Century*. Dublin, 1924, reprinted 1967
Crawford, W.H., 'Landlord-Tenant Relations in Ulster 1609–1820'. *Irish Economic and Social History*, vol. 2, 1975
—— 'The Significance of Landed Estates in Ulster 1600–1820'. *Irish Economic and Social History*, vol. 17, 1990
Cullen, L.M., *Anglo-Irish Trade 1660–1800*. Manchester, 1968
Curtin, Nancy, *The United Irishmen: Popular Politics in Ulster and Dublin, 1791–1798*. Oxford, 1992
Davies, R. R., *Domination and Conquest: the Experience of Ireland, Scotland, and Wales, 1100–1300*. Cambridge, 1990

Dickson, David, *New Foundations: Ireland 1660–1800.* Dublin, 2000

Dolley, Michael, *Anglo-Norman Ireland.* Dublin, 1972

Donnelly, J.S., 'The Whiteboy Movement 1761–5'. *Irish Historical Studies*, vol. 21, 1978

Farrell, Brian (ed.), *The Irish Parliamentary Tradition.* Dublin, 1973

Fitzpatrick, Brendan, *Seventeenth-Century Ireland: the War of Religions.* Dublin, 1988

Froude, J.A., *The English in Ireland in the Eighteenth Century.* London, 1874

Johnston, E.M., *Great Britain and Ireland 1760–1800.* 1963

Lecky, W.E.H., *History of Ireland in the Eighteenth Century.* London, 1892

Lennon, Colm, *Sixteenth-Century Ireland: the Incomplete Conquest.* Dublin, 1994

MacCurtain, Margaret, *Tudor and Stuart Ireland.* Dublin, 1972

MacNoicaill, Gearóid, *Ireland Before the Vikings.* Dublin, 1972

McDowell, R.B., *Irish Public Opinion 1750–1800.* London, 1944

O'Brien, George, *The Economic History of Ireland in the Eighteenth Century.* Dublin, 1918

—— *The Economic History of Ireland in the Seventeenth Century,* Dublin, 1919

O'Connell, Maurice, *Irish Politics and Social Conflict in the Age of the American Revolution.* Philadelphia, 1965.

Richter, Michael, *Medieval Ireland: the Enduring Tradition.* Dublin, 1988

Roebuck, Peter (ed.), *Plantation to Partition.* Belfast, 1981

Sims, J.G., *Williamite Confiscation of Ireland 1690–1703.* London, 1956

Wall, Maureen, *The Penal Laws, 1691–1760.* Dublin, 1961

—— 'The Whiteboys'. In Williams, T.D. (ed.) *Secret Societies in Ireland.* Dublin, 1973

O'CONNELL RELIGION AND POLITICS, 1800–48

Boyce, D. George, *Nineteenth-Century Ireland: the Search for Stability.* Dublin, 1990

Davis, Richard, *Young Ireland Movement.* Dublin, 1988

MacDonagh, Oliver, *The Hereditary Bondsman: Daniel O'Connell, 1775–1830.* London, 1988

—— *The Emancipationist: Daniel O'Connell, 1830–1847.* London, 1989

Macintyre, Angus, *The Liberator: Daniel O'Connell and the Irish Party, 1830–1847.* London, 1965

McCartney, Donal (ed.), *The World of Daniel O'Connell.* Dublin, 1980

Nowlan, Kevin, *The Politics of Repeal: a Study in the Relations Between Britain and Ireland, 1841–50.* London, 1965

O'Connell, Maurice, *Daniel O'Connell: Political Pioneer.* Dublin, 1983.

O'Connell, M.R. (ed.), *The Correspondence of Daniel O'Connell.* 8 vols. Dublin, 1972–80

O'Ferrall, Fergus, *Catholic Emancipation: Daniel O'Connell and the Birth of Irish Democracy, 1820–30.* Dublin, 1985

THE FAMINE, 1845-1852

Bowen, Desmond, *Souperism: Myth or Reality?* Cork, 1970

Daly, Mary, *The Famine in Ireland.* Dublin, 1986

Gray, Peter, *The Irish Famine.* London, 1995

—— *Famine, Land, and Politics: British Government and Irish Society 1843–1850.* Dublin, 1999

Kerr, Donal, '*A Nation of Beggars': Priests, People and Politics in Famine Ireland, 1846–1852.* Oxford, 1994

Kinealy, Christine, *This Great Calamity: the Irish Famine 1845–1852.* Dublin, 1994

Kinealy, Christine and MacAtasney, Gerard, *The Hidden Famine: Hunger, Poverty and Sectarianism in Belfast.* London, 2000

Mitchel, John, *The Last Conquest of Ireland (Perhaps).* 1860

Moykyr, Joel, *Why Ireland Starved: a Quantitative and Analytical History of the Irish Economy, 1800–1850.* London, 1985

Ó Gráda, Cormac, *The Great Irish Famine.* Dublin, 1989

—— *Black '47 and Beyond: the Great Irish Famine in History, Economy, and Memory.* Princeton, NJ, 1999

Póirtéir, Cathal (ed.), *The Great Irish Famine.* Dublin, 1995

Scally, R.J., *The End of Hidden Ireland: Rebellion, Famine and Emigration.* Oxford, 1996

Williams, T.D. and Edwards, R.D. (eds.), *The Great Famine: Studies in Irish History 1845–52.* Dublin, 1956

Woodham-Smith, Cecil, *The Great Hunger: Ireland, 1845–49.* London, 1962

FENIANISM AND THE LAND, 1848-81

Bew, Paul, *Land and the National Question in Ireland 1858–82.* Dublin, 1978

Bull, Phillip, *Land, Politics and Nationalism: a Study of the Irish Land Question.* Dublin, 1996

Clark, Samuel, *Social Origins of the Irish Land War.* Princeton, NJ, 1979

Clark, Samuel and Donnelly, J.S. (eds.), *Irish Peasants: Violence and Political Unrest, 1780–1914.* Manchester, 1983

Comerford, R.V., *The Fenians in Context: Irish Politics and Society, 1848–1882.* Dublin, 1985

Connolly, James, *Labour in Irish History.* Dublin, 1910

Crossman, Virginia, *Politics, Law and Order in Nineteenth Century Ireland.* Dublin, 1996

Devoy, John, *Recollections of an Irish Rebel.* New York, 1926

Donnelly, James S., *The Land and the People of Nineteenth Century Cork: the Rural Economy and the Land Question.* London, 1975

Geary, Laurence, *The Plan of Campaign, 1886–1891.* Cork, 1986

Jones, David Seth, *Graziers, Land Reform, and Political Conflict in Ireland.* Washington DC, 1995

Kee, Robert, *The Green Flag: a History of Irish Nationalism.* London, 1972

Lee, Joseph, *Modernization of Irish Society 1848–1918*. Dublin, 1978
Moody, T.W. (ed.), *Fenian Movement*. Cork, 1968
Newsinger, John, *Fenianism in Mid-Victorian Britain*. London, 1994
Ó Broin, Leon, *Fenian Fever: an Anglo-American Dilemma*. London, 1971
O'Farrell, Patrick, *Ireland's English Question: Anglo-Irish Relations 1534–1970*. London, 1971
O'Leary, John, *Recollection of Fenians and Fenianism*. 1896
Pomfret, J.E., *The Struggle for Land in Ireland, 1800–1923*. Princeton, 1930
Ryan, Desmond, *The Fenian Chief*. Dublin, 1967
Solow, Barbara, *The Land Question and the Irish Economy, 1870–1903*. Cambridge, MA, 1971
Steele, E.D., *Irish Land and British Politics: Tenant Right and Nationality, 1865–70*. Cambridge, 1974
Strauss, Emile, *Irish Nationalism and British Democracy*. London, 1951
Vaughan, W.E., *Landlords and Tenants in Mid-Victorian Ireland*. Oxford, 1994

HOME RULE, 1870–93

Cooke, A.B. and Vincent, John, *The Governing Passion: Cabinet Government and Party Politics in Britain 1885–86*. Brighton, 1974
Dangerfield, George, *The Strange Death of Liberal England*. London, 1935
—— *The Damnable Question: a Study in Anglo-Irish Relations*. London, 1977
Dicey, A.V., *England's Case Against Home Rule*. 1886
Ensor, R.C.K., *England 1870–1914*. Oxford, 1936
Garvin, Tom, *Nationalist Revolutionaries in Ireland, 1858–1928*. Oxford, 1987
Hamer, D., *John Morley: Liberal Intellectual in Politics*. Oxford, 1968
Hammond, J.L., *Gladstone and the Irish Nation*. London, 1938
Hurst, Michael, *Joseph Chamberlain and the Liberal Reunion*. London, 1967
Jackson, T.A., *Ireland Her Own*. London, 1947
Jenkins, T.A., *Gladstone, Whiggery, and the Liberal Party 1874–1885*. Oxford, 1987
Lubenow, William, *Parliamentary Politics and the Home Rule Crisis: the British House of Commons in 1886*. Oxford, 1988
Mansergh, Nicholas, *Ireland in the Age of Reform and Revolution*. London, 1940
Matthew, H.C.G., *Gladstone 1875–1898*. Oxford, 1995
Morley, J., *Life of William Ewart Gladstone*. London, 1903
O'Brien, Conor Cruise, *Parnell and His Party, 1880–90*. Oxford, 1957
O'Brien, R. Barry, *The Life of Charles Stewart Parnell*. London, 1898
O'Day, Alan, *Irish Home Rule 1867–1921*. Manchester, 1998

NATIONALISM, UNIONISM AND IRISH IDENTITY, 1891–1922

Beckett, J.C., 'Ireland Under the Union'. *Topic*, vol. 13, 1967; reprinted in Beckett, J.C., *Confrontations*. London, 1972

Boyce, D.G., *Nationalism in Ireland*. London, 1982, third edition 1995

Bradshaw, Brendan, 'Nationalism and Historical Scholarship in Modern Ireland'. *Irish Historical Studies*, vol. 26, 1989

Buckland, P., *Irish Unionism 1885–1923: a Documentary History*. Belfast, 1973

Collins, Peter (ed.), *Nationalism and Unionism: Conflict in Ireland, 1885–1921*. Belfast, 1994

Coogan, Tim Pat, *Michael Collins: a Biography*. London, 1990

—— *De Valera: Long Fellow, Long Shadow*. London, 1993

Crawford, F.H., *Guns for Ulster*. 1947

Curran, Joseph, *The Birth of the Irish Free State, 1921–23*. University, Alabama, 1980

Davis, Richard, *Arthur Griffith and Non-Violent Sinn Féin*. Dublin, 1974

Dhonnchadha, Máirín ni and Dorgan, Theo (eds.), *Revising the Rising*. Derry, 1991

Dorries, Reinhard R., *Prelude to the Easter Rising: Sir Roger Casement in Imperial Germany*. London, 2000

Edwards, Ruth Dudley, *Patrick Pearse: the Triumph of Failure*. London, 1977

Fitzpatrick, David, *Politics and Irish Life 1913–1921: Provincial Experience of War and Revolution*. Dublin, 1977

Foster, R.F., *W.B. Yeats: a Life. vol. 1: the Apprentice Mage*. Oxford, 1997

Gallagher, Frank, *The Indivisible Island: the History of the Partition of Ireland*. London, 1957

Garvin, Tom, *Nationalist Revolutionaries in Ireland, 1858–1928*. Oxford, 1987

—— *1922: the Birth of Irish Democracy*. Dublin, 1996

Gibbon, Peter, *The Origins of Ulster Unionism: the Formation of Popular Protestant Politics and Ideology in Nineteenth-Century Ireland*. Manchester, 1975

Hepburn, A.C. and Rumpf, E., *Nationalism and Socialism in Ireland*. Liverpool, 1977

Hopkinson, Michael, *Green Against Green: the Irish Civil War*. Dublin, 1988

Hoppen, K. Theodore, *Elections, Politics, and Society in Ireland, 1832–1885*. Oxford, 1984

Hutchinson, John, *The Dynamics of Cultural Nationalism: the Gaelic Revival and the Creation of the Irish Nation State*. London, 1987

Hyland, J.L., *James Connolly*. Dublin, 1997

Jackson, Alvin, *The Ulster Party: Irish Unionists in the House of Commons, 1884–1911*. Oxford, 1989

—— *Sir Edward Carson*. Dublin, 1993

—— *Colonel Edward Saunderson: Land and Loyalty in Victorian Ireland*. Oxford, 1995

Jalland, Patricia, *The Liberals and Ireland: the Ulster Question in British Politics to 1914.* Brighton, 1980

Laffan, Michael, *The Partition of Ireland, 1911–1925.* Dundalk, 1983

—— *The Resurrection of Ireland: the Sinn Féin Party, 1916–1923.* Cambridge, 1999

Lee, Joseph, *Ireland, 1912–85: Politics and Society.* Cambridge, 1989

Loughlin, James, *Ulster Unionism and British National Identity Since 1885.* London, 1995

Lyons, F.S.L., *The Irish Parliamentary Party 1890–1910.* London, 1951

—— *Culture and Anarchy in Ireland, 1890–1939.* Oxford, 1979

Mandle, W.F., *The Gaelic Athletic Association and Irish Nationalist Politics, 1884–1924.* Dublin, 1987

Martin, F.X., 'Eoin MacNeill on the 1916 Rising'. *Irish Historical Studies,* vol. 11, 1948

—— (ed.) *Leaders and Men of the Easter Rising: Dublin, 1916.* London, 1966

McNeill, Ronald, *Ulster's Stand for the Union.* London, 1922

Morgan, Austen, *James Connolly: a Political Biography.* Manchester, 1988

O'Day, Alan, *The English Face of Irish Nationalism: Parnellite Involvement in British Politics, 1880–86.* Dublin, 1977

O'Halpin, Eunan, *The Decline of the Union: British Government in Ireland, 1892–1920.* New York, 1987

Shannon, Catherine, *Arthur J. Balfour and Ireland, 1874–1922.* Washington DC, 1988

Shaw, Francis, 'The Canon of Irish History: a Challenge'. *Irish Historical Studies,* vol. 61, 1972

Sheehy, Jeanne, *The Rediscovery of Ireland's Past: the Celtic Revival, 1830–1930.* London, 1980

Stewart, A.T.Q., *Ulster Crisis: Resistance to Home Rule, 1912–1914.* London, 1967

Thompson, W.I., *Imagination of the Insurrection: Dublin 1916.* London, 1976

Townshend, Charles, 'Modernization and Nationalism: Perspectives in Recent Irish History'. *History,* vol. 66, 1981

Williams, T.D., *The Irish Struggle, 1916–1926.* London, 1966

THE MAKING OF TWO IRELANDS, 1922–66

Barrington, Ruth, *Health, Medicine and Politics in Ireland, 1900–70.* Dublin, 1987

Bew, Paul and Patterson, Henry, *Seán Lemass and the Making of Modern Ireland, 1945–1996.* Dublin, 1982

Buckland, P., *The Factory of Grievances: Devolved Government in Northern Ireland 1921–39.* Dublin, 1979

Collins, Stephen, *The Cosgrave Legacy.* Dublin, 1996

Cronin, Mike, *The Blueshirts and Irish Politics.* Dublin, 1997

Daly, Mary, *Industrial Development and Irish National Identity, 1922–1939.* Dublin, 1992

FitzGerald, Garrett, *Towards a New Ireland*. Dublin, 1972

Heslinga, M.W., *The Irish Border as a Cultural Divide: a Contribution to the Study of Regionalism in the British Isles*. Assen, 1962

McDonald, Henry, *Trimble*. London, 2000

McKittrick, David, Kelters, Seamus, Feeney, Brian and Thornton, Chris, *Lost Lives: the Stories of the Men, Women and Children who Died as a Result of the Northern Ireland Troubles*. London, 2000

Moody, T.W., *The Ulster Question 1603–1973*. Dublin, 1974

O'Brien, Conor Cruise, *States of Ireland*. London, 1972

Quinn, Dermot, *Understanding Northern Ireland*. Manchester, 1993

Routledge, Paul, *John Hume: a Biography*. London, 1997

Sherman, Hugh, *Not an Inch*. 1942

Shirlow, Peter and McGovern, Mark, *Who Are 'The People'?: Unionism, Protestantism and Loyalism in Northern Ireland*. London, 1997

Stewart, A.T.Q., *Narrow Ground: Aspects of Ulster, 1609–1969*. London, 1977

Taylor, Peter, *Brits*. London, 2000

—— *Loyalists*. London, 1999

—— *Provos: the IRA and Sinn Fein*. London, 1997. Published in the United States as *Behind the Mask: the IRA and Sinn Fein*

Tonge, Jonathan, *Northern Ireland: Conflict and Change*. Hemel Hempstead, 1998

Walker, Brian, *Ulster Politics: the Formative Years, 1868–86*. Belfast, 1989

Whyte, John, *Interpreting Northern Ireland*. Oxford, 1989

Wichert, Sabine, *Northern Ireland Since 1945*. London, 1999

PERIODICALS AND JOURNALS

History Ireland. This is a well-written and illustrated history magazine bringing current ideas of Irish history to a general audience.

Irish Historical Studies. The dominant professional history journal in Irish history.

Irish Economic and Social History. A more specialized professional journal than *IHS*.

Index

relief measures 48, 63–4, 65–7,
   68–72, 77–8
and soup kitchens 66–7
farmers *see* tenant farmers
Farrell, Michael 208
Faulkner, Brian 178–80
federalism 99
Fenianism 84–5
   and Gaelic Athletic Association 120
   and Home Rule movement 87–8, 98,
      99–101
   independence demands 73, 85, 97
   interpretations 93–4, 96–7
   and New Departure 88–9
   and sports 85–6, 94
Fianna Fáil
   and Anglo-Irish Treaty 148–9, 166
   in coalition governments 187, 190
   and de Valera 148–9, 152, 156, 163,
      164
   and Easter Rising 137
   and economy 172–4
   and European Community 172
   interpretations 166–7
   and labour movement 149
   and New Ireland Forum 182
Field Day Theatre Company 136–7
fine (extended family) 9
Fine Gael
   establishment 152–3
   in government 156–7, 163, 167,
      172–4, 187
   and New Ireland Forum 182
First World War 130
   and Easter Rising 127–9
   and nationalist opposition 125–6
   and nationalist support for
      Britain 125, 135
   and unionist support for Britain 128,
      143
FitzGerald, Garrett 174, 183, 186, 204
Fitzgerald, Thomas (brother of 8th earl
      of Kildare) 17
Fitzgerald, Thomas (son of 9th earl of
      Kildare) 19–20
Fitzgerald, Vesey 44
Fitzpatrick, David 140
'flight of the earls' 20
Forster, W.E. 90–1
Foster, Roy ix, 57, 110
France
   and England 21, 26, 27–8, 30
   and support for Ireland 31–2, 85, 213
franchise
   and Catholics 43, 45, 106, 150
   and multiple vote system 150, 176,
      177
Free State *see* Irish Free State

French Revolution, effects 29
Froude, J.A. 35

Gaelic Athletic Association
   (GAA) 119–20, 123, 217
Gaelic League 118–19, 123, 217
Gallagher, Frank 137–8, 203
Gárda Siochána 147
Garvin, Tom 136–7, 139
genocide, accusations 75, 76, 78
geography 6–7
George III of Britain and Ireland 29–30,
   37
George IV of Britain and Ireland, as
   regent 29–30
George V of Great Britain 125, 149
Germany
   and Irish nationalism 126–9
   see also First World War; Second
      World War
Gibbon, Peter 138, 142–3, 169, 208
Gibraltar, killing of IRA members 183
Ginkel, Godert de, 1st earl of
   Athlone 25
Gladstone, William Ewart
   and disestablishment of Church of
      Ireland 87
   and Home Rule 100, 102–6, 107,
      108–11, 120, 210
   and land reform 87, 90–1, 98, 102
   and unionism 138
Good Friday Agreement 4, 191–5, 214
   and arms decommissioning 196–200
   cross-border bodies 190, 192–3, 199
   and referendum 193–4
government, local 41, 45, 113, 121–2,
   176, 177
Grattan, Henry 29, 30, 34, 36, 139, 217
Gray, Peter 78
graziers 114
Gregory, Lady Augusta 117
Griffith, Arthur
   and Famine 75
   as head of the Dáil 145, 146
   and Home Rule 131–2
   and Sinn Féin 122–3
gun-running, unionist 124, 142

Hamer, David 110, 111
Hammond, J.L. 109
Hartington, Spencer Compton, 8th
   duke 103
Haughey, Charles 172, 173–4, 181
Healy, Tim 121–2
Heath, Edward 179
Henry II of England 13–14
Henry IV of England 16
Henry VI of England 17